ESOL Tests and Testing

A Resource for
Teachers and Administrators

Stephen Stoynoff and Carol A. Chapelle

Teachers of English to Speakers of Other Languages, Inc.

Typeset in Berkeley with Adelon
by Capitol Communication Systems, Inc., Crofton, Maryland USA
Printed by Victor Graphics, Baltimore, Maryland USA

Teachers of English to Speakers of Other Languages, Inc.
700 South Washington Street, Suite 200
Alexandria, Virginia 22314 USA
Tel. 703-836-0774 • Fax 703-836-6447 • E-mail info@tesol.org •
http://www.tesol.org/

Director of Publishing: Paul Gibbs
Managing Editor: Marilyn Kupetz
Copy Editor: Ellen Garshick
Additional Reader: Sarah Duffy
Cover Design: Capitol Communication Systems, Inc.

ISBN 1-931185-16-6
Library of Congress Control No. 2004097289

Table of Contents

Preface

The genesis of this volume was a conversation in which we concurred on the necessity for a source of reviews of widely used ESOL tests and lamented that the first book devoted exclusively to ESOL test reviews was no longer in print. *Reviews of English Language Proficiency Tests* (Alderson, Krahnke, & Stansfield, 1987), an extensive collection of reviews of commercially produced ESOL tests in use at the time, was an invaluable resource and served as the impetus for this volume.

Since 1987, ESOL tests and test users have changed. First, some widely used tests have been revised, and a number of new tests now incorporate advances in computer technology. Second, many more ESOL practitioners are responsible for selecting and using tests than in the past; therefore, most of the tests reviewed in this volume were selected on the basis of telephone surveys of a random stratified sample of 160 TESOL members. Additional tests were included because they were new and judged to be of potential interest to readers or because they exemplified recent developments in language testing. In view of the way that tests were selected, the contents are slanted toward the tests that are most accessible and of interest to TESOL members, the majority of whom have ties to North America, but we hope the volume will benefit ESOL practitioners everywhere.

The fact that so many more ESOL practitioners are engaged in the testing process in 2005 than in 1987 prompted a second change in the current volume. We felt it was essential for such a volume to serve not only as a source of information on particular tests but also as a means of gaining access to principles, methods, and the language of language assessment. By situating the reviews quite literally in the middle of the volume, rather than in an appendix or as an addendum to chapter 5, we present the chapters in the sequence that approximates how teachers and administrators might respond to the practical assessment challenge of selecting and evaluating a standardized test.

Initially, potential test users need to become informed about current assessment practices and learn about aspects of test purpose, test design, and test method; they also need to understand fundamental test constructs before examining information about a test. Following these preparatory activities, the search begins for an appropriate test. This stage of the process involves obtaining and examining as much information as possible about the tests of interest, including the information contained in test manuals. Having identified the most promising test, potential users need to conduct a comprehensive evaluation of the test's usefulness by evaluating the test and the information contained in the manual, in view of the test setting. Following a usefulness analysis, the test of interest may be judged inappropriate for the target group of test takers or the test setting. In this case, a test must be developed, a process that often requires drawing on additional resources and employing procedures that will lead to construction of a suitable assessment. This volume is designed to guide practitioners through this complex process and to assist them in responding to these assessment challenges.

Chapter 1 establishes a basic framework for the volume by introducing three broad themes that have changed the assessment landscape: new educational policies and practices; advances in measurement theory; and developments in language testing research. We argue that, taken together, these changes require higher standards of assessment literacy on the part of ESOL professionals and require practitioners to assume greater responsibility for selecting, developing, using, and interpreting all forms of tests and assessments. The chapter presents a tripartite approach to considering a test in terms of its purpose, its method, and the justification of its use in a particular situation. Essential test constructs and related terminology are defined in context and integrated into subsequent chapters.

Chapter 2, containing test reviews, is the part of the book that most resembles Alderson et al.'s (1987) publication. In addition to 20 test reviews, the chapter highlights sources of information about language tests as well as how to locate the tests themselves. These sources include reference volumes that list test publishers and test reviews, selected online resources, and specialized serial publications.

Each test review entry is 1,000–2,500 words in length and includes the name, publisher, contact information, publication date, target population, and cost of the test. The narrative is divided into three parts that correspond to the major considerations presented in chapter 1: test purpose, test method, and justification of test use. Under the heading of test purpose, reviewers consider any inferences and types of decisions that can be made based on test performance as well as the impact of the test on test takers and others. Test methods are described in terms of the input test takers receive, response types, and how test performance is scored or evaluated. The final section of each review addresses the issue of justifying the use of the test for particular purposes. This includes considering the validity and reliability evidence presented by publishers and offering judgments about the suitability of the test for various contexts and purposes. Reviewers were encouraged to use the terminology presented in chapter 1 whenever possible to enhance the readability and comparability of the entries.

Test manuals are a crucial source of information on a test, and chapter 3 is intended to help ESOL practitioners utilize this resource effectively. The chapter takes the position that test practices are enhanced when developers and users embrace the same professional standards, and it advocates for the standards promulgated in the authoritative *Standards for Educational and Psychological Testing* (Joint Committee on Standards for Educational & Psychological Testing, 1999). The chapter explains what typically appears in test manuals and offers guidelines that practitioners can use to examine manuals and critically evaluate their contents.

Chapter 4 extends the test analysis activities initiated in preceding chapters and integrates them into a systematic analysis of the usefulness of a test that considers the test, the test manual, and the test setting. Such an approach connects testing theory to testing practices and principles and to the reality in ESOL classrooms and programs. To illustrate how to apply the process to a practical assessment challenge, chapter 4 describes a case in which an ESOL program conducted a usefulness analysis of a test reviewed in chapter 2.

The final chapter confronts the question of what to do when the results of a usefulness analysis favor constructing rather than adopting a test. It presents essential aspects of the test development process, suggests how to evaluate and improve the performance of a test, and emphasizes the importance of considering the impact of a test on individuals and, more broadly, its influence on teaching and learning. The latter consideration recognizes the inherent power of tests and their potential for misuse. Chapter 5 highlights a number of recent publications that ESOL practitioners can consult to improve their ability to develop tests that are useful for themselves and appropriate for their learners.

An annotated bibliography complements the contents of chapter 5 and describes a collection of books written primarily for practitioners. These resources, though not an exhaustive list of what is available, cover the range of issues and basic considerations of significance to language testing. Although some of the entries in the bibliography may be familiar, we hope that including these books encourages you to revisit them and that you will add the other titles to your professional libraries as well.

We are grateful for the cooperation and enthusiastic support we received from many people during the process of compiling this volume. First, we are most grateful to the 21 authors who contributed test reviews to chapter 2: Jay Banerjee, Lindsay Brooks, Norm Brown, Micheline Chalhoub-Deville, Yeonsuk Cho, Caroline Clapham, Tina Scott Edstam, April Ginther, Jeff Johnson, Sari Luoma, Meg Malone, Keith Morrow, Barry O'Sullivan, James Purpura, David Qian, Carsten Roever, Diane Schmitt, Diane Strong-Krause, Carolyn Turner, Jean Turner, and Gillian Wigglesworth. This volume could not have been completed without their cooperation and careful attention to detail. We are also grateful to Marilyn Kupetz and two chairs of the TESOL Publications Committee, Karen Johnson and Julian Edge, as well as the members of the committee and two anonymous reviewers for their very thorough and useful comments on the first draft of the volume. We would also like to thank Neil Anderson for his insight and assistance in the planning stages of the project.

Chapter 1

Understanding Language Tests and Testing Practices

All ESOL teachers come into contact with language assessment in one form or another, yet many find principles of assessment an aspect of professional knowledge that is difficult to update and apply effectively. This chapter, therefore, lays out the critical concepts required for an understanding of the language tests and testing practices outlined in subsequent chapters.

We begin with a brief discussion of the importance of assessment in the broader context of TESOL and education followed by an explanation of the problem that has developed because of the intellectual division between those concerned with language testing and those who teach. We argue that changes in educational practice, measurement theory, and language testing research necessitate bridging that division to meet current and future classroom needs. This chapter begins to build the bridge by deconstructing the dichotomy that narrows the knowledge and responsibility of the language teacher, and by replacing it with a more robust set of concepts for understanding a range of testing practices: test purpose, test method, and test justification. These overarching concepts form the basis for introducing key terms often used to describe language tests.

The Importance of Assessment

Teachers are involved in many forms of assessment and testing through their daily teaching and use of test scores. The significance of testing issues is evidenced in practitioner publications like *TESOL Journal*, which in the mid-1990s published one special issue and a number of articles that reported the successful use of student-constructed assessments in ESOL classrooms (see, e.g., Gardner, 1996; Gottlieb, 1995; McNamara & Deane, 1995; Murphy, 1995; Smolen, Newman, Wathen, & Lee, 1995). For the most part, these assessments were implemented in contexts where teachers were making low-stakes decisions and had the freedom to select the forms of assessment. Even so, all classroom materials, whether they are for teaching, assessment, or both, need to be constructed and administered in a manner that ensures their appropriate use. Assessments that begin as onetime classroom innovations may draw the attention of colleagues, who may ask to borrow them or use the scores for other purposes.

Moreover, teachers are often involved in high-stakes, mandated assessment programs that prescribe forms of assessment, including standardized, traditional forms of assessment. As recently as academic year 1992–1993, 70% of the statewide educational testing programs in the United States were using multiple-choice assessments (Barton & Coley, 1994). The ever-increasing sense of mismatch between educational philosophy, instructional practices, and assessment techniques has some practitioners frustrated with many standardized tests (Herman, Aschbacher, & Winters, 1992) and interested in alternatives. Gottlieb (1995) echoes the sentiments of many ESOL teachers when she states that "rich, descriptive information about the processes and products of learning cannot be gathered by conventional teaching and testing methods" (p. 12). She maintains there has been a "rise of instructional and assessment practices that are holistic, student centered, integrated, and multidimensional" (p. 12).

The Division Between Teachers and Testers

Despite the effect of teacher-initiated practices on classroom assessments, a division continues to exist between language teachers and testers. Many teachers voice dissatisfaction with high-stakes, standardized tests but do not feel qualified to argue effectively against them and propose alternatives. In situations involving classroom assessments or programwide tests, teachers need to be empowered to address questions about the choice, development, and use of traditional tests and other forms of assessment.

Although teachers construct tests and test specialists may teach or have taught ESOL, the daily activities and roles of the two groups are generally different. The division of labor evident in language education is part of a broader phenomenon that began in the educational community in the first few decades of the 20th century and continued unabated for the next half-century. Teaching and testing became separated as the trend toward academic specialization accelerated and culminated in the emergence of a psychometric perspective that was dedicated to developing highly refined, standardized, objective measures (Stoynoff, 1996). Created by testing specialists who worked in universities and research centers, and designed to measure human traits and abilities, these tests were scientifically developed and empirically tested; moreover, some of the more widely used tests have been continuously researched. During this period of language testing, which Spolsky (1978, 1995) referred to as *psychometric-structuralist* or *modern,* society in general—and teachers in particular—vested a great deal of power and authority in testing specialists.

In many respects, this authority was justly earned as the science of educational testing rapidly matured and advanced during the 20th century. Throughout the century, testing specialists extended research methods, improved their ability to develop and empirically evaluate tests (often by applying increasingly sophisticated statistical procedures and techniques to test development), and built more comprehensive theories to explain the abilities they sought to measure. This activity was supported by an academic culture that emphasized basic research, test development, empirical evaluation, and theory building. These activities, moreover, contributed to the refinement of important test constructs and produced sophisticated tests that accurately measured what they were designed to measure. But as the science of testing expanded, so did the gulf between what teachers knew and what testing specialists knew about testing. Educators who worked in schools were consumers of what was produced by those in academe, and the culture of schools emphasized test selection and administration, interpretation of results, and decision making based on test results. This division of labor permitted both cultures to focus on what they did best. Teachers taught, and test specialists developed standardized tests that schools used to evaluate students.

Writing about the use of standardized tests in U.S. schools, Stiggins (1997) observed that

> The paradox is that, as a society (within and outside schools), we seem to have been operating on blind faith that these tests are sound, and that educators are using them appropriately. As a society, almost to a person, we actually know very little about standardized tests or the scores they produce. It has been so for decades. This blind faith has prevented us from understanding either the strengths or the important limitations of standardized tests. (p. 352)

Stiggins explained that the majority of standardized tests used to measure educational attainment, including language tests, are intended to offer general estimates of the learner's ability or achievement in broad content domains or in certain kinds of reasoning. Administrators and teachers are to use the results to sort learners by ability or gauge their general achievement after a substantial amount of learning has occurred. As such, the results are unsuitable for assessing the daily progress of learners or their achievements at the end of a single course.

In other words, the division of labor has produced tests that are useful for some purposes but not for others. But the more systemic result of the division is the partial and fragile knowledge that teachers have about how to collect information systematically for the purpose of making certain determinations about learners, which has led to the perception that testing and assessment are completely distinct educational processes. Ironically, this perception further dichotomizes the classroom assessment that teachers engage in and the testing that is the responsibility of researchers. Despite the value of a strong theory and practice of classroom-based assessment, maintaining the separation between testing and assessment keeps teachers from applying their knowledge of assessment to high-stakes testing.

From Division to Unity

Forging stronger links between teaching and assessment is essential if educators hope to optimize classroom learning. This section highlights some of the salient developments that occurred during the transition to the postmodern period and their effect on the relationship between teaching and testing.

Educational Practices

The educational landscape in the United States changed dramatically in the early 1980s. The U.S. educational reform movement was precipitated by the publication of *A Nation at Risk: The Imperative for Educational Reform* (National Commission on Excellence in Education, 1983). This 32-page report to the U.S. secretary of education documented a decline in the academic quality of U.S. educational institutions (public and private, from kindergarten through university), and it recommended five major reforms to correct the declines in achievement. Two recommendations with implications for testing and assessment were (a) to restore an academic core (called *new basics*) to the curriculum that should reflect a decidedly applied orientation and (b) to implement more rigorous and measurable standards for academic performance. Instructional practices and assessment procedures were modified to conform to the curriculum reforms that followed the release of the report (Linn, 1994). The reform movement gained momentum in the 1990s, when the federal government passed the Goals 2000: Educate America Act (1994), which created a structure and empowered a body to develop guidelines for national education standards and offer states exemplary standards and the assessments to use in achieving these new national standards. Barton and Coley (1994) underscored the shift in assessment as a result of these reforms.

> The nation is entering an era of change in testing and assessment. Efforts at the national and state levels are now directed at greater use of performance assessment, constructed response questions, and portfolios based on actual student work. (as cited in Linn, 1994, p. 5)

With the enactment of Public Law 107-110, widely referred to as the No Child Left Behind Act of 2001 (2002), the federal government increased the pressure on states to adopt challenging academic achievement standards and improve the performance of low-achieving students, including those for whom English is a second language (L2). The legislation compels states to require that students pass state assessments a minimum of once between Grades 3–5, 6–9, and 10–12 in mathematics, reading, and language arts beginning in academic year 2005–2006 and in history and science by 2007–2008. Any nonnative speaker of English who has received 3 consecutive years of schooling in the United States will be expected to pass the same assessments without accommodations (pp. 1449–1451). However, Title III of the act stipulates that, beginning in academic year 2002–2003, schools must assess annually the English language proficiency of all limited-English-proficient students and determine the extent of their progress in acquiring English. Although schools are permitted to select or develop their assessments, measures must be approved by the state and need to assess the "child's level of comprehension, speaking, listening, reading, and writing skills in English" (p. 1701). Moreover, the act indicates that assessments must be consistent with the standards established by the professional testing community and "enable itemized score analyses to be produced and reported" (pp. 1451–1452). Clearly, the educational reforms contained in this legislation will increase the assessment responsibilities of ESOL teachers and program administrators.

The shift toward standards-based education and the assessment of learner performance relative to a set of predetermined outcomes is not limited to the United States. In fact, there is evidence that the language teaching profession is in the midst of a global trend in establishing educational goals and holding teachers and programs accountable for monitoring and documenting learners' achievements (Brindley, 1998). European reforms in L2 education have been especially ambitious and noteworthy over the past 30 years. The Council of Europe—a consortium of 40 nations founded in 1949—has been instrumental in promoting reforms in the teaching, learning, and evaluation of foreign language abilities across Europe's languages by coordinating the activities of educational administrators, curriculum developers, teachers, and testing specialists (Davies et al., 1999; "Towards a European Framework," 1994). Working with the Association of Language Testers in Europe, a professional network of European institutions that develop and administer language examinations, the Council of Europe (2001) created a comprehensive program that includes a common set of objectives and procedures for monitoring learners' achievement and evaluating their ability in a foreign language. The European approach to reforming language learning and testing differs from the legislative approach taken in the United States. Although the Council of Europe encourages member states to adopt the new educational framework, states are not required to do so.

Educational Measurement Theory

Another impetus for change comes from developments in educational measurement theory. In the eyes of the public, government-initiated educational reform may have sparked changes in assessment in the 1990s, but, in fact, expressions of dissatisfaction with theory and practice had been stirring in the educational measurement community throughout the previous decade. Five important papers published in the 1980s and 1990s offer a glimpse into these developments. Fredrickson (1984) pointed out that the overuse of multiple-choice testing could have a negative effect on student learning because of the practice of teaching to the test. In view of this concern and other developments in measurement theory, Messick (1989) published his seminal paper proposing an expanded concept of validity. Validity, he suggested, should be seen as an argument concerning the extent to which test use can be justified for a particular purpose, and one aspect of the argument should include the effects of test use on instruction.

Linn, Baker, and Dunbar (1991) pointed out the importance of the criteria used in developing the validity argument and suggested criteria that would privilege assessments with complex constructed responses over multiple-choice tests. Moss (1992) took up the polemic issue of the relationship between reliability and validity, suggesting that the orthodox view of reliability as essential for validity precluded the acceptance of some forms of assessments, a point that is critical for language testing (Swain, 1993). Concerned with the scope of the theoretically sound validity argument versus the practical needs of test development and use, Shepard (1993) suggested that the use of a particular test needed to figure substantively in the development of its validity argument.

What is apparent from this summary is that educational measurement theory centers on how one defines validity. This makes sense if one considers that the types of evaluative questions test users ask about tests all concern validity (see Table 1.1). The change in how the educational measurement community views validity is reflected in the questions about tests implied by former and current conceptions of validity. In the past, validity was considered a characteristic of a test—the extent to which a test measures what it is supposed to measure—whereas today it is considered an argument concerning test interpretation and use—the extent to which test interpretations and uses can be justified. Reliability was seen as distinct from and a necessary condition for validity, but now reliability is more

**Table 1.1. Past and Current Test Evaluation Questions
(Based on Chapelle, 1999)**

Past	*Current*
Q: Is the test valid?	Q: What makes me think that this test would meet my needs?
Q: Have the experts found this test to be reliable?	Q: Can appropriate types and levels of consistency be shown for this test in my setting?
Q: Have the experts found strong correlations between this test and other measures?	Q: Can I demonstrate that this test performs as I would expect and want it to in my situation?
Q: Have the experts found that the test has one or more of the three validities?	Q: How can I show that the test is valid for my use?

typically seen as one type of validity evidence. In the past, validity was largely established through correlations of a test with other tests, but now validity is best argued on the basis of a number of types of rationales and evidence, including the consequences of testing (e.g., its effect on teaching). Construct validity was seen as one of three types of validity: content, criterion related, and construct. But today, validity is a unitary concept with construct validity as central; content and criterion-related evidence can be used as evidence about construct validity.

These changes are interesting and important for language test users particularly because of three themes that underlie them. First, the changes have resulted in a view of validity as a context-specific argument rather than a test characteristic that can be established in a universal way. As a consequence, a second theme is the view that justifying the validity of test use is the responsibility of all test users rather than a job solely within the purview of testing researchers who develop large-scale, high-stakes tests. A third theme is that one consideration of ESOL test users should be the effects of tests on the teaching and learning of English.

Language Testing Research and Practice

These three themes may have arisen from the U.S. educational measurement scene, but their influence has been substantial in the international community of language testing. This influence is embodied in a common journal (*Language Testing*), an electronic discussion list, an international organization (the International Language Testing Association), and an annual conference (the Language Testing Research Colloquium) as well as in international EFL testing programs such as the Test of English as a Foreign Language (TOEFL) and the International English Language Testing System (IELTS).

As for the first theme of a situation-specific validity argument, recent work in language testing questions whether building generally accepted and valid models of language ability is practical given that language use and testing occur in such varied contexts (Chalhoub-Deville, 1997). Hence, some analysts have suggested that a more useful endeavor would be to develop what Chalhoub-Deville describes as *operational models* appropriate for particular test situations. This conclusion follows logically from the theory of communicative language ability as it has evolved over the past 25 years: Canale and Swain (1980) viewed communicative competence as including the strategies that would come into play during language use; Bachman's (1990) and Bachman and Palmer's (1996) concept of communicative language ability includes the context of language use in the overall schematic of their discussion of communicative language ability; Chapelle's (1998) description of an interactionalist construct definition goes one step further, stating that part of construct definition is context definition; that is, a definition of language ability needs to include the range of contexts of language use. What follows from the situation-specific construct definition—operational or theoretical—is the purpose-specific nature of tests, meaning that the validity of test use clearly rests on the situation of use. The tension between situation-specific construct definition and validation, on the one hand, and the need for general theories and principles, on the other, is defining one focus of language testing inquiry in the postmodern period.

The second theme—that testing not be left solely to the language testing researcher—has been taken up to some degree by the alternative assessment movement, but another less apparent manifestation is the expansion of language testing research to include more than model-fitting studies concerned with issues associated with reliability. A variety of research methodologies have led to important insights into the ways in which test takers' performance varies across test characteristics such as the type of tasks and content of the test (e.g., topics, instructions, genre, text types) and that this variability reflects the variability that exists in L2 performance. Such research requires expertise that extends beyond statistical matters. The ideal expressed in Messick's (1989) reaching discussion of validity inquiry is being realized in language testing research that has explored test score meaning from theoretical perspectives and through qualitative and quantitative methods.

One of these relatively new approaches, the study of testing consequences, addresses the third theme (Alderson & Wall, 1996; Bailey, 1999). Concern for the effects of testing on learning is one aspect of the larger issue of ethical considerations in language testing, which is of growing importance to language testing specialists (Davies, 1997). The ethics of language testing refers to the responsibility of those who develop and choose tests to see that they are used fairly. This discussion builds on the work of Canale (1987), who in the 1980s was an advocate for appreciating that test specialists and practitioners alike have a responsibility to "ensure that language tests are valuable experiences and yield positive consequences for all involved" (Douglas & Chapelle, 1993, p. 3). One of the ongoing issues of the postmodern period is to gain a greater understanding of how test fairness should come into play in the testing process (Kunnan, 1997).

Clearly, recent developments in educational practices, measurement theory, and language testing research offer compelling reasons for ESOL professionals to be *assessment literate,* which means being able to choose and use assessments for all of their purposes (Stiggins, 1997). At one time, the roles of language teachers and testing specialists were highly differentiated, leading many ESOL teachers and program administrators to become increasingly disconnected from the technical developments and practices associated with language tests and different types of assessments. However, the postmodern period is placing more responsibility for selecting, developing, and justifying assessments in the hands of practitioners, many of whom lack sufficient assessment literacy and confidence to fulfill these responsibilities.

Understanding Assessment and Testing

How can language teachers and program administrators take more responsibility for choosing, developing, using, and interpreting all forms of assessments and tests? As mentioned above, one response has been to draw a distinction between traditional testing and alternative assessment, the former being the domain of researchers and the latter the responsibility of teachers. For example, Herman et al. (1992) distinguish between *traditional, multiple-choice testing* and *alternative forms of assessment,* which include interviews, essays with prompts and scoring criteria, documented observations, self-evaluation, and portfolios. Other testing specialists refer to the distinction between *objectively scored, paper-and-pencil tests* and *alternative assessments,* which include compositions, performance assessments such as demonstrations or portfolios, and communicative exchanges such as interviews or conferences (Stiggins, 1997). Brown and Hudson (1998) present a typology for classifying assessments that recognizes differences in the nature of the responses (i.e., selected, constructed, and personal) and assert that personal-response assessments such as conferences, portfolios, and self- or peer assessments should not be considered *alternative assessments* but rather as "alternatives in assessment" (p. 657).

On the surface, the assessment/testing dichotomy appears useful in defining a manageable domain for teachers, but in fact it is regressive in at least three ways. Most important, it attempts to reinforce the historically instantiated division of labor between researchers and teachers, implying that researchers should continue to focus on large-scale testing and teachers should concern themselves with classroom assessments. Second, the fundamental principles of assessing language abilities are the same whether the process is termed *testing* or *assessment*. To compartmentalize the activities is to deny the relevance of teachers' knowledge about assessment and researchers' knowledge about testing to the other group's practices. Third, in practice, it is impossible to draw any clear-cut distinction between testing and assessment. For example, Balliro (1993) reports that the use of the term *alternative assessment* has spread among those working in adult ESOL literacy programs in recent years, but she believes that "the simple distinction between *standardized* versus *alternative assessment* is of limited use" (p. 558). Balliro and others (e.g., Huerta-Macías, 1995) acknowledge the absence of a precise definition for *alternative assessment* but suggest that it represents an alternative perspective to the psychometric tradition, one that relies less on quantitative data and values multiple alternative sources of information in the learning environment. Attempts to apply these fuzzy distinctions, however, raise confusion rather than bring clarity.

To say that the testing/assessment distinction is not productive, however, is not to say that no differences exist among language tests and assessments. The problem is that the simple dichotomy fails to capture the many important differences among assessment possibilities to consider in selecting, constructing, using, and interpreting tests. The simple dichotomy needs to be replaced by a more complex view of the factors involved in addressing a question such as *Why should I use this test for my particular purpose?* These three factors are test purpose, test method, and justification for test use (see Figure 1.1).

Understanding Test Purpose

Test purpose can be defined through three dimensions that capture the important functions of the test. The first is the inferences to be made from test scores or, in other words, what the test is intended to measure. As

Figure 1.1. Three Considerations for Test Choice

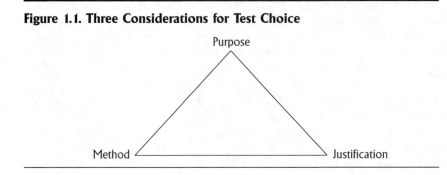

illustrated in Figure 1.2, the inference can be described very narrowly, as it pertains to what is taught and learned in a particular course; very generally as overall language proficiency; or at a number of points along a continuum. At the left end, a very specific inference about learners' ability would be their ability to handle the language of greetings and introductions after they had worked with these functions in a language class. An example of a specific-purpose inference would be the ability to use the language of tourism to guide guests around a city. At the extreme right is general-purpose language ability. The IDEA Proficiency Test (IPT) I—Oral English is an example of a test with results that can be used to make inferences about test takers' English language ability and readiness to enter mainstream classrooms where English is the medium of instruction. Inferences from language tests can be defined in a number of ways, including the areas of language knowledge (e.g., vocabulary) or skills (e.g., listening comprehension) one might infer on the basis of language test performance, and each of these areas can vary in terms of its context specificity.

The second dimension of test purpose is the use to be made of inferences (see Figure 1.3). *Test uses* refer to the types of decisions made on the basis of test scores or profiles, and such decisions are often described in terms of the stakes they hold for test takers. For example, at one extreme are the many self-tests learners can find on the Internet, which allow them to respond to a series of items and then receive a score. Such tests offer

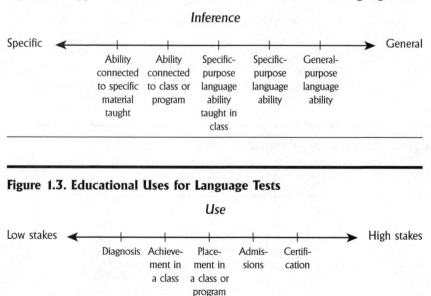

Figure 1.2. Types of Inferences That Can Be Drawn From Language Tests

Inference

Specific ← | | | | | → General

| Ability connected to specific material taught | Ability connected to class or program | Specific-purpose language ability taught in class | Specific-purpose language ability | General-purpose language ability |

Figure 1.3. Educational Uses for Language Tests

Use

Low stakes ← | | | | | → High stakes

| Diagnosis | Achievement in a class | Placement in a class or program | Admissions | Certification |

learners an opportunity to determine how well they know a particular lexical distinction, for example. Based on their score, learners can decide for themselves whether or not they wish to study this point further. Near the other extreme would be a test such as the TOEFL, which is intended to help admissions officers decide whether or not applicants' English is sufficient to undertake postsecondary studies in North American institutions. In other words, scores are used in a process involving great consequences for learners. Medium-stakes decisions include those made on the basis of test results within language classes and programs.

A test's intended impacts refer to the effects that the test designer intends it to have on its users (see Figure 1.4). Entities potentially affected by a test, as Bachman and Palmer (1996) point out, include individuals (e.g., students and teachers), language classes and programs, and society. In the past, those who developed and chose tests might not have thought of positive impact as a concern, but in today's postmodern period, a test's impact should be considered along with its inference and use. For example, in developing the Basic English Skills Test, testers wanted to contribute to the improvement of adult education by providing a mechanism for accurate placement of students. One might argue that appropriate placement was intended to affect not only those involved in the ESOL programs but also the institutions and society in which the learners would be more likely to contribute positively as a result of achievement in ESOL classes.

Developing a test purpose statement should be the first step in choosing or developing a test. For example, a program seeking a test designed for selecting candidates for a training program on farming in the United States might develop their test purpose statement as follows:

> The test is needed to measure candidates' ability to speak about farming in English [inference] in order to select students for a short training program on farming in the United States [use] and to demonstrate to students and their sponsoring agency the level of their field-specific language ability to help focus training [impact].

Figure 1.4. The Scope of Impact of Language Tests

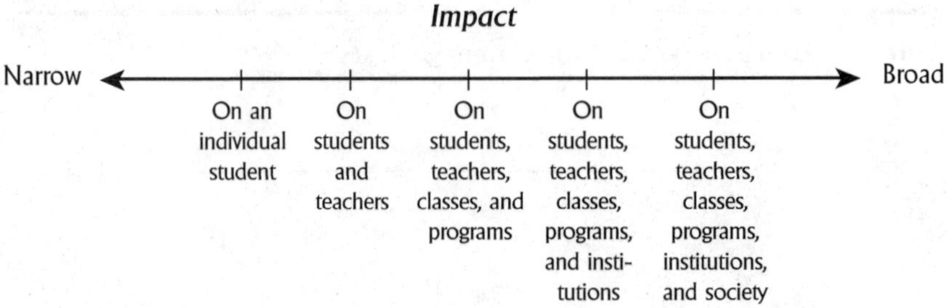

Impact

Narrow ← → Broad

On an individual student	On students and teachers	On students, teachers, classes, and programs	On students, teachers, classes, programs, and institutions	On students, teachers, classes, programs, institutions, and society

Understanding Test Method

A consideration of test purpose is possible only with a clear understanding of test method. It has been conceptualized in a number of different ways in work on language testing (e.g., Brown & Hudson, 1998; Cohen, 1994; Weir, 1990), but the most productive way of gaining new insight into test method is to draw from the perspective that treats tests as analyzable components or facets rather than as a menu of two or more types, such as alternative versus traditional or cloze versus multiple choice. This need was first addressed by Bachman (1990). In this book and a subsequent one (Bachman & Palmer, 1996), he outlined five facets of test method (also called test task characteristics) as a way of defining the important characteristics of language tests: the test setting; the testing rubric, which includes procedures for test taking expressed in the instructions as well as those for response evaluation; characteristics of the input to the learner; characteristics of the expected response; and the relationship between the input and the expected response. These facets of test method are useful for analyzing existing tests, describing the design of new tests, and envisioning possibilities for revising existing tests to better serve their purpose. In the interest of simplicity, however, in this chapter we describe existing tests by highlighting three aspects of the test method facets: the characteristics of the input; the characteristics of the expected response; and two aspects of the rubric, degree of examinee control over rubric and method for response evaluation.

Input to the Examinee

Input on a language test refers to the aurally and visually presented materials that are given to the examinee as part of the test tasks. For example, in the IELTS listening module, examinees listen to short monologues and conversations and respond to questions, often by filling in a diagram or gaps in a chart. The aural input is what examinees listen to, and the written input is what appears on the page. The aural input is for the most part linguistic whereas the written input is linguistic and nonlinguistic.

Bachman (1990) and Bachman and Palmer (1996) introduced a number of relevant categories for detailed analysis of the input, but in this simplified account, the characteristic of the input we consider is the length of any linguistic input that the test presents (see Figure 1.5). At one end of the continuum are tests composed of individual questions, such as one finds on the Combined English Language Skills Assessment in a Reading Context, a multiple-choice cloze test of grammatical knowledge and comprehension of language meaning in context. On the other end are tests that require the learner to comprehend and integrate ideas in the target language. The TOEFL reading subtest, with its reading passages and comprehension questions, is an example of a test near that end.

Figure 1.5. A Range of Possible Input in Language Tests

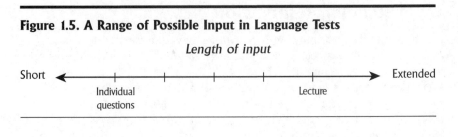

Length of input

Short ← — — — → Extended

Individual   Lecture
questions

Examinees' Responses

Messick (1994) cautioned against making a dichotomous distinction between *multiple-choice items* and *open-ended performance tasks* and argued that they represent "different degrees of response structure" (p. 15). Similarly, the dichotomy *selected* versus *constructed* (see Figure 1.6) is too clear-cut a distinction to describe response types meaningfully. Messick submitted that multiple-choice assessments constitute one end of a continuum whereas "student-constructed products or presentations" (p. 15) form the other.

Characteristics of the Rubric

The rubric includes all aspects of the procedures for administering and taking the test as well as the methods used to evaluate the examinees' responses. Two aspects of the rubric are of concern here: the role of the examinee in structuring the response and the method of evaluating responses. The amount of responsibility the learner has for structuring responses can vary from no responsibility to full responsibility (see Figure 1.7). For example, examinees may respond to a restricted set of alternatives that have been structured for them. Other examples of less traditional test methods, nonetheless structured, include use of a fixed-response protocol, checklist—to assess either a product or a process—inventory, or scale. In other cases, learners construct responses or complete tasks that are partially structured for them, such as fill-in-the-blank, cloze procedure, short-answer, essay response to a prompt, and dictation or dictocomp. Partially structured forms of the open-ended protocol, checklist, inventory, or scale permit learners to respond to structured items and construct responses to open-ended items. Forms of assessment such as projects,

Figure 1.6. A Range of Possible Response Types in Language Tests

Response types

Selected ← — — — → Constructed

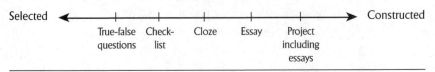

True-false Check-   Cloze   Essay   Project
questions   list   including
                                                    essays

14

Figure 1.7. A Range of Possible Levels of Responsibility for Learners

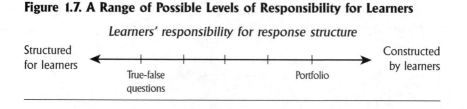

Learners' responsibility for response structure

Structured for learners ⟷ Constructed by learners

True-false questions

Portfolio

demonstrations, interviews, conferences, reflection journals or learning logs, portfolios, and open-ended introspective assessments represent responses that are structured, largely or completely, by the learner.

The method of evaluation can vary in terms of three factors: who does the scoring, whether the result is a single value or a profile, and whether the score is obtained by counting the number correct, judging the level of performance, or identifying the difficulty of items that examinees can consistently answer correctly. Table 1.2 shows how these three scoring options are combined in various tests. An assessment can be scored by, for example, an independent assessor, a teacher, a peer, or the learner. Most

Table 1.2. Factors in Scoring Various Tests

Factor: How is the test evaluated?	Factor: Who evaluates?			
	Independent assessor	Teacher	Peers	Learner
Number correct	Test of English as a Foreign Language (TOEFL): Reading Test (SS)	Woodcock-Muñoz Language Survey: Reading/Writing (SS)	—	—
Judgment of level	Basic English Skills Test: Interview (PP)	Maculaitis Test of English Language Proficiency II: Speaking/Writing (SS)	—	Canadian Academic English Language Assessment: Self-assessment (PP)
Difficulty of items correct	TOEFL Computer-Based Test: Grammar (SS)	—	—	—

Note. SS = single score; PP = profile of performance.

commercially produced forms of assessment call for structured responses scored by an independent assessor (often a machine) or a teacher. However, other forms of assessment can be scored by learners in ways that replicate the language and activities they engage in when they are learning or using the language in real or simulated ways. A third option for scoring concerns the actual result of the scoring process, that is, whether it results in a single score or a profile of performance.

Understanding Justification of Testing Practice

The third critical component of an assessment is the way in which the assessment is justified for its intended purpose. As described in the section Language Testing Research and Practice above, this justification refers to the validity argument that presents evidence for the appropriateness of test use in a particular situation. We gave some background for this approach to considering validity in the section Educational Measurement Theory above. The approach can be summarized as a set of principles, as shown in Table 1.3. These principles help guide the process of justifying test use, first by clarifying what validity is (i.e., an argument) and what it is not (i.e., a quality that is either present or absent in a test). The second principle asserts the primary authority of work in applied linguistics for developing a

Table 1.3. Principles for Justifying Language Test Use Through a Validity Argument (Chapelle, 2001)

Principle	Implication
Validity is an argument about the appropriateness of test use.	Tests are not valid or invalid; a test use is more or less valid depending on the evidence that supports the use.
Validation criteria for evaluating language tests should be based on work in applied linguistics.	The specific practices of language test evaluation are best guided by theory and research in language testing.
Validation criteria must be applied in view of test purpose.	The purpose of a test must be clearly specified in order to consider questions about validity.
Construct validity is central in test evaluation.	The construct that the test is intended to measure must be clearly defined, and other evaluative issues about a test should be secondary.
Tests need to be evaluated through logical and empirical analyses.	Methodologies for examining the test method and the performance are needed.

validity argument. This, of course, includes perspectives from the L2 classroom, such as the need to use tests that are consistent with instruction. The third principle links the validity argument to test purpose as defined above. Because the validity argument pertains to test use in a particular context, the purpose of the test in that context figures into the validity argument.

The fourth principle is related to the third. *Construct validity* refers to the extent to which evidence suggests that the test measures the construct it is intended to measure, in other words, that the inference specified as one facet of test purpose is justified. Construct validity is considered central because the test needs to measure what the user intends to measure if the test is to be used appropriately and have the intended impacts. The fifth principle refers to how validity arguments about test use are developed. It suggests that tests should be examined and that judgments should be made about test methods and test performance. Chapter 4 describes these methodologies in greater detail; here we explain important concepts associated with these analyses.

Essential Vocabulary

A full consideration of language tests and testing requires a working knowledge of the terminology used to express and develop knowledge of this domain. In this section we define the vocabulary used to discuss and evaluate language tests and test results. Of course, these terms are also associated with the three essential components of testing described above: test purpose, test method, and test justification.

Test Purpose Vocabulary

Because test purpose is central to all language testing, a number of specialized terms exist for talking specifically about it. As we have noted, test purpose consists of three components: the inference, the use, and the intended impact of the test. The inference that the test user wants to make about the examinee's language ability (e.g., listening comprehension, grammatical competence) can be defined in several different ways, one of which is called a *trait*. A trait is an unobservable construct that is expected to be constant across different situations. A score awarded for grammatical competence on the Michigan English Language Assessment Battery (MELAB), for example, is thought to indicate something about the examinee's general grammatical knowledge and ability to use that knowledge to perform certain language tasks, such as writing an academic essay or reading a journal article on the Web.

Another way of defining the inference to be made from a test is through *performance,* which refers to the language that the learner produces in a particular test. This use of the term *performance* is tied to the expression *performance assessment,* which refers to a test requiring learners to construct extended responses. Like so many of the concepts discussed in this chapter, the inference can be defined as a continuum, with the trait-type definition at one end and the performance-type at the other.

What lies between the two is an *interactionalist* construct definition, that is, an ability as it is expected to come into play in a particular set of circumstances (Chapelle, 1998). This way of defining inferences is probably the most interesting and useful. After all, very few language teachers would expect learners to call on the same grammatical competence when they order a pizza as when they write a letter of application to a chemistry department. At the same time, the idea that a learner's performance on a language test is a single, never-to-be-repeated event is untenable. The assumption must be that one is teaching and testing for some language use that extends beyond the educational events in which learners engage. The essence of an understanding of language testing is the nature of the inference to be made based on the test performance, although considerable attention has been directed to test use as well.

As a consequence, the discussion of test use involves a number of terms, including those associated with test scores, their description, and their interpretation. A *score* represents a summary of an examinee's performance across one or more tasks on a test. A score may be a single number or a profile describing performance on various components of the test. A score is often expressed as a number, but some test developers consider this appearance of precision to be misleading, and, indeed, it is, because a score should be viewed as indicating a point within the range where the examinee's true ability is likely to fall. To reflect this idea more explicitly than a single score does, some test developers report performance summaries within a band or range. Such reports are called *band scores.*

The examination and interpretation of test results is important and is predicated on the ability to understand certain terms and concepts. Test results are typically discussed in terms of selected statistical characteristics of a group of test scores. We describe many of the most basic terms in the balance of this chapter; these terms are used to describe the tests reviewed in chapter 2 and inform the discussion of test manuals presented in chapter 3. A more complete set of statistical definitions may be found in introductory statistics books and in books on testing.

Perhaps the most widely used statistical expression is *mean score,* which refers to the arithmetic average of all the scores within a group. A high mean score indicates that the test was easy relative to the ability of the examinees who took it. Another way of describing a set of scores is through their dispersion, or *variance,* in other words, how spread out they are. If all test takers score within 1–2 points of the mean, the variance for that group would be small; however, if test takers' scores fell within a wide range, say, within 80 points of the mean, the variance would be large. The common statistical term used to express the variance is the *standard deviation,* which refers to the average distance of scores from the mean.

An elaborate science has developed around the investigation of the characteristics of groups of test scores. The most familiar aspect of this work is that associated with the *normal distribution*; this term refers to a natural tendency for scores to disperse in a particular pattern, with the greatest number of scores clustering near the middle (i.e., the mean) and fewer distributed toward the ends of the scale. In fact, the normal distribution is characterized by a certain percentage of scores that should fall near the mean (i.e., 68% within 1 standard deviation). A normal distribution of test scores is the desired outcome for most tests used to make decisions about admissions or placement because decision makers want a test that shows differences in examinees' abilities. Imagine a director of an intensive English program who gives a placement test to 85 incoming students only to find that all learners have obtained a perfect score. This lack of distribution would indicate that the test did not identify any differences among learners' abilities and was therefore not at all useful for dividing the group of learners into meaningful clusters that might be used to place them in classes.

Such a decision about examinees' placement in classes is called a *norm-referenced* decision because it is made based on a comparison of an individual's abilities with those of other individuals who took the test. When the test has been taken repeatedly by examinees for whom it was intended, an individual's score can be compared with that of a larger *norm group,* a group from which typical performance statistics, or *norms,* have been obtained. Tests used in this fashion are often called *norm-referenced* tests. Another type of decision made on the basis of test scores is called a *criterion-referenced* decision. This term refers to a decision that evaluates an examinee's performance relative to a predetermined criterion, such as a particular score or level of performance on a test. Unlike the norm-referenced decision, in which an examinee's test score is compared with the scores of other examinees, for a criterion-referenced decision the score user sets a *cutoff score.* Examinees with scores above this cutoff are considered to have demonstrated a requisite level of ability.

Test impact refers to the effects of the test on those who use it. Since the 1980s, as language testers have become increasingly concerned with the broad scope of consequences of test use, the term *backwash* (or *washback,* which means exactly the same thing) has been coined to denote the effects of a test on test takers and particularly on teaching. Discussion of backwash has revealed that it is particularly potent (e.g., potentially dangerous) for *high-stakes* tests—tests that are used to make important decisions about examinees' lives. Tests used for certification of proficiency for employment, for example, are considered high stakes because results from such tests determine examinees' access to employment opportunities.

Test Method Vocabulary

In addition to the terms introduced in the section Understanding Test Purpose, another important term is *authenticity,* which, simply put, refers to the degree to which the test tasks, including the language, resemble those that examinees will encounter beyond the test setting. Authenticity is typically argued to be a desirable quality for a test, as we explain in chapter 4. Two other terms that have become widely used in describing language test methods are *discrete (point)* and *integrative. Discrete* refers to test tasks that aim to measure a single aspect of language knowledge, whereas *integrative* refers to those that require examinees to call on multiple aspects of language knowledge simultaneously. Authenticity is not necessarily connected to discrete or integrative test methods.

Test Justification Vocabulary

Test justification, or validation, entails a number of rational and empirical procedures for analyzing the appropriateness of a test for its intended purpose. As a consequence, the process of test justification draws from a set of concepts and terms for describing the characteristics of tests. Chapter 4 explores this broader conceptualization in considerable detail. In this section we define several important types of analyses that are used to establish reliability and validity evidence during test development.

The term *test item* is often used as if its meaning were clear-cut and well known. Most test designers would agree that a single question on a multiple-choice test represents an item, but what about a question (prompt) to which the examinee must respond by composing an essay? Or a portfolio composed of several essays? Because different types of tests ask examinees to respond to a variety of problems, language test designers and researchers often refer to a unit of activity on a test as a *task*. In other words, the terms *item* and *task* on a test are functionally equivalent.

One way of investigating the quality of a test is to examine test takers' responses to each of the test tasks in a process called *item analysis*. This process can entail a variety of qualitative and quantitative procedures, one of which is calculation of *item discrimination*. An item discrimination calculation shows the relationship between examinees' performance on a single item and their performance on the test as a whole. A good item is one that the low-ability test takers tend to answer incorrectly and that the high-ability test takers answer correctly.

A *correlation*—one of the most widely used calculations in test analyses—is an estimate of the strength of the relationship among two or more sets of performance. A *correlation coefficient* represents the statistical summary of the relationship between two sets of performances and permits the analyst to determine how strongly related or how similar they are. The type of correlation calculated depends on the type of data used, and its interpretation depends on the purpose for calculating it. For example, a *point-biserial correlation* is a discrimination index for dichotomous items (i.e., items with responses of *0/1*). The calculation estimates the relationship between the response to an item and the overall score on a test. *Spearman rank-order correlations* are used when one or both members in a set of data are ordinal, such as scores derived as a level of judgment rather than as a total number correct, if the number of cases is very small, or for any other reason a normal distribution of scores cannot be expected. *Pearson product–moment correlations* are used for sets of interval data when a near-normal distribution can be expected.

Also in the family of correlational techniques is the *multiple regression analysis,* a statistical procedure used for looking at relationships among sets of scores. Unlike simple correlations, it can be used to determine which combination of variables can best predict performance. *Factor analysis* is another powerful statistical procedure that is used to reduce a large number of variables (e.g., test or questionnaire items) to a smaller number (thought to represent the underlying abilities the test developer is seeking to measure) of variables. To achieve this reduction, the test developer clusters highly correlated variables to form *factors* and then subjectively identifies these factors as representing specific abilities (e.g., grammatical ability or listening ability). The developers of the MELAB utilized a factor analysis procedure to provide construct validity evidence for the overall test by analyzing the similarity of the scores within two components of the test (i.e., grammar/vocabulary/reading and listening) and across two forms of the test.

Reliability (discussed further in chapter 4) as the term is used in testing manuals can be construed as the consistency of the test scores or the absence of error from a set of test scores. A test score is said to contain error if it reflects more than what the test developer wishes to assess; for example, in the case of a language test, error would be anything other than language ability. Measurement error can be attributed to a variety of sources: noise in the test environment, cheating, or the fact that examinees have jet lag, for example. The statistical index that expresses the amount of error estimated to be present in a set of scores is the *standard error of measurement.* This concept is a convenient way to account for the imprecision in a test, and it allows test users to estimate the range within which a test taker's true score is likely to lie.

The opposite of error, *reliability,* is expressed as a coefficient between the values of 0 and 1. It can be calculated in several different ways, and each method of calculating reliability provides a different type of information about the reliability of the scores. *Internal consistency reliability* (e.g., using the *Kuder–Richardson [K-R] 20* statistical procedure) estimates the degree of consistency reflected in the test scores that is due to variation among the test tasks and other factors internal to the test. Because internal consistency is based on item variance, it is dependent on the number of test items and on the range of ability of the test population. An *interrater reliability* analysis shows the degree of consistency between scores based on raters' judgments. *Intrarater reliability* indicates the degree of consistency among judgments made by the same raters on two different occasions. *Test-retest reliability* indicates the degree of consistency between test performance at two different times. For this type of reliability to be calculated, the examinees have to take a test twice.

Some of the terms associated with the study of validity are changing as the shifts in ideas about validity mentioned above gain acceptance. Because the investigation of validity is really a process of considering evidence for and against test interpretations and uses, the terms used today generally refer to types of evidence rather than types of validity, as in the past. Many test manuals, however, continue to refer to types of validity rather than validity evidence.

Concurrent validity, or concurrent evidence, is established when strong positive correlations exist between the test of interest and another test or criterion of the same construct. *Concurrent* in the expression means that the other test scores have to be obtained at the same time as the score on the test of interest. *Criterion-related validity evidence* is similar to concurrent validity but is established by comparing performance on a specific test with performance on an external criterion (which may be another test or assessment, e.g., teacher judgments or course grades). High correlations between the test of interest and the specified criterion may be offered as *predictive evidence for validity.* Predictive validity is achieved by establishing how well performance on the test of interest predicts performance on some other test or criterion. *Content-related validity* is obtained by systematically collecting the judgments of experts who agree the test items are good indicators of what the test is intended to measure. This kind of validity evidence can refer to either or both of two conditions: the adequacy of the sample language being tested or the judgment of experts regarding whether the items assess what the test developer claims the items are intended to test. Evidence for *construct validity* can be drawn from any data that support the hypothesis that the test measures the construct as defined in the statement of test purpose (i.e., the inference). One of the many ways to find this evidence is through studies that demonstrate that particular examinees score systematically better than others for reasons other than the language ability tested. Such systematic error is referred to as *test bias.* Test bias can result from test methods, test takers' characteristics, or other factors.

A term that still appears in the language testing literature but has little if any technical meaning is *face validity.* This term has been used to denote that test users and test takers feel that the test is a fair and reasonable test of what it is intended to measure. However, it is not clear how this quality should be documented or whether positive attitudes toward a test should be considered a form of validity evidence at all.

Conclusion

This chapter has laid the groundwork for examining current ESOL tests and assessments. We have reviewed the historical division that exists between language teachers and language testers as well as the changes over the past 20 years that make such a division untenable for both groups in the postmodern period of language testing. In order to reconceptualize testing and assessment in a more productive way, we have rejected the distinction between the two and introduced concepts and terms for understanding the notions within the domains of *test purpose, test method,* and *test justification.*

Chapter 2

Locating English Language Tests and Test Reviews

We begin this chapter with an overview of useful sources of information on language testing followed by reviews of 20 language tests. Although these tests represent only a sample of the tests used worldwide to assess English language ability, the reviews are a useful starting point for anyone interested in learning more about such tests.

Limitations of Published Resources

All published test references have certain limitations. Clearly, one of the most frustrating is that no single reference contains a review of every language test. Even the most comprehensive and authoritative reference, the *Mental Measurements Yearbook* (MMY) series, does not include a review of every published language test. Of the 369 tests reviewed in the 13th edition (Impara & Plake, 1998), less than 6% (21) are English language tests, and only 3 of these are ESOL tests (Comprehensive Adult Student Assessment System [CASAS], IDEA Reading and Writing Proficiency Tests, and Woodcock-Muñoz Language Survey [WMLS]). The 12th edition (Conoley & Impara, 1995) reviews 4 ESOL tests (Language Assessment Scales, Listening Comprehension Test [LCT], and Woodcock Language Proficiency Battery— Revised), and the 11th edition (Kramer & Conoley, 1992) reviews three (Basic English Skills Test [BEST]; Test of English for International Communication [TOEIC]; and ELSA: English Language Skills Assessment in a Reading Context, the precursor to the Combined English Language Skills Assessment in a Reading Context [CELSA]). *Test Critiques,* another respected source of test reviews, reviews only 7 ESOL tests (Bilingual Syntax Measure [BSM] II, LCT, Henderson-Moriarty ESL/Literacy Placement Test, IDEA Proficiency Test [IPT] I and IPT II—Oral English, Test of Written English, and Woodcock Language Proficiency Battery) through Volume 10 (Keyser & Sweetlands, 1994). In contrast to general resources like *MMY* and *Test Critiques*, the collection of tests in this chapter is one of the most comprehensive available for widely used and significant tests of ESOL.

A lesser limitation of most collections is the fact that each entry is prepared by a different author, which often leads to considerable variation in the organization, content, and style of test review entries. To enhance the comparability of the reviews in this chapter, the contributors adopted the same terminology and format, and a style consistent with general academic writing.

Finally, during the lag between the preparation and publication of a reference, the price, contact information, and even ownership of a test can change. Given the inherent limitations in compiling a set of published test reviews, test users are advised to consult a variety of sources when investigating a particular test.

Useful Resources in Language Testing

The resources outlined in this section are important sources of information on a wide range of ESOL tests and test reviews. An additional resource is the annotated bibliography at the back of this volume.

Online Resources

With the advent of the Internet, information on a particular test is often only a keystroke away. Moreover, Web sites are proliferating at such an astonishing rate that it is impossible to compile a current list of every site containing relevant information. In addition to the sites maintained by test publishers, useful Web sites include those operated by nonprofit organizations and some individuals. The information available on the Internet varies widely, and a site's content reflects the biases of the people who designed and maintain it. A thorough investigation of any test should combine information obtained from online sources with that gleaned from credible published resources.

One of the most useful nonprofit sites is the National Clearinghouse for English Language Acquisition and Language Instruction Educational Programs (http://www.ncela.gwu.edu/). This site has links to other sites where related information is available.

Federally supported educational research centers, usually associated with universities, are another online resource. The National Center for

Research on Evaluation, Standards, and Student Testing at the University of California, Los Angeles (http://cresst96.cse.ucla.edu/), is a good example of a federally supported, university-based site. Web sites maintained by individuals can be helpful, too, and some offer connections to other related sites. Glenn Fulcher, a language testing specialist at the University of Dundee, has maintained the *Resources in Language Testing Page* (Fulcher, 2004, http://www.dundee.ac.uk/languagestudies/ltest/ltr.html) since 1995, and it has many useful links.

To find test publishers or test reviews, begin by accessing the Web sites of test publishers. The Buros Institute (http://buros.unl.edu/) advertises its products and services on its Web site. You can also locate a test publisher by visiting the Association of Test Publishers' site (http://www.testpublishers.org/) or the Educational Testing Service (ETS) site (http://www.ets.org/), where directories of tests and their publishers are posted. Buros and ETS have combined their resources to support test and test review locators.

Print References

Printed testing references are a crucial source of impartial information on tests. Although testing specialists prepare the resources, they are intended for both specialists and nonspecialists, that is, educators, students, and other consumers of tests.

Four of the most significant references are published by the Buros Institute (distributor of *Tests in Print* and *MMY*) and Pro-Ed (publisher of *Tests: A Comprehensive Reference for Assessments in Psychology, Education, and Business* and *Test Critiques*). All are available in most large academic libraries. These comprehensive indexes operate as sets; Buros' *Tests in Print* and Pro-Ed's *Tests* each inventory published tests that can be purchased by test consumers, and each is complemented by its respective companion volume, *MMY* and *Test Critiques*. The test inventories contain abbreviated, descriptive information about a test, including its name, publication date, purpose, publisher, cost, and scoring method. *Tests in Print* is cross-referenced to the corresponding *MMY* edition(s), where a more detailed description of the test appears with an evaluative review and additional references. *Test Critiques* includes a cumulative index back to Volume 3 (1984) in each new volume; the most current at the time of writing is Volume 10 (Keyser & Sweetlands, 1994). The cumulative test index is located in the back of the volume, and each entry is followed by the corresponding volume in which a test review appears. Each new edition of *MMY* includes only new tests or previously reviewed tests that have been substantially revised. Therefore, the most efficient way to search for a specific test is by consulting the cumulative index in *Tests in Print* and, after determining that the test is included in the resource, to select the *MMY* edition in which the test is reviewed.

Another source of impartial ESOL test reviews is the international journal *Language Testing,* which is dedicated to the study and dissemination of research on language testing, especially ESOL testing. The journal publishes test reviews prepared by qualified test specialists who proffer valuable appraisals of tests of interest to ESOL teachers and programs. Although the journal is not widely circulated, it is found in a number of academic libraries, and individuals may purchase subscriptions. *Language Testing*'s primary audience is test specialists, but the test reviews are expected "to inform prospective users and decision-makers of the appropriateness of the assessment for the intended uses, likely consequences of use, relative costs, and known limitations of the assessment of and potential misuses and misinterpretations of score information . . ." ("Notes on the Test Review Feature," 1999, p. 127).

ETS Bulletins, Monographs, and Research Reports

ETS distributes *Test Bulletins,* which announces updates and includes useful information on the tests that the organization publishes. ETS also sponsors and conducts in-house research on its products. Although the primary audience for ETS's monographs and research reports is researchers and testing specialists, many of the publications are available to any interested reader and offer thorough examinations of the scholarship on a current topic of interest to test developers and ESOL program administrators. Monograph 15 (Bailey, 1999), titled *Washback in Language Testing,* for example, considers washback and its implications for the Test of English as a Foreign Language Computer-Based Test (TOEFL CBT).

TOEFL Research Reports are technical studies of specific tests or topics. One report (Ginther, 2001) examines the effect of using different visuals on examinees' performances on the Listening component of the computerized version of the TOEFL, and another (Powers, Schedl, Wilson-Leung, & Butler, 1999) discusses the validity of a revised form of the Test of Spoken English (TSE).

Handbook of English Language Proficiency Tests

Handbook of English Language Proficiency Tests (Del Vecchio & Guerrero, 1995, http://www.ncela.gwu.edu/pubs/eacwest/elptests.htm) is an interesting example of a resource devoted to a small subset of ESOL tests. Despite its seemingly comprehensive title, this free online resource includes descriptions of only five language tests (Basic Inventory of Natural Language, BSM I and II, IPT, Language Assessment Scales, and WMLS). The authors justify their focus on these particular tests because they are used in U.S. K–12 school systems to determine students' eligibility for bilingual education services (under Title VII of the Elementary and Secondary Education Act). This resource, however, gives only descriptive information and offers no evaluative appraisals of the tests. Entries include the title of the test, the publisher, contact information, and a brief summary followed by a more detailed description of the test's purpose, target population, administration time, cost, item types, scoring, design and theoretical assumptions, and reliability and validity evidence. At the end of each entry, the authors cite any published test reviews.

Reviews of English Language Proficiency Tests

Alderson, Krahnke, and Stansfield (1987) edited the first and most comprehensive resource devoted exclusively to ESOL tests. Their book was an ambitious undertaking that included descriptive and evaluative information on 46 of the most widely used commercial ESOL tests in use at the time. An extremely popular and valuable reference for practicing ESOL professionals, *Reviews of English Language Proficiency Tests* is the impetus and inspiration for this chapter.

In the preface to *Reviews,* the editors explain the criteria they used to select the tests and the process employed to produce the reviews. Two criteria guided their selections: The test had to be available to users who wished to purchase it—in effect, it had to be a published test—and it had to be "relatively widely used" (Alderson et al., 1987, p. i). The editors indicated that they gradually compiled a list of tests on the basis of informal discussions with a number of test users. The list was circulated among testing professionals, in particular those active in ESL/EFL testing, over a period of several years to determine whether tests should be added or deleted.

Two of the editors shared the responsibility for commissioning reviews. Each invited qualified reviewers and communicated to them the format and expectations for preparing test descriptions and evaluations. These two editors critiqued the reviews prepared by each of their respective reviewers, and the third editor verified the information in each entry. Completed reviews were sent to other test review authors for an independent assessment, which in some cases led to revisions. Finally, each review was sent to the relevant test publisher, which sometimes resulted in additional revisions to the review.

Each review had two parts. The first consisted of an abbreviated overview of the test, including the name, purpose, target population, cost, publisher information, author, date of publication, and pertinent specifics on administering and scoring the instrument. The second part offered a 900- to 2,500-word description and evaluative commentary on the test.

The Reviews in This Volume

The tests in this volume were selected on the basis of the same criteria used in *Reviews* (i.e., the tests are commercially available and widely used).

However, in addition to using the judgments of various test users and test specialists in determining the latter, we conducted a telephone survey of a random, stratified sample of 160 current TESOL members to learn which commercial language tests were most widely used in the respondents' ESOL programs. The survey results led us to include reviews of several tests that we otherwise might not have included. Finally, we applied a third criterion: the ability of a test to illustrate important concepts presented in other chapters of this book.

The process of preparing test reviews for this volume was nearly identical to the one followed in *Reviews*, except that entries did not undergo independent peer evaluation. Entries in this volume range from 1,000 to 2,500 words and include the test's name, publisher and contact information, publication date, target population, and cost.

The narratives are divided into three parts that correspond to the major considerations presented in chapter 1: test purpose, test methods, and test use. Under the heading of test purpose, reviewers consider inferences and types of decisions that can be made based on test performance as well as the impact of the test on test takers and others. Test methods are described in terms of the input test takers receive, the response types, and the way test performance is scored or evaluated. The final section of each review addresses the issue of justifying the use of the test for particular purposes, including a consideration of the validity and reliability evidence presented by publishers and judgments about the suitability of the test for various contexts and purposes. Reviewers were encouraged to use the terminology presented in chapter 1 whenever possible to enhance the readability and comparability of entries.

All printed material is subject to change, and the tests and the reviews of them in this chapter are no exception, although every effort was made to ensure that the information in this chapter was accurate and current at the time of writing. Some tests (e.g., the IPT I and the Maculaitis Assessment of Competencies Test of English Language Proficiency II [MAC II]) are revised and sometimes superseded by new ones. The Michigan English Language Assessment Battery (MELAB) and the TOEFL CBT represent alternatives to previous tests (the Michigan English Language Proficiency Test and the TOEFL) distributed by their respective publishers. Even when the content of a test remains the same, the price and contact information often change. Consequently, the information in this chapter should not be considered apart from other sources, including current information available from the publisher and more recent reviews. Most, but not all, publishers maintain Web sites that are a convenient source of the latest contact information, price, and updates. Moreover, many sites contain order forms that can be printed or submitted online, and some publishers even post technical reports on their tests.

ACT ESL Placement Test

Reviewed by Sari Luoma

Publisher:	ACT Educational Services Division, 2201 North Dodge Street, Iowa City, IA 52243-0168 USA; telephone 319-337-1000; fax 319-337-1790; http://www.act.org/esl /index.html
Publication Date:	1999
Target Population:	ESOL students at postsecondary educational institutions in the United States. The product is sold to institutions, which can use it to place students into ESOL or mainstream courses.
Cost:	Included as an option within the COMPASS/ESL assessment system. US$450.00 per campus for COMPASS/ESL annual license plus US$1.10–$1.30 per administration for 1–4,999 units. Institution-specific descriptive reports and placement analysis services are available for supplementary fees.

Test Purpose

The ACT ESL Placement Test is a computer-adaptive test that guides the placement of non-English-speaking students in postsecondary education into appropriate English support programs or into mainstream classes. According to the publisher, institutions can also use the system to measure students' progress and obtain advice on enrollment and retention patterns (ACT, 2000c, pp. 2, 4). Institutions can localize the placement reports by adding information and advice relevant to their setting.

The ACT ESL package contains three tests: Grammar/Usage, Reading, and Listening. Scores are reported separately for each test. Institutions may use any or all of them and may combine the package with local, performance-based assessments.

All the ACT ESL tasks are presented on the computer in a multiple-choice format; students respond by clicking on the computer's mouse. Each test is typically 10–15 items long (ACT, 2000b, p. 103). The tests are not timed, but they typically take approximately 20 minutes each.

The test assesses students' abilities to recognize, understand, and manipulate standard American English (ACT, 2000c, p. 4). The Grammar/Usage test focuses on sentence elements such as verbs, subjects, modifiers, and conventions, and on sentence structure and syntax. The Reading test assesses reading explicitly stated material and inferential reading, and the Listening test assesses the ability to understand explicitly and implicitly stated information in standard American English. The language use contexts range from everyday situations to academic texts and classroom discourse.

31

Scores are reported in terms of five levels and as a more detailed score (1–99) that estimates the proportion of items in the item pool that the student would answer correctly.

The proficiency descriptors describe what typical students at each of five levels can recognize or understand and how consistently they can do so. The Grammar/Usage descriptors focus on language forms, and the Reading and Listening descriptors give more emphasis to text types and content areas. For example, according to the information brochure (ACT, 2000c), students at Grammar/Usage Level 1 "typically recognize simple present tense, plurals, correct word order in simple sentences, and simple pronominal references" (p. 7). At Reading Level 2, students "typically are able to read brief prose composed of short, simple sentences related to everyday needs," such as street signs and simple instructions, and at Level 4 they can typically "read for many purposes at a relatively normal rate with greater comprehension, and they can read materials that are increasingly abstract and grammatically complex" (p. 8). Students at Listening Level 3 "are able to understand most discourse about personal situations and other everyday experiences" and "can understand most exchanges which occur at a near-normal to normal conversational rate" (p. 9). No assumptions are made about test takers' ability to use English in interaction.

The main intended uses of the ACT ESL Placement Test are placement and diagnosis, which means that the test can be categorized as medium stakes. The principal parties affected by test use are students, teachers, classes, and programs within institutions that use the test. The potential positive impacts of the test for students are that they get appropriate English instruction in a group with shared learning goals, and once they proceed through an English program within an institution, they will be able to cope with the demands of the mainstream courses in the institution. Potential negative impacts include the possibility that test takers are incorrectly placed and either face a class that is too demanding for them or have to spend more time learning English than they need. These potential negative impacts can be alleviated by institutional policies that encourage teachers to conduct informal classroom assessments during the first few lessons to confirm that learners are placed correctly. Responsibility for such proce-dures, however, rests with the test user rather than the test developer.

Test Methods

The ACT ESL Placement Test focuses on language comprehension and manipulation. The test input ranges from short phrases or utterances, to paragraph-length texts and brief conversational exchanges, to multi-paragraph texts and short academic lectures designed to simulate language used in college classrooms. The test items are highly structured, as only the selected-response item formats of gap filling and traditional multiple choice are used.

Test performances are scored automatically while the test is in progress.

The results are calculated by determining the difficulty of items answered correctly and are expressed as an estimate of the proportion of the item pool that the student would get correct. The estimate is also converted into a level score.

Justifying Test Use

Based on procedures for COMPASS/ESL Writing Skills, Reading, and Mathematics tests, which have been available since 1994, the *COMPASS/ESL Reference Manual* (ACT, 2000b) explains in detail how placement validity indices will be calculated for the ESOL tests evaluated here. The methodology relies on logistic regression, which accounts for student placement into developmental courses versus the standard course and for students' degree of success in the standard course—the variable of interest in placement. Once operational data for the ESL test exist, these indices will provide useful predictive validity information. Although the 2000 *Reference Manual* does not contain this information, indications at the time of writing were that ACT was collaborating with institutions to supply it in the future. After the writing of this review, ACT (2001) released an updated version of the *ACT ESL Placement Test Research and Data Report* that includes an analysis of more than 22,000 student data sets, each test having been taken by over 7,000 students. The report also includes a case study from one college that indicates support for using the test in course placement.

A detailed report on the development of the ACT ESL tests (ACT, 2000b) indicates that the developers followed the guidelines presented in *Standards for Educational and Psychological Testing* (Joint Committee on Standards for Educational & Psychological Testing, 1999). This statement lends credibility to the content validity argument that ACT can present for the ESL test. The argument could be strengthened further by conceptual analyses of the relationship between test content and the level descriptors. ACT (2000a) indicates that the scale development was based solely on experiential/intuitive methods (for alternatives, see, e.g., Council of Europe, 2001, pp. 207–211). Qualitative content analysis of the test items to see if the skills tested correspond to the descriptors at various scale ranges, a content analysis of the response patterns of students scoring within specified score ranges, or both, might enhance the construct validity argument for the test, especially because the items in the ACT ESL item pools have already been placed on a common measurement scale.

The reliability figures reported for the ESL tests are .85 (ACT, 2000b), which is sufficient for classifying students into four categories. In the absence of data from operational use, the figures are based on a calibration study encompassing 7,285 students, on simulation studies, or on both. Conditional standard errors of measurement (CSEMs) are also reported, and these figures will be useful once data from operational administrations become available. The current CSEM estimates are approximately half a band wide.

Based on the careful reporting of test development, a promising approach to reporting validity and reliability information, and a willingness on the part of the developers to collaborate with test users and support localized validation studies, the ACT ESL Placement Test seems suitable for placement purposes in postsecondary education in the United States. However, further studies of operational use of the test would lend more support to this recommendation. Because no studies have been published on the use of the ACT ESL Placement Test in progress testing, test users should take a cautious, experimental approach to its use for that purpose.

Basic English Skills Test (BEST)

Reviewed by Gillian Wigglesworth

Publisher:	Center for Applied Linguistics, 4646 40th Street NW, Washington, DC 20016 USA; telephone 202-362-0700; fax 202-362-3740; http://www.cal.org/
Publication Date:	1984, 1989
Target Population:	Adult learners of English
Cost:	US$150

Test Purpose

The BEST is designed to provide information about the oral and literate language development of adult learners of English. The test measures the extent to which they have attained the language skills necessary to communicate their daily basic needs; these learners may not yet have the language skills that might be expected for employment purposes.

The BEST offers useful information for users who work in English language programs. The test can provide information on student placement or progress, or it can give feedback on students' linguistic and sociolinguistic knowledge. In addition, the test may indicate learners' readiness for more advanced courses of study or, when used as a pre- and posttest, may contribute to evaluating programs of instruction.

Test Methods

The test consists of two components—an Oral Interview and a Literacy Skills section—and takes approximately $1\frac{1}{4}$ hours to complete. This review is based on an examination of complete sets of materials for Forms B and C. Scaled scores are comparable across the two forms.

The Literacy Skills component of the test, which takes 1 hour to complete, can be administered individually or in groups. Items assessing reading and writing are interleaved. The reading test consists of varied everyday activities designed to elicit basic language skills, which include identifying dates from a calendar, noting prices from price labels, finding telephone numbers in excerpts from directories, and reading timetables. In addition, test takers must select appropriate vocabulary from a group of three alternatives in the context of a reading passage. A variety of simple texts (e.g., appointment cards, advertisements or notices of various kinds) serve to test text comprehension through multiple-choice items. Writing skills are evaluated through filling out forms, writing checks and addressing envelopes, and reading short functional texts and responding to a simple prompt.

All reading items are scored as either correct or incorrect. Scoring for writing items, however, varies with the task. For example, achieving a full score on the task of writing out a check requires supplying five pieces of information. On the envelope task, obtaining the score of 2 requires addressing the envelope accurately and legibly; partial scores are not given. The short texts are scored 5, 3, 1, or 0. Responses are scored as a whole according to descriptors exemplified below:

5 An extensive amount of relevant, comprehensible information is conveyed. Accuracy in grammar or spelling is not required. If a letter was requested, letter form is NOT required.

3 A reasonable amount of relevant, comprehensible information is conveyed; examinee shows an attempt at elaboration.

1 Only "bare bones" information is given in response to the question. This score should be awarded if any amount of relevant, comprehensible writing is present.

0 Some writing is present, but it is either irrelevant to the question or completely incomprehensible; no writing at all is present.

The test manual (Kenyon & Stansfield, 1989) includes a number of writing examples, with explanations as to score achieved, to assist in the scoring process.

The oral component of the test is designed to evaluate speaking and listening. It is administered individually and examined concurrently by the interviewer. The test taker is given a booklet with picture prompts. The interviewer's booklet has considerable detail about the conduct of the interview, possible test taker responses, and score options. The Oral Interview can be administered in its full extended version or as a short form, which is a subset of the original. The short form is designed as a 5- to 7-minute pretest that can be used for placement purposes in large programs already using the BEST. The two versions are considered comparable, and a table allows the conversion of scores from the short form to scaled scores on the extended version.

Both interview versions use a range of questions and picture prompts to elicit responses. In the extended version, individual items are scored for listening comprehension, communication, or fluency, although several items may occur within a single task, such that all three abilities are tested within the task. A holistic score is given for pronunciation. In the short form, only fluency and communication are assessed. Fluency items are generally preceded by unscored introductory items that serve as a warm-up. As with the Literacy Skills module, the items are designed to reflect the kind of language test takers might reasonably be expected to use in real-life situations, such as asking for directions (e.g., "Where's the market?") or asking about prices. Other tasks ask learners to respond to the interviewer's questions about specific picture prompts, such as a doctor's waiting room or the scene of an accident. Some items (identified in the interviewer booklet) request elaboration; for example, the learner might be asked to compare some activity (e.g., visiting the doctor) in the United States with that activity in the learner's native country. The final task in the Oral Interview invites the test taker to complete a form (name, address, and date). This is scored before the interviewer decides whether to proceed to the literacy section of the assessment and may serve to exclude test takers from that section when it is likely to be inappropriate.

Scoring the oral test is somewhat complex. Listening skills are scored dichotomously, communication on a 3-point scale (0–2), and fluency on a 4-point scale (0–3). Each skill set relates to separate questions, and the examiner's task is simplified by the use of coded score slots in the test booklet and on the score sheet (e.g., a triangle for listening, a circle for fluency). On completion of the interview, the examiner gives an overall score for pronunciation on a 3-point scale (1–3).

The Oral Interview is supported by a training video (Clackamas Community College, 1993) that focuses on the short form and gives instructions for preparation, administration, and scoring. The video gives explanations and examples of oral performances to describe the scoring procedures, and finishes with two practice tests for trainee examiners to score and compare with the given scores. The video is a suitable training forum for both forms and is designed to enhance rater reliability.

Justifying Test Use

Although the Literacy Skills and the Oral Interview sections are scored independently, the result is a total score that relates to eight levels of performance (0–VII), each described as a general descriptor. The manual (Kenyon & Stansfield, 1989) also contains more detailed descriptions of each skill (listening, oral, writing, and reading) at each level as well as technical information related to the validity and reliability of the BEST. Each form of the test was field tested on about 300 learners, and the analysis of the results indicates high reliability for the total test and the subscales. Interrater reliability coefficients, although based on only two independent raters, are also high. Statistical information related to the test validity is also satisfactory, and the use of real-life language attests to the BEST's high face validity.

The BEST adopts a thorough yet practical approach, although it is somewhat dated (e.g., the calendars used are from 1984, and prices are quite unrealistic). The test is relatively easy to administer, with detailed instructions given. In sum, the test may be a useful tool for evaluating adult learners in second language (L2) programs that focus on developing learners' functional English. (Note that the BEST Oral Interview section is being replaced by the computer-adaptive, computer-assisted BEST Plus; see http://www.best-plus.net/ for details.)

Bilingual Syntax Measure (BSM) I and II

Reviewed by Lindsay Brooks

Publisher: Harcourt Assessment, 19500 Bulverde Road, San Antonio, TX 78259 USA; telephone 800-211-8378; http://harcourtassessment.com/

Publication Date: 1975 (BSM I), 1978 (BSM II)

Target Population: Students in Grades K–2 (BSM I) and 3–12 (BSM II)

Cost: US$449.50 for BSM I or BSM II, including 35 picture booklets, English child student response booklets, and Spanish child student response booklets; English manual; Spanish manual; class record; and technical handbook

Test Purpose

The BSM is designed to assess children's oral syntactical proficiency in English, Spanish, or both languages. The BSM I is for children in Grades K–2, and the BSM II is for children or adolescents in Grades 3–12. In the test manuals (Burt & Dulay, 1978; Burt, Dulay, & Hernández Chávez, 1975, 1976; Burt, Dulay, Hernández Chávez, & Taleporos, 1980), the publishers state that the BSM measures structural proficiency in English or Spanish as an L2, relative proficiency with respect to basic syntactic structures, and degree of maintenance or loss of basic Spanish structures. (The test could theoretically be used to determine the degree of maintenance or loss of basic English structures, although the publishers mention that this is less likely in the context of the United States.) Another stated application of the BSM is for eliciting natural speech samples for language acquisition research.

The BSM I and II are based on two fundamental concepts about language development. The first is that language structures are acquired hierarchically, with some grammatical structures (or morphemes) learned before others, and the second is that children's language acquisition occurs through "creative construction" (Burt et al., 1980, p. 3), whereby children create their own linguistic rules in the process of their language development. These two concepts form the framework for the test construction and scoring procedures. Although morpheme acquisition research was prominent in the 1970s and early 1980s, when the BSM was developed (see, e.g., Dulay & Burt, 1973), it has since come under criticism for, among other shortcomings (see Cook, 1993), presenting a limited view of language and language acquisition.

In the BSM, the only criterion for language proficiency is syntax, or grammar; inclusion of vocabulary, pronunciation, or functional uses of languages was rejected in the test development stage. Syntactical proficiency is defined in terms of a limited set of morphemes and structures. Because the test focuses narrowly on discrete syntactic points, inferences from the test are limited to the test taker's ability to respond accurately to questions in English, Spanish, or both using the prescribed grammatical structures the test was designed to elicit.

According to the test publishers, the test can determine test takers' structural proficiency and accuracy as well as their language dominance or relative language proficiency. Decisions about the syntactic proficiency of students are criterion referenced in that the cutoff scores can be used for placement into, for example, programs for students with limited language proficiency. This intended use of the test is medium stakes to even high stakes, as placement into such language programs can have a broad impact. Other uses of the test scores, such as for formative and summative evaluation, are low stakes, with a relatively narrow impact limited to the students and their teachers.

Test Methods

The BSM is administered individually, with the tester, usually the teacher, sitting beside the test taker. Designed to simulate a natural conversation, the test involves the tester asking a series of approximately 25 structured questions (depending on the language and level of the test) that are based on cartoonlike pictures. The pictures for the BSM II are considered more appropriate for older children than are the pictures used for the BSM I, and they contain a story line with a beginning, middle, and end. With several test items associated with one picture, each discrete-point test item is designed to elicit a certain grammatical response. The tester reads the items and in some cases points to aspects of the picture. Test responses are completely constructed; students can respond in a single word, a phrase, or a sentence. If the student points instead of responding verbally, the tester prompts the test taker to give an oral answer.

During the administration of the test, the tester records the test taker's responses verbatim in the student response booklet. To warm students up, the tester asks a series of preliminary questions, but the responses are not recorded or scored. The BSM takes approximately 10–15 minutes to administer in each language. The publishers recommend waiting several hours between tests if administering the English and the Spanish versions to the same child.

After the test, the tester hand-scores the test items as either grammatical or ungrammatical in the context of the question. For example, in a question in the BSM I, the tester points to baby birds and asks, "What are those?" to which a grammatical response, "ducks," would receive a score of 1 because the child used the plural /s/. An ungrammatical response, "duck," would be scored as 0 (Burt et al., 1976). No response or the response "I don't know" is scored as 0, as are responses that are partially in another language or conversationally inappropriate. Mispronunciation and conversational forms are acceptable.

In scoring the responses, testers are instructed to allow for regional or social group variations and "forms like 'theirselves' would be considered syntactically correct" as they "might be used by an adult native speaker of English" (Burt & Dulay, 1978, p. 6). The tester evaluates the test taker's responses to groups of questions and, at the end of the scoring procedure, arrives at one of five proficiency bands for the BSM I and one of six proficiency bands for the BSM II.

For Levels 1 and 2, *no English* and *receptive English only,* respectively, the number of questions answered is used to determine the level. For *survival, intermediate, proficient I,* and *proficient II,* corresponding to Levels 3–6, the number and type of grammatically correct answers is used. The results are reported in the form of a band level corresponding to a proficiency profile. The first five proficiency levels of the BSM I and BSM II correspond in that the test questions for each level represent the same syntactic hierarchies. However, the test developers caution that, when interpreting Level 5, users must consider which test they are giving. That is, a Level 5 on the BSM I, the highest level of proficiency, means that the test taker has mastered the syntactic structures expected from the age group represented in that test, but a Level 5 on the BSM II does not indicate mastery of the structures of proficient speakers in Grades 3–12. The highest proficiency band for the BSM II is Level 6, which reflects more complex grammatical structures. Additionally, the sixth level of BSM II is subdivided into two groups: *6N,* indicating native proficiency in nonstandard forms of English, and *6S,* which corresponds to native proficiency in the standard forms.

The possible uses of the BSM are listed in the test manuals, which briefly describe how the test results can be used. In the technical manuals for BSM I and II, through test-retest data, the test developers provide some empirical support for the use of the tests for placement purposes and the ability of the tests to determine students' language proficiency. Also provided are recommendations on test cutoff bands for use by schools to classify students as limited English proficient, non–English speaking, limited English speaking, and fluent English speaking. For students scoring not higher than 4 on either the English or the Spanish test, the publishers recommend that the school conduct further testing. The technical manuals include some construct validity and content validity evidence, but the evidence is weak and insufficient to support the use of the test for placement or diagnostic decisions, which are two of the intended uses of the test, according to the publishers. As evidence of construct validity, the test developers cite (a) the psycholinguistic research on natural sequences of language acquisition, (b) the acquisition hierarchy and scoring procedures they developed, and (c) the fact that the BSM classifications "reflect the relationships expected to be found among bilingual children" (Burt et al., 1976, p. 32). Despite the test developers' call for more research to add to the validity evidence, at the time of writing the publishers had not updated the technical manuals since they were originally published in 1976 (for BSM I) and 1980 (for BSM II).

As reliability evidence, the test publishers provide test-retest reliability for a sample of children who took the Spanish and English versions of the test two times approximately 2 weeks apart. For the BSM I—English version, one third of the 147 children were classified into different proficiency levels based on the two administrations of the test. Almost a quarter of the 143 children taking both administrations of the BSM I—Spanish version tested at different proficiency levels. The kappa coefficients of .62 and .64 for the English and Spanish tests, respectively, are considered low for decision-making purposes. Alpha coefficients of internal consistency reliability for the BSM II were .90 and .82 for the English and Spanish versions, respectively. Test-retest reliability evidence for the BSM II was determined in a study similar to that conducted for the BSM I. Almost one third of the 85 children taking the BSM II—English version in the study were placed in different levels on a subsequent administration of the test. The results for the Spanish version were more accurate, with 89% of the 80 children classified at the same level of proficiency over the two test administrations. In addition to test-retest reliability, other external factors such as interrater reliability need to be considered, but no interrater reliability evidence is provided for the BSM II. However, among the top three levels of the English and Spanish versions of BSM I, interrater reliability was 83.8% and 80.1%, respectively. These figures, however, take into account only the top three levels of the test because the first two levels are determined based on the number of answers only.

Justifying Test Use

Because of the limited validity and reliability evidence available, the BSM would be best used in the context of low-stakes, classroom-level formative assessment. That is, the test could be used to identify the strengths and weaknesses of some aspects of the students' grammar. The test would also be appropriate for diagnostic purposes, but only as a starting point to identify some of the gaps in the students' syntactical proficiency, as the test provides no clear diagnostic information.

Because of its theoretical constraints and because it elicits only a limited range of grammatical structures, the BSM should not be used as the only source of information about students in making medium- to high-stakes placement decisions, such as placement in an English support program. Although the publishers claim that the BSM represents a natural conversation, the speech elicited from the test is artificial in that the number and nature of the test questions restrict the range of responses. This limitation is particularly salient if the test user intends to use the proficiency scores or bands for decision making. The proficiency bands reflect whether the students have mastered the expected syntactic structures elicited by the test at one moment in time, which may or may not reflect the learners' actual grammatical proficiency. The test developers clearly state that the test measures syntactic proficiency, but the bands themselves are general descriptors of proficiency, including aspects of communication not included in the test. Test users should bear in mind that the BSM tests an extremely limited range of syntax; pronunciation, vocabulary, and strategic, discourse and sociolinguistic competence, important in determining a student's language proficiency, are not considered. Therefore, the BSM should not be used in isolation for individual placement or even diagnostic decisions. Gaining a rich overall picture of language proficiency requires multiple measures and tasks, which the BSM cannot provide.

Business Language Testing Service (BULATS) Language Tests

Reviewed by David D. Qian

Publisher:	Business Language Testing Service, University of Cambridge ESOL Examinations; see http://www.bulats.org/ or e-mail bulats@ucles.org.uk for information on local agents.
Publication Date:	1997–1998 (Standard Test, Writing Test, and Speaking Test), 2000 (Computer Test)
Target Population:	Business employees who need to use English in their work; job applicants looking for business-related employment requiring the use of English, and business trainees on English language courses
Cost:	In Hong Kong, HK$350 (£32) each for the Standard Test and Writing Test, HK$450 (£41) for the Speaking Test, HK$330 (£30) for the Computer Test. Discounts are available for groups of 50 or more.

Test Purpose

The BULATS English language tests are used to evaluate the English level of company employees and job applicants, place business trainees, and screen candidates for business training courses. All four tests can be considered high stakes because the results are mainly used for evaluating the English language ability of company employees, selecting new employees, and placing business trainees. Decisions based on BULATS test results can directly affect test takers' future careers. The tests are all administered outside the United Kingdom by local BULATS agents in various countries and regions. BULATS clients are usually companies and organizations rather than individuals.

Test Methods

In the following sections, the four tests are discussed separately.

BULATS Standard Test. The Standard Test is intended to make inferences about the test taker's overall English language ability in the business workplace by measuring listening and reading performance and knowledge of grammar and vocabulary. Like the results of other BULATS tests, results of the Standard Test are reported in individual score reports based on a scale of 0–5 linked to the Association of Language Testers in Europe (ALTE) Framework of Levels for Language Ability (ALTE, 2004b): upper advanced (Level 5), lower advanced (Level 4), upper intermediate (Level 3), intermediate (Level 2), elementary (Level 1), and beginner (Level 0). The score report of the Standard Test contains a brief description of the level the test taker has achieved, such as "Candidates at Level 4 are lower-advanced level, with a good operational command of English in a range of real world situations" (BULATS, 2000b, p. 1).

The test, which lasts 110 minutes, is composed of two sections: Listening, and Reading and Language Knowledge. In the 50-minute Listening section, test takers receive aural input (which includes brief conversations and monologues, telephone messages and conversations, and an extended dialogue or monologue, among other types) and written input in the form of prompts and rubrics in the test booklet. All items in the section are highly structured. With the exception of the telephone messages and conversations, which require partially constructed answers to fill the blanks, all other items basically involve only selected answers.

The 60-minute Reading and Language Knowledge section, in which test takers receive only visual input, consists of 10 subsections totaling 60 questions. Of these, 26 questions test reading comprehension based on a collection of notices, figures, charts, tables, discrete sentences and texts of various lengths (normally in the range of 10–450 words), and 24 questions measure knowledge of grammar and vocabulary in a variety of item formats, such as gapped sentences with multiple-choice tasks, open cloze, multiple-choice cloze, and contextualized error correction. Test takers are expected to provide selected answers to some items and construct short answers for others.

The test papers are hand-scored by independent assessors selected and trained locally by BULATS agents according to criteria set by University of Cambridge ESOL Examinations. The results are computed based on the total number correct. The score report contains an overall score, an ALTE level based on the overall score, and all sectional scores. Scores are not adjusted for difficulty because all versions of the test have been pretested for equal difficulty. Based on the following information provided by the Cambridge ESOL Research and Validation Group for a sample of 2,300 test takers before March 2001 (A. Geranpayeh, personal communication, July 2001), the distribution of scores appears reasonable.

Band level	Test takers (%)
5	1
4	8
3	20
2	30
1	30
0	11

All BULATS items are selected from the pool of University of Cambridge ESOL Examinations' item-banking system, where the items are quality checked, reviewed, banked, pretested, and then kept in the Live

Bank for administration (Beeston, 2000; A. Geranpayeh, personal communication, July 2001). The reliabilities of the test are reported in the range of .92 (Rasch) to .93 (alpha) (Jones, 2000).

The test is appropriate for business workers, business job seekers, and business trainees who need to demonstrate proficiency in English listening and reading comprehension and knowledge of English grammar and vocabulary. Because the test contains a variety of structured items, some more context dependent than others, it may have mixed washback effects on language learners. For example, some types of multiple-choice items can cause negative effects whereas some contextualized items may result in positive effects on language learning.

BULATS Computer Test. The Computer Test was developed as an alternative version of the Standard Test. Users of the Computer Test normally buy the number of tests they want to use on a CD-ROM controlled by a dongle that allows the user to run as many tests as have been bought. The program can be run from a networked CD-ROM drive or a server hard disk. When the user needs more units of the test, the dongle can be recharged by University of Cambridge ESOL Examinations via e-mail or courier. For organizations that regularly assess their employees' language ability, the Computer Test is probably preferable because it is efficient and saves substantial individual testing time.

The test is adaptive. Before it begins, the test taker is given an opportunity to practice on-screen. During the test, the computer program selects a more difficult or an easier subsequent question based on the result of the previous answer given. The questions are presented on-screen and the test taker answers them by using the computer keyboard and mouse. The test usually takes about 50 minutes and normally involves answering approximately 50 items. The types of questions used in this test are generally similar to those in the Standard Test, except that no test booklets are involved. However, once test takers complete a question and move onto a new screen, they are not allowed to return to the previous screen. The candidates are warned about this restriction before they begin the test. Test results, which include an overall score (out of 100) and an ALTE level, are generated on-screen immediately after the test. A full score report, containing the same information as in the score report for the Standard Test, can also be obtained on-screen. However, the test supervisor can opt to conceal the results from the test taker.

The reported average reliability for the current Computer Test is .94 (Jones, 2000). At the time of writing, University of Cambridge ESOL Examinations was developing a new, slightly longer version of the Computer Test that contained some item types different from those in the Standard Test. A study ($n = 81$) of the new version using the test-retest method obtained satisfactory r values between .93 and .94 (Geranpayeh, 2001). The study also found a higher test-retest correlation for the Computer Test (.93, *n* = 81) than between the Computer Test and the Standard Test (.86, *n* = 79, reported by Jones, 2000), which suggests that the mode of test administration has an effect on the results (Geranpayeh, 2001). Research also shows that candidates tend to perform better on the Standard Test than on the Computer Test and that scores on the Standard Test tend to have a narrower spread than those on the Computer Test (Jones, 2000). However, for practical purposes, it appears that University of Cambridge ESOL Examinations will maintain both formats.

BULATS Speaking Test. The Speaking Test is intended to make inferences about ability to speak English in performing business tasks by directly measuring the test taker's English-speaking performance. Based on test performance measured on the ALTE scale, proficient test takers are presumed to be able to communicate comfortably in a variety of business situations. For example, a Level 4 candidate is presumed to be able to talk persuasively, engage in long conversations, make clear presentations, and use the telephone for most purposes (BULATS, 2000a).

The Speaking Test is a face-to-face test conducted by a BULATS examiner, who evaluates the performance of the test taker holistically. The performance is audiotaped for a second assessor to evaluate later according to five criteria, namely, range of language use, language accuracy, pronunciation, ability to express opinions, and ability to interact. In the case of rater discrepancy of more than one band level, the performance is assessed by a third rater.

The test, which lasts 12 minutes, consists of three parts. In Part 1, the test taker and the examiner role-play an interview. The test taker answers questions about background, work, and interests. In Part 2, the test taker gives a short presentation based on a choice of written prompts supplied by the examiner. After the presentation, the test taker answers questions relevant to the topic. In Part 3, the examiner engages the test taker in a discussion of views and information on a topic related to Part 2. The score report contains a profile of the candidate's speaking ability in the business context, in the form of an ALTE level (0–5) with a brief description of the level, subscores on the above five specific criteria, and a *can-do* statement describing what the candidate is able to do in English. For example, Level 3 candidates can typically

- explain their point of view clearly, if it is on a familiar topic

- engage in conversation on general topics with a visitor

- give a simple, prepared presentation

- use the phone for familiar tasks (BULATS, 2000a, p. 1)

The test is appropriate for business workers, business job applicants, and business trainees who need to demonstrate their English-speaking ability to company employers or business trainers. The speaking tasks are communicative and require extensive use of constructed responses from the test taker, so they will likely have a positive effect on language learners because, to prepare for the Speaking Test effectively, learners will have to engage actively in oral communicative activities, which can be a natural part of language activities and facilitate their learning.

However, the usefulness (Bachman & Palmer, 1996) of the Speaking Test appears to be limited because the test requires highly trained examiners to ensure test quality. BULATS agents sometimes have difficulty summoning enough qualified examiners to assess a large number of examinees within a short timeframe.

BULATS Writing Test. The Writing Test is intended to make inferences about test takers' ability in business English writing by directly measuring their performance on business writing tasks. Based on test performance as measured on the ALTE scale of 0–5, proficient test takers are presumed to be able to write business correspondence of various types. For example, a Level 4 candidate will be able to "write most letters and correspondence needed in the course of work" and "write reports that communicate the desired message" (BULATS, 2000c, p. 1).

The test, which lasts 45 minutes, contains two parts. In Part 1, the test taker is given a short text of a business nature, often a memorandum or a letter, as well as instructions on constructing a reply of 50–60 words to the original prompts. Prompts for Part 2 usually contain two contextualized writing tasks. The test taker selects one of the tasks and writes a 180- to 200-word business text, such as a short report or a company profile.

The writing scripts are marked by two trained, independent raters. Test takers are assessed on language use, organization of ideas, and the overall effectiveness of their writing. In the case of a score discrepancy of more than one band level, a third rater is called on to assess the script. The score report contains a profile of the candidate's writing ability in the business context, including an ALTE level with a brief description of the level and a detailed can-do statement.

The test is appropriate for business workers, business job applicants, and business trainees who need to demonstrate their proficiency in business English writing to company employers or business trainers. Because the writing tasks are basically contextualized and test takers are required to construct extended answers based on limited written prompts, the test will likely have a positive effect on language learning activities by encouraging learners to work creatively in constructing their writing. However, there are obvious gaps between these writing tasks and real-life situations. The companies in the tasks are generally faceless (anonymous and without a geographic location), and writing prompts are often brief and general. Although this generality gives test takers much room to demonstrate their ability to create details, it may remind test takers that they are actually taking a writing test instead of using English in a real-life workplace.

Justifying Test Use

The four BULATS English language tests reviewed will likely make an important impact on test takers as well as test users, because requiring company employees, job applicants, and business trainees to take the BULATS tests will likely motivate test takers to engage in English language learning. In turn, this involvement will improve their English proficiency levels and enable them to contribute more to society by using English effectively in their work. In Hong Kong, the government's Workplace English Campaign (WEC), which aims to enhance the English language competency of the Hong Kong workforce, has used the BULATS tests to assess company employees' English proficiency levels. The long-term significance of the BULATS tests in Hong Kong will depend on how WEC evolves and especially on how favorably employers view these tests in the long run.

Most item types in the BULATS tests reviewed are context dependent. In particular, the Speaking Test and Writing Test are largely task-based, communication-oriented performance tests. Although there is still room for improvement, these characteristics have distinguished the BULATS tests favorably from some traditional language proficiency tests still in use.

If the Computer Test is viewed as an equivalent, or alternative, version of the Standard Test, the inventory of BULATS English tests actually consists of three independent measures (Standard Test, Speaking Test, and Writing Test), each with a somewhat different construct. Although there is some construct overlap among the three tests, these tests primarily measure different traits. A recent study (Lumley & Qian, 2001) has found some moderately strong correlations between the Standard Test and the Writing Test ($r = .70$, $R^2 = .49$, $n = 43$) and between the Standard Test and the Speaking Test ($r = .72$, $R^2 = .52$, $n = 39$). These figures, however, also indicate that the Standard Test cannot fully replace the other two tests in predicting candidates' English writing and speaking abilities in the workplace. Therefore, it is not justifiable to state that the results from the Standard Test alone can fairly reflect a candidate's writing or speaking ability; both are important language skills in the business workplace. In Hong Kong, however, when this review was prepared, taking the Standard Test was a prerequisite to sitting for the BULATS Writing Test or Speaking Test. The sponsoring organization is therefore strongly advised to find out the local situation before registering its employees for BULATS tests, especially when the organization has a tight budget.

Canadian Academic English Language (CAEL) Assessment

Reviewed by Carolyn E. Turner

Publisher: Carleton University; contact Usman Erdosy, CAEL Assessment Testing Manager, Testing Unit, CAEL Assessment Office, 220 Paterson Hall, Carleton University, 1125 Colonel By Drive, Ottawa, ON Canada K1S 5B6; telephone 613-520-2600 ext. 2271; fax 613-520-7872; cael@carleton.ca; http://www.cael.ca/

Publication Date: 1989; new versions published periodically

Target Population: Students whose first language is not English and who are planning to study in English-medium colleges and universities

Cost: Can$110 at Canadian sites; for cost at sites outside Canada, see http://www.cael.ca/

Test Purpose

The specific purpose of the CAEL Assessment is to evaluate English in use for English for academic purposes (EAP). It serves to verify whether a person's level of English language proficiency is adequate to meet the demands of academic study at the college or university level. It stands apart from other well-known standardized tests (e.g., the TOEFL and the MELAB) that are global proficiency measures, in that it is a context-specific (college and university), criterion-based, topic-based performance test that focuses on EAP. Through an integrated set of language tasks it purports to measure a person's EAP skills in reading, writing, listening, and speaking. It claims to provide opportunities that generate test taker performance in the following areas and therefore to yield information for making inferences about the test taker's ability in these areas:

- extensive *reading* of a range of academic texts, for synthesis of key ideas, note-taking, paraphrasing, and responding in writing to questions that arise from the information;

- *listening* to lectures, for note-taking, synthesizing the information and responding;

- *academic writing* across modes (i.e., personal and argumentative), in speeded and nonspeeded situations, and involving both extended and short answer responses;

- *speaking for academic purposes* across tasks (i.e., prepared and spontaneous), in speeded and nonspeeded situations, involving both extended and short answer responses. (Fox, 2000, p. 10)

The results of the CAEL Assessment provide information to help in high-stakes decisions concerning college or university entry. They are used to (a) help identify students capable of meeting the academic language demands of full-time study, (b) place students who do not fully meet those demands into EAP courses while they are concurrently enrolled in part-time study, and (c) identify students who do not meet the demands and place them into full-time EAP courses prior to their acceptance into academic studies in postsecondary institutions.

Ongoing research and development concerning the CAEL Assessment takes place at Carleton University. Due to its collaborative in-house test development effort, which links and serves the needs of language teachers and students, and the university at large, all three of the above uses can be implemented there. The CAEL Assessment is administered in other institutions as well, however (e.g., across Canada, Asia, Europe, the Middle East, and South America). Whether such institutions have EAP courses would dictate the extent to which uses (b) and (c) above could be implemented.

Because of the decisions that are made using CAEL Assessment results, the test can be classified as a high-stakes test with a relatively broad impact. Students' success on the test determines their future in an academic institution of higher learning (e.g., admission status), which in turn affects the classes, programs, and institution as a whole.

Test Methods

The CAEL Assessment claims to reflect the demands of introductory, first-year undergraduate university classroom contexts. It uses a variety of response formats and tasks that are sampled from university classes and span the four language skills (i.e., reading, writing, listening, and speaking).

Most of the content is based on authentic material. Again, the test stands apart from other well-known standardized tests (e.g., the TOEFL and the MELAB) in that it maintains a central topic throughout the reading, listening, and writing sections. This topic is not integrated into the speaking section, however, because not all overseas sites can offer that section. There are three stages to the CAEL Assessment: registration; Oral Language Test (OLT), 25 minutes; and CAEL Written Test (which includes reading, listening, and writing), 2 hours. In the first stage, in addition to typical registration procedures, test takers are requested to fill out a self-assessment questionnaire and write a short personal essay. The information from all three stages is used to develop a language ability profile of each test taker.

The test taker is assigned a specific testing date and time before the CAEL Written Test to do the OLT. The OLT is a semidirect test administered through an audiotape recorder. It claims to include tasks representing EAP. The test taker must produce a short oral presentation; relay information from a lecture, an academic document, and an academic text (to read aloud); and explain a choice for participation in a group project. Trained raters give scores for each task, first using analytic scales and then rating the task holistically. Scores are summed, and the raw total score is converted to a criterion-related band score that ranges from 10 (very limited) to 90 (expert).

The third stage consists of the CAEL Written Test, which is administered in a university classroom setting. At the outset of the test, the central topic is presented in the form of an essay question. Test takers are asked to agree or disagree with the statement. The test procedure goes on to present readings, a lecture, and tasks that help develop the test topic. Once these tasks are completed, the test taker is asked to respond to the initial essay question and to use the information in the test to develop the answer. The reading component includes two readings taken from such sources as textbooks, newspapers, and government publications. The CAEL Assessment moves away from the traditional selected-response types in general and requires constructed responses, such as summarizing main ideas, responding to short-answer questions, and transferring information read to charts and diagrams. Trained raters score the test using a marking key and focusing on test taker comprehension. As with the speaking test, raw scores are converted to criterion-related band scores ranging from 10 to 90.

The listening component is a tape-recorded lecture adapted from a first-year university course. The tape is played once. Response types vary from constructed to selected (e.g., short answer, completion of tables, note-taking, multiple choice). Scoring procedures are similar to those for the reading component.

The final writing component is the most critical. The test taker is asked to write a response to the essay question presented at the outset of the test. Three trained CAEL Assessment raters do the marking collaboratively. Much research has been done on this marking protocol, which is called the *collaborative read-aloud marking protocol*. The scores are expressed as criterion-related bands (with ranges of 10–90).

The results of a test taker's performance are given in a score report, which gives subtest results on English proficiency in the four skill areas noted above. In addition, an overall score is provided. The latter, however, is not a simple average of the subtest scores because each subtest result is weighted. The score report also includes evaluation of the self-assessment and personal essay administered at the first stage of registration.

Justifying Test Use

The research that has been carried out to support the quality of the CAEL Assessment (the instrument and the scores) is considerable, valuable, and readily available (see Fox, 2000, 2002a; Language Assessment and Testing Research Unit, n.d.). An ongoing research agenda began with close attention to the construct of EAP at the test development stage. The test is based on current theories of language use, psycholinguistic and sociolinguistic research, and a needs analysis and documentation of EAP at Carleton University. The operationalization of the tested construct is well investigated and described in detail, and considers scoring criteria, test methods, version comparison, reliability, and validity issues. The research adheres to the definitions of reliability and validity articulated in the *Standards for Educational and Psychological Testing* (American Educational Research Association, American Psychological Association, & National Council on Measurement in Education, 1985), and the approach to validity reflects the work of Messick (1989), that is, that validity is an evolving characteristic and validation is an ongoing process.

Fox (2000, 2002a) provides evidence of interrater reliability for all components of the test because they consist mainly of constructed responses. The writing component uses teams of three raters. For rater teams using the collaborative read-aloud marking protocol, 86.9% of writing scores were exactly the same or within one band score of each other (calculated by means of a Spearman rank-order correlation). Interrater reliability coefficients for the various components range from .86 (Oral Language Test) to .97 (reading). The coefficient for the listening component was .96. The users' guide describes all scoring procedures in detail. The overall score given by review committees is periodically monitored as well. Recent reports indicate an obtained coefficient of .95 across two review committees.

The validity of the CAEL Assessment is reported by Fox (2000, 2002a) for four areas (i.e., ensuring construct representation, investigating construct irrelevant variance, gathering criterion-related evidence of validity, and consequences of use). To address construct representation, the developers performed an in-depth needs analysis before developing the test specifications. Follow-up studies are done periodically.

Investigating construct-irrelevant variance has been a challenge for the CAEL Assessment developers mainly because each written version of the test focuses on one topic, which could generate test bias. The issue at stake is the effect of the topic on test takers' performance (i.e., the topic effect). Are test takers advantaged or disadvantaged because of their background knowledge or lack of knowledge concerning the topic? In a topic-based test, the developers must ensure that the information needed to complete all tasks is contained in the materials. The results of a study by Jennings, Fox, Graves, and Shohamy (1999) indicated that test performance was not significantly different across test takers who were given a choice of topic and those who were not.

To gather criterion-related evidence of validity, the developers have conducted follow-up studies of test takers who have scored at various proficiency levels on the CAEL Assessment. Results showed that the vast majority of students who took the test were performing at an acceptable academic level. Evidence to indicate consequences of test use is gathered through test taker questionnaires and teacher feedback. Students and institutions have indicated high satisfaction with the test. Positive washback in teaching to the test appears to support and complement student EAP learning (Fox, 2000, 2002a). The CAEL Assessment Web site (http://www.cael.ca/) offers information to assist test takers in preparing for the CAEL Assessment, including academic strategies. *The CAEL Assessment Test Takers' Preparation Guide* (Fraser & Brisson, 2003) augments information available on the Web site. The PreCAEL Academic Diagnostic and Placement test (PreCAEL ADAPT; Fox, 2002b) has been published to meet the needs of students at the lower level of English proficiency.

Users of the CAEL Assessment must be aware of two issues. First, the format of the test, in keeping true to the construct, contains interdependent parts. This interdependence violates an important assumption in psychometric analysis, that is, local independence. The developers have dealt with this issue by investigating reliability indicators that are more relevant to the purpose of the test. Another point to keep in mind is that students in EFL contexts where multiple-choice, objective response formats are typical and expected may be disadvantaged on the CAEL Assessment, resulting in test bias against this group.

Overall, however, the CAEL Assessment represents an innovative approach to testing EAP and makes information on development, scoring, and research issues available to the test user.

Certificate of Proficiency in English (CPE)
Reviewed by Keith Morrow

Publisher: University of Cambridge ESOL Examinations, 1 Hills Road, Cambridge CB1 2EU, United Kingdom; telephone 44-1223-553355; fax 44-1223-460-278; ESOL@ucles.org.uk; http://www.cambridgeesol.org/

Publication Date: 1913, revised in 1984; current version introduced in 2002

Target Population: Mainly adults aged 18–25 looking for an internationally recognized qualification of a high level of competence in English

Cost: Set by each approved test center

Test Purpose

The CPE, which is widely recognized throughout the world by universities, by professional bodies, and in commerce and industry, is intended to provide evidence of a very high level of general competence in English. There are five components:

1. Reading (1 hour 30 minutes) aims to assess candidates' ability to understand the meaning of written English at the word, phrase, sentence, and whole-text level.

2. Writing (2 hours) aims to assess candidates' ability to write specified text types with a range of functions. Examples of text types required are an article, a report, an essay, and a letter. These texts may involve functions such as persuading, narrating, making recommendations, and summarizing.

3. Use of English (1 hour 30 minutes) aims to assess candidates' ability to demonstrate knowledge and control of the language systems.

4. Listening (40 minutes) aims to assess candidates' ability to understand the meaning of spoken English, to extract information from a text, and to understand speakers' attitudes and opinions.

5. Speaking (19 minutes) aims to assess candidates' ability to produce spoken English using a range of functions (e.g., speculating, evaluating, comparing) in a variety of tasks (e.g., sharing personal information and opinions with the examiner, discussing material with a fellow candidate).

The test is designed to provide evidence of language ability at Level 5 of the ALTE framework. Level 5, the highest level of the framework, is linked to a series of *can-do* statements setting out what language users are actually able to do. Summary statements at this level include the following:

- *Listening/Speaking:* Can advise on or talk about complex or sensitive issues, understanding colloquial references and dealing confidently with hostile questions.

- *Reading:* Can understand documents, correspondence, and reports, including the finer points of complex texts.

- *Writing:* Can write letters on any subject and full notes of meetings or seminars with good expression and accuracy. (ALTE, 2004a, n.p.)

The CPE is a medium- to high-stakes test; success is likely to be significant to candidates in identifying them as high-level users of English. It has a broad impact on the design of courses and the production of published materials to prepare candidates.

Test Methods

Each component of the CPE consists of a number of parts. Reading has structured items. Part 1 includes three short texts, each with six four-option multiple-choice gap-fill questions; Part 2, four short texts, each with two four-option multiple-choice questions; Part 3, a text with seven gaps into each of which candidates must insert one of eight given paragraphs; and Part 4, a long text (approximately 700–850 words) with seven four-option multiple-choice questions.

The Writing component consists of constructed items. Part 1 includes one compulsory task, and in Part 2 test takers choose one of four tasks (one of which includes one task related to each of three set texts).

The Use of English component includes mainly structured items. Part 1 is a modified open cloze with 15 items, Part 2 is a short text (approximately 200 words) with 10 word-formation questions, Part 3 includes six sets of three gapped sentences, Part 4 has eight word transformations, and Part 5 consists of two texts with a total of four questions plus a summary-writing task.

The Listening component features structured items. Part 1 includes four short extracts (approximately 1 minute each) with two three-option multiple-choice questions on each, and Part 2 has one long text (approximately 4 minutes) with nine sentence completion questions. Part 3 consists of one long text (approximately 4 minutes) with five four-option multiple-choice questions, and Part 4 has one long text (approximately 3 minutes) with six matching questions.

The Speaking component consists of constructed items. Part 1 includes examiner-led questions to each candidate, Part 2 is a collaborative task with a fellow candidate or candidates, and Part 3 consists of individual long turns and follow-up discussion.

Each component is equally weighted. The Reading component and parts of the Listening component are scored through computer scanning of answer sheets. Parts 1–3 of the Use of English component and parts of the Listening component are clerically marked using an answer key. Parts 4 and 5 as well as Questions 40–43 of the Use of English component are marked by examiners using an answer key. The Writing component, the Speaking component, and Part 5, Question 44 of the Use of English component are marked by the examiner using criterion-referenced assessment scales.

Successful candidates are issued a certificate showing their grade of A, B, or C with a graphical profile of their performance on each component. To gain a grade of C, candidates must typically achieve 60% of the total marks.

Justifying Test Use

Because of its long track record, the CPE has achieved almost iconic status in many parts of the world. Having "the Proficiency" is recognized as meaning that one has a high level of competence in English and the ability to demonstrate it in a challenging examination context.

Since the 1984 revision, the test publisher has invested considerable resources in establishing and maintaining the reliability of the examination. The development of standardized rubrics and formats, and rigorous pretesting of items, have ensured consistency of test difficulty from administration to administration.

The major innovation in the 2002 revision is the explicit linking of the test to the external ALTE framework and specifically to the *can-do* statements. This linking is clearly intended to enhance the perceived value of the test by indicating the range of competencies that a successful candidate can perform. However, I note two significant problems, which the test publisher glosses over in the published documentation:

1. The ALTE framework itself, and specifically the *can-do* statements, are evolving constructs that are open to multiple interpretations.

2. The competencies set out in the ALTE framework are not used directly in the specification of the test content. This means that relationships between test performance and *can-do* statements are indirect; a major cross-validation exercise would therefore be necessary to confirm the status of ALTE *can-do* claims made on the basis of performance on this test. Such an exercise has not been carried out.

Combined English Language Skills Assessment in a Reading Context (CELSA)

Reviewed by Diane Strong-Krause

Publisher: Association of Classroom Teacher Testers; contact Pablo Buckelew, 1187 Coast Village Road, Suite 1, PMB 378, Montecito, CA 93108-2794 USA; telephone 805-569-0734; actt@cappassoc.com; http://www.assessment-testing.com/

Publication Date: 1993

Target Population: Literate ESOL high school students and adults (especially immigrants)

Cost: US$95 (1–60 students) to US$795 (751–1,200 students) for annual license; US$400 per year for software for computer-based administration; US$600 per year for scanning software to score paper test

Test Purpose

The CELSA is designed to place literate adult ESOL learners into classes at the beginning of a program. In addition, the publisher suggests that the CELSA can be used to assess students for promotion into higher levels and to provide accountability data for programs by analyzing gain scores, comparison data of new and continuing students, and comparison data on levels of instruction in different programs. The test has also been used in community college, university, and high school ESOL programs. The test is intended to measure general English language skills, specifically reading and grammar in context.

The CELSA is designed as a relatively low-stakes test with a narrow impact, although decisions based on test results may change the nature of the stakes and impact. For example, the CELSA is approved by the U.S. Department of Education for use in determining ability to benefit (ATB). ATB determination is a federal requirement stipulating that every student who does not possess a high school diploma or equivalent must be assessed with a U.S. Department of Education–approved measure to be eligible to apply for Title IV federal financial aid. When using CELSA results to determine ATB, the impact is broader and the stakes higher.

Test Methods

The CELSA has two equivalent forms for its paper-based and computer-based versions. Each form consists of three multiple-choice cloze passages with 25 items, for a total of 75 items per form. The passages increase in difficulty, with one in dialogue format and the other two as narratives. Examinees read the passages and mark their answers on a separate answer sheet. The entire test takes 45 minutes to administer and is easily scored by hand or by machine, if appropriate answer sheets are used. The number correct is calculated and compared with a conversion table that indicates seven levels of student ability (low beginning, high beginning, low intermediate, high intermediate, low advanced, high advanced, and advanced plus).

Each site license includes permission to administer the test, a master copy of the two forms (which can be reproduced as many times as the number of students covered by the site license), a master student answer sheet (which can be duplicated as needed), a master answer key for both forms, and placement information. A user's guide (Ilyin, 1993) gives more details about the forms and their intended audiences and uses, gives directions for test administration, and reports findings from field testing.

The computer-based version of the test is the same as the paper-based version (i.e., it is not adaptive) and can be used in a standalone or network environment (i.e., it is not Web based). In addition to delivering the tests, the software automatically scores them and divides students into levels based on the cutoff scores users have set. In the case of ATB students, the software converts obtained scores to scaled scores (as required by the U.S. Department of Education) and produces an ATB report.

Justifying Test Use

Field tests provide evidence of the CELSA's reliability and validity. Reliability indices are high. Internal reliability using Cronbach's coefficient alpha was reported as .95 for both forms. Test-retest reliability estimates were .93 (Form 1) and .96 (Form 2). The equivalent test form reliability estimate was .94. Test users at different field-test sites reported that in general the tests rank-ordered the groups as expected. The CELSA has also been correlated with other ESOL tests. Correlations with reading and structure tests were quite high (.82–.94) and with listening tests were generally moderate to high.

A limitation of the test is the inability of the test results to discriminate at very low levels of language ability. If the ability range of the group of examinees is quite narrow at the lower end, the author suggests using another test, such as the BEST. Similarly, if most of the examinees are clustered at an advanced level, another test designed for higher proficiency examinees is recommended.

Another limitation is the absence of information about listening, speaking, and writing skills, as acknowledged by the author, although at the time of writing a companion listening comprehension test was expected to be released soon. Using other measures of language ability that assess these areas along with the CELSA might yield a more rounded view of examinee ability.

In sum, the CELSA is a good option for test users looking for a fairly quick, easy-to-administer-and-score assessment to use as a low-stakes placement test. It is also the only test approved by the U.S. Department of Education for determining ESL ATB status.

Comprehensive Adult Student Assessment System (CASAS)

Reviewed by Micheline Chalhoub-Deville

Publisher: CASAS, Foundation for Educational Achievement, 5151 Murphy Canyon Road, Suite 220, San Diego, CA 92123-4440 USA; telephone 858-292-2900; fax 858-292-2910; http://www.casas.org/

Publication Date: 1980–2001

Target Population: Young adults and adults

Cost: Available from the publisher

Test Purpose

CASAS is an integrated curriculum, instruction, and assessment program employed nationwide for vocational preparation, workplace literacy, adult basic education (ABE), and ESOL with adult and high school–level students. This review focuses on the assessment component of the program.

CASAS is not a single test but includes more than 140 instruments developed from an extensive item bank. The various manuals (CASAS, 2000b, 2000c, 2001) point out that there are two main series of tests: Life Skills and Employability. Within these series, three types of assessments are available: appraisal, monitoring, and certification. CASAS appraisal instruments help identify the appropriate testing level. The CASAS Test Referral Chart identifies, based on the appraisal test score, the appropriate follow-up and progress tests to be administered. CASAS monitoring tests diagnose and document students' learning progress (operationalized in terms of pre- and posttest design). Finally, certification tests are intended to establish learners' proficiency level for promotion to the next instructional level or for exit from the CASAS instructional program. CASAS instruments employ paper-and-pencil (multiple-choice and written response) and performance-based (demonstration/simulation and observation/checklist) modes of assessment to measure a variety of skills, including the four modalities as well as math and critical thinking.

CASAS instruments measure a range of abilities. The standardized scoring scale ranges from 150 (learners with severe learning deficits) to 250 (advanced secondary-level learners). CASAS instructional-level designations and skill descriptors describing performance in real-life contexts accompany the scaled scores. According to the CASAS ESL scale, a score of 180, for example, is designated as *beginning literacy/pre-beginning ESL,* a score of 220 is *high intermediate ESL/Level B,* and a score above 245 is *proficient skills/ Level E.* A similar chart is available for the ABE system. Performance-based tests do not yield scaled scores. Instead, results are reported as a perform-ance score based on a standardized competency rubric.

In addition to the tests themselves, CASAS provides a variety of supporting documents, including technical manuals, test administration manuals, and scoring packets. Reports, instructional guides, and regularly published newsletters are available from the publisher. Navigating through the extensive CASAS materials and tests could prove to be a challenge, even for test users with considerable instructional and testing experience. CASAS offers regular institutes and workshops intended to provide professional development as well as training and certification for professionals using or interested in employing CASAS materials and tests. A training CD-ROM is also available.

This review focuses on the ESL Appraisal Form 20 module of CASAS. For other CASAS reviews, see the *Thirteenth Mental Measurements Yearbook* (Impara & Plake, 1998). ESL Appraisal Form 20 is intended primarily for English language learners. Its content focuses on general life skills and not employability. According to the *Test Administration Manual/Life Skills* (CASAS, 2000c), "tests in the Life Skills Series contain items drawn from the CASAS item bank of over 6,000 field-tested and calibrated multiple-choice items" (p. 5). The ESL Appraisal is composed of listening and reading comprehen-sion test items. The writing and oral screening sections are optional.

Test Methods

For the Listening section, an audiotape provides the cues. The Listening section includes 23 three-option (A, B, or C) multiple-choice items divided into three parts, each beginning with a practice item. The first 8 questions are based on pictures (e.g., of clocks, envelopes) and one- to two-sentence aural cues. The second part contains 7 questions. The test takers listen to three to four sentences of dialogue and then must choose the appropriate response to complete the dialogue. The last part includes 8 questions based on dialogues/monologues. On average, students take 25 minutes to com-plete the listening section.

The Reading section begins with two practice samples. The 10 reading texts include, for example, instructions, forms, letters, and stories. Two multiple-choice items (with four options) accompany each text for a total of 20 items. On average, learners complete the section in 25 minutes.

The optional Writing section, which takes about 5 minutes to complete, includes two dictation items/sentences. Items are scored holistically on a 3-point scale. The Oral Screening section comprises a one-on-one oral interview that includes six questions on familiar topics. The 3-point scoring rubric focuses on grammatical accuracy and the ability to understand and communicate simple ideas. These productive skill measures cannot be said to represent real-life performance assessments. They are intended to screen for minimal English proficiency and determine the appropriate follow-up test, such as the Beginning Literacy Reading Assessment or the Level A Listening Test.

Examples of CASAS performance assessments are the Oral Communication Applied Performance Appraisal and the Functional Writing Assessment. These instruments include a variety of tasks that assess students' skills in functional, real-life settings. Score interpretation is based on the CASAS Competency List, which identifies the basic skills adults need to function in daily life and in the workplace. This Competency List is said to be "revalidated annually by the CASAS National Consortium" (CASAS, 2000b, p. 7). Unfortunately, the publisher possesses no printed information on this validation effort.

Justifying Test Use

The *Technical Manual* (CASAS, 2001) provides item-bank calibration statistics and a variety of reliability, bias, and validity analyses to support the multiple uses of CASAS. This work complies with the Joint Committee's (1999) Standards 1.1 and 13.2. Classical item and item-response (Rasch model) theory is employed in the analyses. Acceptable reliability (Kuder–Richardson 20) indices of .84–.93 are reported for the Life Skills Series. Although the publisher provides item statistics information and bias analyses for a variety of Life Skills test forms, such information is conspicuously absent for Form 20, which is the locator test (appraisal) for the Life Skills Series. Also, information is sketchy regarding the ESOL examinees who participated in the calibration and other research undertaken. This lack of information violates Standards 1.5 and 6.4, which emphasize a detailed description of the sample from which validity/norming evidence is obtained in order to ascertain the relevant population to which findings can be said to generalize.

CASAS promotes sound practices in different facets of its operation. A strength of CASAS is its integrated approach to instruction and assessment. CASAS developers work closely with educators to improve instructional, curricular, and assessment materials. For example, the *CASAS ESL Appraisal* (CASAS, 2000a) states that the "skills levels are based on many years of achievement data and experience with students enrolled in Basic Education programs, and are valid for . . . non-native English speakers" (p. 18). Another instance of sound practice is the emphasis in CASAS publications that test users supplement standardized assessments with information from other sources when making significant decisions that affect students.

Even though various CASAS reports document that the developers frequently undertake research to support CASAS' proposed purposes, these disparate publications do not indicate whether such research is part of a principled research agenda or inspired more by ad hoc needs. For example, it is unclear how often CASAS conducts renorming studies to help ensure appropriate score interpretation (Standard 4.18). The *Technical Manual*

(CASAS, 2001) indicates that the item bank was calibrated in the early 1980s and that "item calibration and field testing for *most* [italics added] test forms has continued on a continuous basis to the present" (p. 18). Information is lacking on these calibration efforts, however. Resources need to be allocated for a research team to construct a coherent research program that corresponds in scale to the magnitude of the CASAS operation. Such an articulated agenda should drive continuous and principled research and publications to document and support the validation arguments.

Comprehensive English Language Test (CELT)
Reviewed by Yeonsuk Cho

Publisher: McGraw-Hill College Division, 1750 South Brentwood, Suite 280, St. Louis, MO 63144-1312 USA; telephone 800-338-3987; fax 614-759-3644; http://www.mhhe .com/

Publication Date: 1986

Target Population: Intermediate- and advanced-level nonnative English speakers in high school, college, and adult ESL/EFL programs

Cost: US$157 for 10 packs of test books (Form A or B), audiotapes, scoring keys, exam kit booklet, answer sheets

Test Purpose

CELT is a standardized test intended to measure the English proficiency of nonnative English speakers in high school, college, and adult ESOL programs. The test should be particularly useful for determining placement and achievement in language programs.

Test Methods

The test has two comparable forms (A and B). Each has three sections of discrete multiple-choice test items: Listening, Structure, and Vocabulary. The Listening section, which takes approximately 40 minutes to administer, has 50 items consisting of short statements, questions, and short dialogues designed to measure the ability to comprehend spoken English. Test takers choose an answer among four written options after listening to each recorded question once. The Structure component of the test, which takes 45 minutes to administer, has 75 sentence-completion items (written in the test booklet) that measure knowledge of the structure of spoken English text. Test takers select the option that completes a sentence of a short dialogue grammatically. The Vocabulary section, which takes 35 minutes to administer, has 75 items that measure the ability to understand meanings of lexical items. Test takers identify the word that best completes a sentence or corresponds to a phrase or word given in the question. The time required for the administration of the complete CELT is approximately $2\frac{1}{4}$ hours, but the publisher states that each section can be administered separately without much loss of reliability.

For all three sections, test takers mark their answers on a separate answer sheet. The test can be scored by hand using punched answer keys or by machine. Each answer is either correct or incorrect; no partial credit or penalty is applied to an incorrect answer. Test scores are reported as the percentage of items answered correctly for each section. (The answer keys include a conversion table.) The section scores are combined to yield the total score.

Justifying Test Use

Many aspects of CELT should appeal to institutions or teachers seeking a practical, reliable test. First, the test demonstrates a high degree of reliability, that is, a high reliability coefficient and a small standard error of measurement (*SEM*). For the three sections of CELT, reliability indices range from .82 to .97, and the values of *SEM* are below 5.86. Test reliability is expected to be slightly higher when it is based on total scores (.98 for reliability and 7.05 for *SEM,* as cited in the technical manual (Harris & Palmer, 1986).

Second, the technical manual (Harris & Palmer, 1986) provides some validity-related evidence for CELT. The test items fairly well represent the content of CELT that test developers aim for, which contributes to the content validity of the test. The Listening section includes simple *wh-* and *yes/no* questions and comprehension questions based on simple statements and dialogues. The Structure section focuses on word order and choice of word forms and conjunctions. Lexical items included in the Vocabulary section are chosen based on the word frequency. A drawback, however, is that the target content of CELT is so narrowly defined that it weakens the construct validity of the test. Concurrent validity is established by studies that showed CELT to have a substantially positive relationship with other major standardized English proficiency tests: a correlation of .79 with the TOEFL and .81 with the Michigan Test of English Language Proficiency. Furthermore, the vigilant test development process described in the technical manual supports the procedural validity of CELT.

Third, the test is highly practical. Because the test materials are inexpensive and reusable, CELT is cost-effective. In addition, because the administration of CELT is easy and requires few resources, any testing setting can accommodate its use.

These merits do not come without limitations. One is the lack of authenticity of the test tasks. Discrete recognition tasks on the test have very little resemblance to real-life language tasks. For example, the ability to select an appropriate answers to a *wh-* question in an isolated context does not necessarily mean that test takers can actually produce an appropriate response to the same question. There is no evidence that performance on CELT can predict test takers' real-life language ability. I point out, however, that the publisher does not make this claim directly. The publisher implies, rather, that CELT scores reflect language skills attainable in classroom instruction (Harris & Palmer, 1986, p. 19).

Another limitation of CELT is the absence of measures of productive language skills, such as speaking and writing, which are an important aspect of language ability. Considering that the functions of language include perception and production, and that a primary goal of a proficiency test is to determine a test taker's ability to use language in performing tasks in real contexts, it is difficult to infer an individual's language ability only from performance on a multiple-choice test.

The lack of authenticity in the test tasks and the lack of a measure of speaking or writing ability restrict the amount of information that CELT can provide about test takers' language ability. As a consequence, these limitations raise questions about the validity of CELT and its ability to assess language proficiency. Another weakness is that test items may not be challenging enough to differentiate among more advanced-level English learners. Even though the publisher indicates that the test targets these speakers, the content and tasks of the test appear insufficiently challenging for them.

Overall, CELT is a highly reliable, practical, well-developed objective test of English proficiency. It can be administered in various low- to moderate-stakes testing settings (e.g., as a diagnostic or achievement test in language programs or classrooms) but may not be appropriate for a high-stakes testing situation because the test is easy to obtain and has only two forms. However, the test is cost-effective and user-friendly; the technical manual gives test users sufficient information regarding test administration and the characteristics of the test. Because all three sections of CELT are discrete, the test might be considered for use in testing contexts where the course curriculum is structured in a similar discrete way. The use of CELT as a sole measure of English proficiency is, however, not advisable if the test user aims to obtain a comprehensive picture of a test taker's English proficiency. In such a case, CELT should be supplemented with other tests or tasks that focus on language performance.

ESL Computerized Adaptive Placement Exam (ESL-CAPE)

Reviewed by Carsten Roever

Publisher: Department of Linguistics and English Language, Attn:
Diane Strong-Krause, Brigham Young University, Provo,
UT 84602-6278 USA; telephone 801-422-3970; fax
801-422-0906; http://creativeworks.byu.edu/hrc/

Publication Date: 1999

Target Population: Adult ESL/EFL learners

Cost: US$995

Test Purpose

The ESL-CAPE is a computer-adaptive placement test for nonnative speakers
of English at the tertiary level, developed at Brigham Young University
(BYU). The test is intended to assess nonnative-English-speaking students'
proficiency in American English listening, reading, and grammar, and is
intended for placement decisions only.

   Like most placement tests, this test can be described as medium stakes
with relatively narrow impact, although such stakes and impact depend on
institutional decisions with regard to what courses ESOL students are
allowed to enroll in. For use as a placement instrument in a language
program other than BYU's, the authors suggest pretesting the test with
groups of learners of known proficiency levels to derive standards for
placement decisions (Strong-Krause, Larsen, & Smith, 1999).

Test Methods

The test consists of three sections (Reading, Listening, and Grammar) and
draws on an item bank of about 150 grammar items, 150 reading items,
and 80 listening items. Items are tagged as belonging to one of six difficulty
levels, corresponding to the levels of BYU's ESL program. All questions are
in multiple-choice format and are immediately and automatically scored.
The item selection algorithm is based on a one-parameter Rasch model and
selects items solely on the basis of their difficulty after initially gauging test
takers' ability by displaying one item from each difficulty level. No set
number of items is displayed; rather, item selection ceases when the
adaptive algorithm converges, so that different test takers may be administered tests of different length.

   In keeping with the oft-neglected item response theory (IRT) requirement that all adaptive tests be absolute power tests, there are no time limits
on the Grammar and Listening sections; and only the Reading section is
limited (to 50 minutes). The entire test should take about 90 minutes but

no more than 2 hours to complete. Test results are collected in a separate file and can be displayed to the test taker on completion of the test if the examiner desires.

Justifying Test Use

The vast majority of items belong to the nebulous realm of general English rather than being part of a specific academic discourse domain. Items in the Reading section consist of a reading passage of 60–150 words (on average 100 words) and several questions, testing comprehension of referent structure and ideas, multiword expressions, and the main idea of the text. The Listening section requires test takers to draw inferences based on the whole passage as well as listen for details. The Grammar section contains gap-filling and error identification questions, and covers a wide and varied range of grammatical phenomena.

The test is easy to set up and allows testers to choose the sequence in which to administer the sections and which kinds of personal data to collect. These settings can be easily changed, and the test screens themselves are clear, uncluttered, and easily navigable. Results for each student and section are accessible only to the test administrator, either as a summary score or a detailed report including the student's answer and score for every item.

The major limitation of this test, as the authors clearly point out in the manual (Strong-Krause et al., 1999) is the absence of speaking and writing items, so that no inferences can be drawn from test scores in terms of a test taker's abilities with regard to those skills. Additionally, two caveats must be raised regarding the discourse domain from which items are sampled and the unusual *I don't know* option as the fifth choice for every item.

As noted, the vast majority of items come not from the discourse domain of EAP but rather from general English, and only some of the most difficult items approach simple academic English. This is not necessarily a shortcoming if the test is used with learners of low proficiency, but it would probably be far too easy for learners scoring in the medium ranges of tests like the TOEFL.

The inclusion of an *I don't know* option is possibly the only serious concern from a measurement perspective. At the beginning of the test, test takers are instructed not to guess but rather to select this option, which is always the fifth choice, whenever they do not know an answer. This answer is considered an incorrect answer by the scoring algorithm. From a practical point of view, it seems doubtful that any moderately testwise test takers would ever choose *I don't know,* knowing full well that they would not receive points for choosing it. More important, it is not clear what conclusions could be drawn from test takers' selecting the *I don't know* option. Do they not have any knowledge of the issue tested so that none of the choices appealed to them? Or do they have some latent knowledge but were unable to decide between two attractive choices?

The *I don't know* response also raises a psychometric problem because the scoring algorithm simply considers them as incorrect. If a test taker chooses *I don't know* for reasons other than lack of knowledge about the feature tested (e.g., not understanding the vocabulary of a grammar item, disliking the content of an item, or simply being bored), the response gives misleading information.

In general, the ESL-CAPE is an attractive and easily administered test that provides relatively quick insight into low-level students' abilities in listening, reading, and grammar.

IDEA Proficiency Test (IPT) I-Oral English, Form E

Reviewed by Tina Scott Edstam

Publisher: Ballard & Tighe, Inc., 480 Atlas Street, Brea, CA 92821 USA; telephone 714-990-4332, 800-321-4332; fax 714-255-9828; http://www.ballard-tighe.com/

Publication Date: 2001

Target Population: English learners in Grades K–6

Cost: US$137.00 for Form E or F Oral Test set (including test pictures, 50 level summaries and consumable test booklets, examiner's manual, and technical manual); as individual components, US$36.50 for 50 test booklets, or 50 diagnostic answer sheets with 1 test booklet, or 50 scannable answer sheets with 1 test booklet; US$46.50 for Form E or F pictures; US$25.00 for examiner's manual; US$28.00 for technical manual; US$10.50 for 50 level summaries; US$7.50 for 50 group lists

Test Purpose

The IPT I—Oral English, Form E, is designed to measure the English oral language proficiency of nonnative English speakers, yielding three designations (non–English speaking [NES], limited English speaking [LES], and fluent English speaking [FES]). These designations can be used for initial program placement, redesignation of students into the mainstream program, or diagnostic purposes related to specific language domains, concepts, and skills.

The IPT I—Oral English is intended to measure the areas of syntax, morphological structures, lexical items, and phonological structures that are reflected in a matrix of test items assessing the skill areas of verbal expression, grammar/syntax, comprehension, and vocabulary. Test items reflect the publisher's intent to include "a measure of the basic or minimum language capabilities students must possess in order to succeed in the mainstream classroom alongside native speakers of English" (Ballard, Dalton, & Tighe, 2001b, p. 6). If the resulting classifications alone are used to make initial programming decisions, the IPT I—Oral English K–6 test could be deemed a high-stakes test; for purposes of redesignation when continued monitoring took place, it would have medium-stakes significance. Used for purely diagnostic purposes by the classroom teacher, it would be considered a low-stakes test. When the test is used to identify K–6 English language learners who need additional instructional support or to place them in classes where they receive special services, the results could have a broad impact on school districts that are required to use a norm-referenced standardized oral language proficiency test to comply with state- and federally funded mandates.

Test Methods

With a 14-minute average, the time for individual administration of the IPT I—Oral English can range from several minutes for the NES child to 20 or more minutes for the FES child. Test takers listen to four types of input: (a) basic prompt-only items consisting of an individual question, (b) prompts with pictures, (c) prompts that require a student to display an action or follow a direction, and (d) prompts with a story stimulus.

Test takers' responses to the 83 test items include nonverbal responses, individual words, phrases, complete sentences, question construction, sentence repetition, retelling of main ideas, and auditory discrimination. Test takers' responsibility for structuring their oral responses ranges from giving a picture-prompted verbal prediction of future events (e.g., "What do you think will happen?") to an open-ended verbal description of abstract human attributes (e.g., "Tell me three things that make a good friend"). Although several test items require direct repetition, the majority of responses are orally constructed by the test taker.

The test examiner scores the test by checking the appropriate box (*correct* or *incorrect*) next to each test item in the booklet immediately after hearing or observing the test taker's response. The acceptable student responses are printed to the right of each item in the test booklet.

The test items are divided into six levels (A–F), with A being a designation only if a student fails to answer more than 50% of the correct items in Level B. At the end of each level, the examiner determines the number of errors based on the error threshold noted in the test booklet and either designates that level as the test taker's appropriate one or continues to the following levels until a level classification is determined. Using the score conversion table printed in each test booklet, the test examiner cross-references the test taker's grade level and score level (e.g., A, B, or C) to locate the intersecting point that indicates the NES, LES, or FES designation. The *IPT I Oral Grades K–6 Examiner's Manual* (Ballard, Dalton, & Tighe, 2001a) satisfactorily explains the basic testing, scoring, and rating procedures; see Ballard & Tighe's Web site (http://www.ballard-tighe.com/) for information on online in-service training.

Justifying Test Use

The *Technical Manual* (Ballard et al., 2001b) provides a variety of statistical information on the authors' national research and analysis of data related to the test, noting issues of validity and reliability. The spring 2000 field-testing and norming of the IPT I included 891 students ranging from 6 to 14 years of age (approximately half male and half female) from 12 states and 23 school districts. The test takers in this norming sample represented

55 countries and 28 different languages, with Spanish (66.5%) and English (13.1%) representing the most prevalent first languages.

Validity evidence offered by the publisher is of three types: content, criterion, and construct. Content validity appears adequate based on the relationship between the test items and the percentages of these found in each of the six domains (syntax, lexicon, phonology, morphology, comprehension, and oral expression). The percentages in the two parallel forms (E and F) are similar as well. A possible concern again is that the test does not truly measure comprehension if a test taker understood the question but was unable to supply the correct English term to reflect this understanding (McCollum, 1983).

Criterion—specifically concurrent—validity is demonstrated by correlating teachers' predictions of the IPT score level by IPT results, yielding a correlation of .73 (Pearson's; Ballard et al., 2001b), a relatively strong, positive relationship between the two. Additional tables addressing a teacher's opinion of a student's academic abilities correlated with an IPT score level show positive low-moderate to moderate correlations (.27, .42, .40). The test developers assert construct validity based on six theoretical beliefs with additional commentary on their understanding of language competency addressed through linguistic performance. Evidence of construct validity includes correlating age and grade level with IPT level and obtaining correlations of .43 and .43 (Pearson's), respectively. Correlations with teacher opinion of oral language ability by IPT level resulted in a correlation of .63 (Pearson's) for the combined E and F forms, showing a moderately strong correlation.

Reliability studies (Ballard et al., 2001b) show a correlation of .99 (Cronbach's alpha), reflecting an excellent level of internal consistency reliability. Test-retest reliability (.85) and alternate form reliability (.88) provide further evidence of the test's precision as a measurement instrument.

A test of authentic oral language proficiency is perhaps by its very description an oxymoron. How does one truly test natural language in an unnatural setting? Yet school districts need to determine how best to serve their English language learners by accurately assessing their language proficiency as soon as they enter the public school domain. ESOL practitioners recognize that they have neither the luxury of time nor the statistical expertise to make these high-stakes decisions in a vacuum.

The IPT I—Oral English, Form E, provides teachers with an easy-to-administer instrument that appears to have high face validity and moderate criterion validity coupled with high reliability. It makes some attempts to simulate authentic oral language use and gives the examiner immediate results through its straightforward scoring procedure. Initial identification and placement of every K–6 English language learner is, in itself, a high-stakes event for that child and should be carried out with the care and caution that such a procedure calls for. Noting that the publishers see their tests as "an integral part in helping to determine the level of instruction ELL [English language learning] students need in the classroom" (Ballard et al., 2001b, p. 3), schools and districts would be wise to view the IPT I as one of several measures to be used in the decision-making process.

International English Language Testing System (IELTS)

Reviewed by Barry O'Sullivan

Publisher: University of Cambridge ESOL Examinations, the British Council, and IDP: IELTS Australia. Subject Manager, University of Cambridge ESOL Examinations, 1 Hills Road, Cambridge CB1 2EU United Kingdom; telephone 44-1223-553355; fax 44-1223-460278; ielts@ucles.org.uk; http://www.ielts.org/. Manager, North America, Cambridge Examinations and IELTS International, 100 East Corson Street, Suite 200, Pasadena, CA 91103 USA; telephone 626-564-2954; fax 626-564-2981; bmeiron@ceii.org; http://www.ielts.org/

Publication Date: 1989 (introduced as ELTS in 1980–1981)

Target Population: Students for whom English is not a first language and who wish to work or attend university in an English-speaking country

Cost: Varies greatly by location of test center; see http://www.ielts.org/ or the IELTS handbook (University of Cambridge ESOL Examinations, 2003). In general, costs are Australia, A$160; United Kingdom, £72; United States, about US$100.

Test Purpose

The purpose of IELTS is to provide a measure of the English language ability of people whose first language is not English and who wish to work or study in an environment where English is used as the language of communication. Until recently, the test, which is offered in more than 100 locations, has been primarily targeted at students planning to study in Australia, the United Kingdom, and to a lesser extent New Zealand. However, interest in IELTS has been increasing in the United States and Canada, to the extent that over 230 universities in those countries now recognize IELTS.

IELTS is not just a single test. Test takers choose one of two test routes depending on their own purpose in taking the test (see Figure 2.1). The *academic* route is designed for test takers who are planning to enter university or are applying for membership in professional organizations (many such organizations, e.g., the Institute of Engineers in Australia, have a language requirement that can be satisfied by reaching a set IELTS level). The *general training* (GT) route is taken by students who wish to study at

Figure 2.1. The Different IELTS Routes

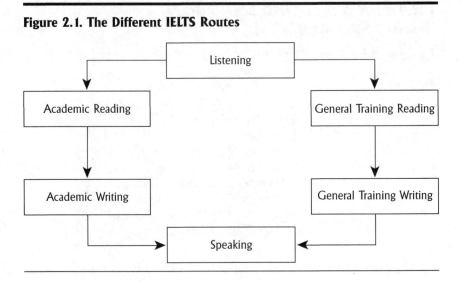

secondary (high school) level or participate in work or training activities. The GT modules are also used for immigration purposes in Australia and New Zealand. The two routes, therefore, are designed to allow the end-user to draw somewhat different inferences, although the skills tested and levels of performance expected are similar.

IELTS is designed to describe performance in the four skills at a range of levels. The levels are reported using a 9-point band descriptor scale—benchmarked with the ALTE (2004a) framework. The typical minimal achievement level required by universities (for participation in courses in which the linguistic requirements are relatively low) is 6.5, corresponding approximately to ALTE Level 4. A summary of ALTE study statements for this level is shown in Table 2.1. (The test taker will be expected to meet the descriptions of all levels up to and including this level.)

Table 2.1. ALTE Study Statements Summary, Level 4 (ALTE, 2004a)

LEVELS	Listening/Speaking	Reading	Writing
C1 Level 4	CAN contribute effectively to meetings and seminars within own area of work or keep up a casual conversation with a good degree of fluency, coping with abstract expressions.	CAN read quickly enough to cope with an academic course, to read the media for information or to understand non-standard correspondence.	CAN prepare/draft professional correspondence, take reasonably accurate notes in meetings or write an essay which shows an ability to communicate.

The scores on IELTS test modules can be used in making high-stakes decisions relating to study, training, or employment, with different organizations setting levels of attainment that satisfy their own requirements. For example, the University of California, Berkeley, in the United States, requires overall scores of 7.0, and the University of Toronto, in Canada, requires an overall score of 6.5 (with a minimum of 6.0 in each module). Similarly, the Australian Medical Council requires an overall score of 7.0 (academic), and the New Zealand Immigration Service requires an overall 5.0 (GT).

Although the high-stakes nature of IELTS will have an undoubted impact on the test taker directly, the test may have some impact in other areas, including teaching materials and methods (on IELTS preparation courses and academic preparatory post-IELTS courses) and academic subject teachers and tutors. There is also potential for impact on university admissions. For example, a set of guidelines aimed specifically at admissions officers was under development at the time of writing. Exactly how this impact is evidenced is the subject of an ongoing major study by University of Cambridge ESOL Examinations.

Test Methods

Table 2.2 describes the range of input that test takers are expected to respond to when performing test tasks. Although all of the items are structured in terms of input, the nature of performance testing means that the responses, particularly those involving language production (writing and speaking) are, to a large extent, constructed by the test taker. In the other modules, the response types range from being selected by the test taker, in the case of true–false–not given or multiple-choice items, and partially constructed, in the fill-in-the-blank and short-answer items.

All IELTS tests are scored and performance levels established at the test administration center (allowing a turnaround time of 2 weeks from test to report). The Speaking and Writing modules are marked by trained and accredited raters, and the Reading and Listening modules are marked by trained clerical markers using a specified key. Scores are then interpreted in terms of a set of band descriptors (Levels 1–9, with half-level distinctions for Reading and Listening but no half-level distinctions for Writing or Speaking), one for each of the four modules taken, and a final, overall descriptor and level score (an average of the levels achieved in the four modules reported on a scale of 1–9, with half-level distinctions possible). All score data are returned to University of Cambridge ESOL Examinations for after-the-fact analysis.

The final report contains a profile based on the results obtained in the four modules as well as an overall level score. The profile and the overall score are presented as a mark and a written descriptor of a typical performance at the level attained.

Table 2.2. Typical IELTS Tasks

Module	Input	Response	Time
Listening	6 recordings (played once): single utterances, short monologues, and brief conversational exchanges	Complete tables or programs of events, respond to written (and spoken) prompts, select correct information (multiple-choice format), locate written prompts on a map	30 minutes (10 minutes at the end to transfer answers to answer sheet)
Academic Reading	3 passages (2,000–2,750 words in total), 38 items	Give mostly short answers, focus on overall meaning and on details, answer small number of yes/no items, label diagrams	60 minutes
Academic Writing	Task 1: input from chart, graph, or table Task 2: written input	Write a report Write a discussion (using own ideas, knowledge, and experience)	150 words, 20 minutes 250 words, 40 minutes
General Training Reading	2,000–2,750 words total; short descriptive passage Section 1: advertisements, information sheets/notices Section 2: short passage Section 3: longer passage	Scan for details Identify letter or number Quote from passage For example, identify details and determine true, false, or not given	40 items in 3 sections, 60 minutes
General Training Writing	2 written prompts	Write letter (typically written in response to a problem), offer opinion in response to set topic	150 words, 20 minutes; 250 words, 40 minutes
Speaking	Part 1: basic introductions and verbal questions on familiar topics Part 2: written input (general instruction and content-focused prompt) Part 3: verbal questions (with thematic link to Part 2)	Take part in short interview (one examiner) Produce individual long turn Take part in interactive discussion	4–5 minutes 3–4 minutes (including 1 minute for preparation) 4–5 minutes

Justifying Test Use

The test publisher provides a comprehensive set of publications, including a set of specimen materials (including benchmark performance levels for Writing and Speaking—on CD), a comprehensive test handbook (University of Cambridge ESOL Examinations, 2003) an annual review (giving demographic and score data, outlining IELTS development initiatives, and reporting on related research), a detailed introduction to IELTS for admissions personnel, and an annual volume of research reports commissioned by the IELTS partners.

University of Cambridge ESOL Examinations claims evidence of construct-related validity through the use of expert judgment in operationalizing the construct (matching test items and tasks to the construct definition) in addition to empirical evidence provided through statistical analysis of test responses. In the case of content-related validation, the publisher refers to the representative nature of the test writers in terms of their nationality, institutional affiliations, and familiarization with the test, and to the quality control procedures adopted to ensure that the tasks selected for inclusion in an IELTS version offer an appropriate balance of texts, tasks, and items across each module. As evidence of criterion-related validity, the publisher cites a large number of research studies claiming a high degree of correlation between test scores and test outcomes (i.e., predictive validity). Although there is relatively little evidence of concurrent validity, the publisher refers to an ongoing attempt to establish a relationship between IELTS performance and the *can-do,* self-rated responses of test takers.

Reliability estimates are reported for the modules testing listening and reading, as is an overall composite reliability estimate. Table 2.3 contains the most up-to-date estimates at the time of writing (IELTS, 2004). The overall estimates of reliability for the 1999 administrations are reported as .94 (*SEM* = .36 bands) for academic modules and .94 (*SEM* = .35 bands) for the GT modules (IELTS, 2004). In addition, Shaw (2004) reports reliability estimates in the range of .77 to .85 (p. 5) for a series of research studies carried out during the writing paper revision project.

IELTS has clearly been developed for a set of specific purposes. The evidence reported above seems to support the claims of its publishers that it offers a valid and reliable measure of the abilities it claims to be measuring.

Table 2.3. Reliability Estimates for the IELTS Modules (IELTS, 2004)

Module	M	SD
Listening	.90	0.02
Academic Reading	.85	0.02
General Training Reading	.90	0.02

Evidence also supports the use of the test for high-stakes decisions related to education, training, and work. Since the 1990s, the academic test route has been very well established as a suitable measure of a test taker's ability to cope, in terms of language, in an academic environment, and there seems to be a growing acceptance that the GT route offers an acceptable measure of a test taker's ability to cope in an English-speaking environment, particularly in the Australian and New Zealand contexts.

Because IELTS tests the four skills, with each seen as being of equal importance, a positive washback effect is likely on teaching and on test takers. The length of the test (more than 160 minutes) may mean that test takers are more physically challenged than they are, say, in the case of a computer-adaptive test (which might last just 20–30 minutes), but test takers (and many of their teachers) appear to believe that such a wide-ranging test of their language ability has a greater degree of face validity. Ultimately, the greatest benefit to using this test is that test takers have a great opportunity to display the full range of their language ability under conditions that closely mirror those in which they may find themselves in an academic, training, or work environment.

As with any test, using IELTS presents a number of potential problems:

- The test is time-consuming; although it may offer a broad profile of language ability, it does not do so quickly.

- There are relatively few examination centers, with just 14 in the United States in 2004 (see http://www.ielts.org/), though this situation is changing as the test gains in prominence there. As many students tend to sit for IELTS in their home country, this is not a major problem.

- Reliability estimates for the performance modules are relatively low. The low reliability for the Speaking module was addressed through the introduction in July 2001 of a revised format, which uses an interlocutor frame to establish a more consistent input. The Writing module is scored by a single rater, but if the Writing or Speaking module score varies significantly from the mean of the Reading and Listening scores, the particular performance is marked by a second assessor.

Listening Comprehension Test (LCT)

Reviewed by Jean Turner

Publisher:	Testing and Certification Division, English Language Institute, 3020 North University Building, University of Michigan, Ann Arbor, MI 48109-1057 USA; telephone 313-764-2416; fax 313-763-0369; http://www.lsa .umich.edu/eli/testing.html
Publication Date:	1972
Target Population:	Adult nonnative speakers of English
Cost:	US$70 for all three available forms (20 test booklets, 100 answer sheets, 3 scoring stencils, manual, and audiotape)

Test Purpose

The LCT is a retired component of the Michigan English Proficiency Battery, a set of instruments intended to measure general language ability for the purpose of college admission. The LCT itself is a norm-referenced test designed to measure aural comprehension of specific features of English grammar. It supports a general-purpose notion of language ability. Documents supplied by the publisher (English Language Institute, Testing & Certification Division, 1986, 1994, 1998) indicate that the LCT can be used to determine whether students admitted to an English-medium university or college need supplementary ESOL, place students in a multilevel ESOL program, or measure ESOL students' progress in a language program. These documents note that, as a retired, nonsecure instrument, the LCT should not be used as an admissions test or as a component of an admissions test; therefore, the types of decisions made on the basis of LCT performance range from low to medium stakes.

When the Michigan battery, including the LCT, was first published, the battery had a broad impact, influencing what was taught in L2 programs, what students learned, and even how language ability was perceived. However, in the current era, influenced by models of communicative competence, the LCT should have a narrow impact because it does not reflect current thinking regarding L2 ability. Given the LCT's distance from current notions of language ability and the fact that the test is norm referenced, it is unlikely to be an effective measure of students' progress in a language program. As a norm-referenced test, the LCT discriminates among levels of knowledge and thus might be used for sorting students into levels, but the lack of congruence between a postmodern curriculum and the construct measured by the LCT, aural comprehension of grammar, may result in somewhat meaningless distinctions. The same can be said of the

LCT's potential usefulness for identifying students who might need supplementary ESOL instruction.

Test Methods

Each of the three forms of the LCT has 45 three-option multiple-choice items, presented via audiotape and requiring 15 minutes' administration time. Each multiple-choice item is based on a brief, single utterance. The utterances are of two types, questions and statements. The question type requires the examinees to select the grammatically appropriate response to a question from among the three options presented in the test booklet. The statement type requires the examinees to select the grammatically appropriate paraphrase from among the options. All three forms use the same test booklet. That is, each option for an item is the correct response on one of the LCT forms, though across the three forms the item measures different grammatical points.

The LCT is scored using stencils provided by the publisher. Raw scores are adjusted using an equation table of standardized scores. These standardized scores allow placement of raw LCT scores on the scale for the component tests of the Michigan battery.

Justifying Test Use

Chapter 1 of this volume asserts that test justification employs rational and empirical analyses of a test to determine the appropriateness of a test for its intended purposes. The analyses of the LCT reported in the test manual (English Language Institute, Testing & Certification Division, 1986) reflect the psychometric-structuralist era in which the LCT was developed and the approaches to test justification that were respected practice at that time, including establishing the internal consistency reliability of the test and reporting on investigations into the test's content validity and concurrent validity.

The internal consistency reliability of the LCT, based on a sample of 1,486 people who took one of the three forms of the official Michigan battery in 1983, is K-R 21 = .80, which is acceptable though moderate. The equivalent form reliability of the three forms is not reported, though evidence of their comparability is provided through means and standard deviations. The North American sample of 1,486 examinees, taken when the LCT was part of a secure, high-stakes test battery, may not inform current use of the test. The current test population may include international students and many students, North American and international, whose knowledge of English reflects a model of communicative competence rather than a structuralist model.

Following accepted practice in the psychometric-structuralist era, establishing content validity involved verifying that the content of the LCT is a representative sample of the domain to be measured, that is, aural comprehension of specific grammatical features of English. The LCT manual

(English Language Institute, Testing & Certification Division, 1986) reports that this was done by referring to the two core texts used in the ESL program at the English Language Institute at that time. The results of a concurrent validity study, also reported in the manual, show that performance on the LCT is correlated with performance on the Michigan battery and its various components, including more recent versions of the LCT. All correlations are moderate (.60–.76), but the highest correlations are with other tests of grammar, and the lowest are with reading, vocabulary, and composition tests or test components. In the postmodern era, none of the information in the manual is evidence of the LCT's validity because there is no evidence in support of the LCT's usefulness for any of the suggested purposes.

Maculaitis Assessment of Competencies Test of English Language Proficiency II (MAC II)

Reviewed by Norman Brown

Publisher: Touchstone Applied Science Associates, Inc. (TASA), 4 Hardscrabble Heights, PO Box 382, Brewster, NY 10509-0382 USA; telephone 800-800-2598; fax 845-277-3548; http://www.tasa.com/

Publication Date: 2001

Target Population: K–12 nonnative speakers of English

Cost: Up to US$222 for a test packet for one level, including administration manual and scoring overlay plus 25 test booklets, writing sample forms, answer sheets, and student record forms

Test Purpose

The MAC II is a revision of the original (1982) MAC, which was created by Jean Maculaitis at New York University, in the United States. Compared with the MAC I, the updated version is intended to be more modern, streamlined, logically sequenced, and instructionally relevant. As did its predecessor, the current instrument evaluates the English language proficiency of K–12 English language learners in four areas (speaking, listening, reading, and writing), with grade-specific tests at five levels (Red for K–1, Blue for Grades 2–3, Orange for Grades 4–5, Ivory for Grades 6–8, and Tan for Grades 9–12) yielding formal quantitative/qualitative proficiency scores and data for year-to-year progress tracking.

According to the publisher, the MAC II is designed for both pre- and posttesting (with alternate forms at each level) and serves four functions: identifying student proficiency (as criteria for placement/exit decisions), diagnosing classroom instructional needs, evaluating schoolwide programs, and measuring progress in developing English proficiency. National norms (from data collected in 2000–2001) are given for each level and for each modality.

As described in a thorough and informative handbook (Maculaitis, 2001b) accompanying the instrument, the emphasis of the MAC II is on the functional/communicative use of language; hence it draws heavily from the work of Savignon (1997) and Cummins (1979) and reflects the three goals published in *ESL Standards for Pre-K–12 Students* (TESOL, 1997) (using English to communicate socially, academically, and appropriately). Based on test performance, lower level test takers are presumed to possess certain basic interpersonal communication skills (BICS) (e.g., survival skills such as the ability to ask questions); higher level examinees may demonstrate more advanced cognitive academic language proficiency (CALP) (e.g., in essay writing) as well as BICS.

Given the variety of ways in which this test may be used, its varied impact is not surprising. At one end of the spectrum, diagnostic information provided by the MAC II may underlie low-stakes decisions within the classroom; at the other extreme, the use of this test to make program entrance or exit decisions is typically of great importance to the stakeholders.

Test Methods

The MAC II is a traditional tool with a variety of structured items (e.g., multiple choice, true-false, matching) and—in the upper levels—partially structured items (e.g., cloze, fill-in-the-blank, essay with prompt). Test administration may begin with the Green level, an optional 10-minute screening test for English language learners entering any grade. All five levels of the MAC II offer speaking, listening, reading, and writing components.

The Red (K–1) level test is individually administered and marked by the tester, and includes four sections:

1. The Speaking Test requires about 4 minutes and consists of 16 items intended to elicit verbal responses (e.g., naming things, telling a story) through pictorial prompts and by posing verbal conversational questions.

2. The Listening Test takes about 6 minutes and includes 18 items meant to elicit verbal responses (e.g., identifying picture and story details) through pictorial and verbal prompts and by posing text-based questions.

3. The (optional) Reading Test lasts about 10 minutes and involves 32 items designed to elicit verbal responses (e.g., identifying correct letters, words, or sentences) through written prompts (as well as some oral and pictorial prompts).

4. The (optional) Writing Test takes about 5 minutes and has 11 items intended to elicit written responses (e.g., the test taker's name, common vocabulary words) through verbal and pictorial prompts.

Beyond the Red level, the MAC II is mostly group administered except for the individually given Speaking Test, with fairly consistent test times (e.g., for the Tan level, typical times are 6 minutes for Speaking, 30 for Listening, 45 for Reading, and 40 for Writing). As test levels advance, however, the percentage of written prompts increases (e.g., in the Tan level, to 78 of the 113 items). Specifically, the Tan (9–12) level includes three components:

1. The Speaking Test consists of 11 items meant to elicit verbal responses (e.g., posing questions and telling stories) through verbal and pictorial prompts. The Answering Questions and Asking Questions parts of the test are rated by means of a rubric with 0–2 possible points. The Sustained Oral Production part of this test is rated by means of a rubric with 0–4 points each on several dimensions.

2. The Listening Test includes 24 items designed to elicit written responses through a variety of prompts (oral questions and multiple-choice answer prompts, oral dialogue and *yes/no* question prompts, and oral instruction with oral/written multiple-choice question prompts).

3. The Reading Test involves 56 items intended to elicit written responses (e.g., selecting synonyms, filling in blanks) through written prompts (multiple-choice vocabulary word prompts and degrees-of-reading-power [DRP] passages with modified cloze questions).

4. The Writing Test has 20 written (modified cloze) sentences covering vocabulary and grammar followed by two partially structured writing activities (completing a job application form and an essay with a prompt). These writing samples are scored using rubrics with 0–4 possible points on each of several dimensions.

As a predominantly structured-response (traditional) test, the MAC II is fairly straightforward in its scoring. Testers have the option of machine scoring (by TASA or one of several third parties) or local hand-scoring using transparent overlays supplied by the publisher. Scoring time is supposedly under 2 minutes per student, but this time will likely be longer for speaking and writing activities using rubrics (the publisher supplies additional training materials to help improve a scorer's rating proficiency and reliability; see Maculaitis, 2001a).

National norms are given for each of the four subtests (as well as for the entire test) along with tables for converting raw scores to stanines or English competency levels in the four modalities. In addition, for Grades 4–12, the results of the Reading Test may be converted into DRP scores, which indicate students' reading abilities on a scale of text difficulty; local scores can be compared to the DRP scores of native-speaking students throughout the United States. Thus, descriptions of student performance on the MAC II may be either proficiency based or norm referenced.

Justifying Test Use

Chapter 5 of the *MAC II Handbook* (Maculaitis, 2001b) provides extensive evidence justifying the use of this instrument, including a detailed description of the norming procedure. First, in the area of reliability, the developers note their concern for

- *internal consistency:* Three forms of the test were developed at each level for the norming study, generating internal consistency reliability coefficients (alpha) ranging from .82 to .97.

- *reliability of scoring:* Three readers were assigned to rate 4,000 writing items (across all test levels). The readers were in exact agreement on 73.1% of the items and within 1 point on 95.7% of the items.

In addition to establishing reliability, the authors of the MAC II went to great lengths to establish the test's validity (content, construct, and criterion related). Content validity (appropriateness) was generated not only from the test's basic design features (e.g., its emphasis on discourse-based instruction and TESOL's 1997 standards) but also from a careful review of the test items by a panel of 13 knowledgeable ESOL educators (to reduce confusion, bias, and offensiveness) and extensive field testing in 1999–2000. Likewise, construct validity (consistency with theoretical language constructs) and criterion-related validity are high, as indicated by students' scores on other widely used tests. For example, Pearson product–moment correlations of the MAC II (reading and writing) and the DRP range from .75 to .82; the MAC II Reading Test is also strongly correlated with the Secondary Level English Proficiency (SLEP) Reading Test (.77) and with the Stanford Diagnostic Reading Comprehension Test (.75). The MAC II Writing Test, meanwhile, is strongly correlated (.77) with the writing portion of the Language Assessment Scales Writing Test. Because of this evidence, the developers of the MAC II feel confident that their individual tests accurately measure the intended language domains.

Perhaps the most impressive aspect of the MAC II development involves the care with which this test was standardized. During the fall of 2000 and the spring of 2001, more than 8,200 English language learners (50.5% of them males, from 36 school districts in 19 widely scattered states, representing some 35 primary languages, and having a range of 0–8+ years of English instruction) completed the MAC II. Their scores were used to generate average standard scores, percentile ranks, and stanines for the various test modalities and levels. Because of this large sample drawn from both genders and a variety of nationalities, grade levels, and English language learning backgrounds, this test should be deemed appropriate for most English learner populations.

To be sure, several issues may cloud the effectiveness of the MAC II. Content validity may be questionable in the Listening Test, which also requires reading or memory skills (e.g., needing to choose from a list of four oral multiple-choice answers). Likewise, reliability may be negatively affected by the inclusion of oral prompts given by the tester (as opposed to audiotaped prompts) and by the use of (subjective) scoring rubrics in certain of the Speaking and Writing subtests; any inconsistencies on the part of the tester or scorer will color the results. In addition, although many primary languages are represented in the norming sample, in some cases the size of these groups is not clear (e.g., a Somali sample of <0.1 could mean anything from 1 to 69 students). What remains clear is that the overwhelming majority of participants in the norming sample (85.5%) were Spanish speaking; a more equitable distribution of nationalities would have given the instrument an even broader application. Finally, the initial cost, as well as the need to administer portions of the test individually (requiring more time), may make the MAC II impractical for some test situations.

Despite these potential problems, the flexibility and wide application of this proficiency test should make it attractive to a great many elementary and secondary school teachers. Indeed, the MAC II appears to have great potential as a multipurpose language assessment tool.

Michigan English Language Assessment Battery (MELAB)

Reviewed by James E. Purpura

Publisher: Testing and Certification Division, English Language Institute, 3020 North University Building, University of Michigan, Ann Arbor, MI 48109-1057 USA; telephone 313-764-2416, 313-764-3452; fax 313-763-0369; melab@umich.edu; http://www.lsa.umich.edu/eli /testing.htm

Publication Date: 1985

Target Population: Adult nonnative speakers of English who will be using English for academic or professional purposes

Cost: In Ann Arbor, US$35 (plus US$15 for the interview); outside Ann Arbor, US$50 (plus US$15 for the interview)

Test Purpose

The MELAB is a standardized English language proficiency test designed to "evaluate the advanced level English language competence of adult nonnative speakers of English" (Briggs & Dobson, 1994, p. 1). Inferences from MELAB scores are general in nature, given their intent to provide users with an assessment of the examinees' overall English language proficiency as well as a specific evaluation of their writing ability, listening ability, and combined ability in grammar, vocabulary, and reading. The MELAB Speaking Test is optional. MELAB results are used to make high-stakes decisions about the English language proficiency of students applying for university admission or professionals applying for employment or other opportunities. Given the role this exam plays in admissions and in certifying professionals, its impact is very broad.

Test Methods

The MELAB contains three sections. Section 1 is designed to measure writing ability by means of a 200- to 300-word composition in which examinees are given 30 minutes "to take a position on a topic and defend it, to describe something from a personal experience, or to explain a problem and offer possible solutions" (Briggs & Dobson, 1994, p. 3). Examinees choose from two prompt options. Two independent raters score the composition according to a 10-point, holistic rubric. The scale descriptors address "clarity and overall effectiveness, topic development, organization, and range, accuracy and appropriateness of grammar and vocabulary" (p. 3). Ratings that differ by more than one interval are adjudicated by a third rater. Besides assigning numerical scores, raters may give formative feedback to examinees by coding essays for salient features (e.g., topic especially well developed). If two raters report the same feature, it is reported to examinees.

Section 2 intends to measure listening ability by means of short utterances and extended discourse followed by 50 discrete multiple-choice items delivered via a 25-minute audiotaped recording. The short-utterance tasks involve one- or two-turn questions or statements. Test takers indicate the most logical literal meaning or pragmatic interpretation of the input. The extended discourse tasks involve a 3- to 4-minute minilecture and a 4- to 5-minute conversation revolving around a simplified map or graph. Note-taking is permitted. Items aim to measure textual knowledge, lexical knowledge, and a range of pragmatic meanings. Scaled scores range from 30 to 100.

Section 3, the Grammar/Cloze/Vocabulary/Reading (GCVR) section, presents four tasks and 100 multiple-choice questions. The grammar task contains 30 discrete items designed to measure morphosyntactic form; the cloze task presents 20 items in one passage intended to measure "elements of coherence and cohesion and elements of grammar and semantics" (English Language Institute, Testing & Certification Division, 1995, p. 39); the vocabulary task contains 30 discrete items designed to measure "the understanding and use of lexis" (p. 39); and the reading section presents four or five short passages drawn from the humanities and the social, physical, and biological sciences followed by 20 items designed to measure comprehension of information explicitly and implicitly communicated. Pragmatic inference questions relate to gist, author's stance, and rhetorical relationships between portions of the text. Scaled scores range from 15 to 100.

The Speaking Test involves a 10- to 15-minute interview with the examiner designed to measure examinees' ability to communicate effectively in English with relation to their academic, professional, or technical subject area. The interview begins with a warm-up, followed by questions to elicit extended discourse on a familiar topic, and a closing. Examinees are evaluated on their overall spoken English defined in terms of their (a) fluency/intelligibility (i.e., rate of speech, pauses or hesitation, articulation, prosodics); (b) grammar and vocabulary (i.e., utterance length and complexity, lexical range, morphological control, grammatical accuracy); (c) functional language use and sociolinguistic proficiency (e.g., initiative, elaboration, sustained topic development, interactional facility, sensitivity to cultural referents); and (d) listening comprehension, based on the degree to which the interviewer needs to make accommodations involving rate of delivery, complexity, topic exploration, or frequency of repetition. Speaking performance is scored on a 12-point holistic rubric (4+, 4, 4–, . . . 1–). The MELAB recommends, but does not require, that speech samples be audiotaped. Performance samples are scored by only one person, the examiner, who unfortunately fulfills the role of interviewer and evaluator simultaneously. Judges receive rating instructions, but no measures are taken to ensure that raters have been adequately trained for accurate and consistent scoring.

The MELAB score report contains scaled scores for Composition, Listening, GCVR, and Speaking (optional) as well as a final overall score (excluding the Speaking section). The report also includes comments on the essay as well as clear and useful information on score interpretation and use.

Justifying Test Use

The MELAB is useful to the extent that score-based inferences can provide trustworthy and meaningful information for making appropriate decisions about the English language proficiency of adult nonnative speakers of English wishing to use English in academic or professional contexts. To justify the appropriateness of the MELAB for these purposes, the technical manual (English Language Institute, Testing & Certification Division, 1995) provides a considerable amount of documentation on the qualities of the test. In addition to a full description of the exam and information on test administration, scoring, interpretation, and intended uses, it supplies interested audiences with statistical information on the test along with a clear and thorough discussion of reliability and validity. To the authors' credit, the documentation is presented in a way that is comprehensible to most test users.

All in all, the MELAB appears to provide useful information about test takers' overall English language proficiency. Given the combination of selected-response and extended production tasks, it gives examinees the opportunity to demonstrate their explicit and implicit knowledge of the language. More specifically, it tests their receptive knowledge of grammar, vocabulary, listening, and reading and their productive skills in writing and speaking.

In terms of reliability, the MELAB reports several methods for estimating the consistency of test scores, each producing relatively high estimates (.82–.95) for each required section of the test and relatively low *SEMs*. Reliability estimates for the Speaking section are unfortunately not given, casting some doubt on the trustworthiness of those scores. Of some confusion is the way the reliability analysis of the Listening and GCVR sections were carried out. Instead of examining the homogeneity of items with regard to a common trait (e.g., grammatical knowledge), items were grouped in many cases according to test method (e.g., cloze) or type of input (e.g., lecture listening task). Of further confusion is the theoretical rationale for combining the reading scores with the grammar, cloze, and vocabulary scores. If this decision was based on the results of exploratory factor analyses in which the Composition, Listening, and GCVR components were analyzed together (English Language Institute, Testing & Certification Division, 1995, p. 55), then one might question why the Composition score was not combined with the GCVR scores. Despite the high reliability estimates, the MELAB lacks a theoretical rationale on which to map inferences from these statistics, making interpretation difficult. This is the obvious disadvantage of constructing a test around tasks as opposed to rooting test construction in an overarching model of English language proficiency.

In terms of test usefulness, the authors of the *MELAB Technical Manual* (Briggs & Dobson, 1994) have gone to great lengths to provide evidence of validity. For each section of the test, content-related evidence of validity takes the form of a thorough description of the traits being measured, the test development procedures, and the items. A description of item coverage across forms is also supplied. Of equal interest would be the results of the item analyses or a discussion of item fit (and misfit) in the test. The authors demonstrate construct-related evidence of validity indicating how various components of the MELAB are intended to measure the different components of language ability proposed by Bachman and Palmer (1996). Unfortunately, however, no analyses have been produced to demonstrate empirically how data from the MELAB might fit this model of language ability. As further evidence of construct validity, the underlying structure of the MELAB is examined by means of exploratory factor analysis. A comparison of MELAB scores with TOEFL scores provides criterion-related evidence of validity. Finally, MELAB scores and teacher rankings of students were compared, producing some agreement between the two.

Although the MELAB appears carefully designed with high reliability estimates, it is likely to be severely criticized from the perspective of authenticity and interactiveness, as described by Bachman and Palmer (1996). In terms of authenticity, the selected-response format is highly unlikely outside the most controlled testing or instructional situations; nonetheless, it can be argued theoretically that this format provides a means of measuring the examinees' receptive knowledge of a wide content domain. Given that examinees also demonstrate their productive use of this knowledge in the writing and speaking tasks, the dependence on selected-response tasks, in my view, is not such a liability. However, in the grammar and vocabulary sections, the discrete nature of the items, which jump from topic to topic, is distracting and inauthentic. Many of these same items could be assessed in the context of situated events or coherent themes of interest to the test reference groups. For example, lexis, particles, and gerunds could be assessed in the context of a doctor's office visit, thereby increasing the authenticity of the test for medical professionals. Content-rich input in these sections might also engage the examinees' individual characteristics (i.e., their language knowledge, topical knowledge, strategic competence, and affective schemata) to a greater degree, thereby increasing the interactivity of the test.

In sum, the MELAB is carefully constructed, reliable, and comprehensive. Given the range of tasks, the instrument assesses examinees' receptive knowledge and their full production skills in English. As in many standard-ized exams, the discrete nature of the Listening and GCVR tasks could profit from more contextualization, and the input, especially in some Listening tasks and in the reading passages, could be lengthened to better match potential tasks in the target language use domain. To be reliable (and trustworthy), the Speaking task should be audiotaped and scored by trained or certified raters. Finally, the provision of formative feedback on composi-tions should be required rather than optional. This would significantly increase the benefits of taking the test to examinees and teachers. Despite these limitations, the MELAB is a credible English language proficiency exam, and test users have sufficient information to decide for themselves if this exam can serve their purposes well.

Secondary Level English Proficiency (SLEP) Test

Reviewed by Jeff S. Johnson

Publisher: SLEP Program Office, Educational Testing Service,
                         PO Box 6155, Princeton, NJ 08541 USA; telephone
                         609-771-7206; fax 609-771-7835; http://www.toefl.org
                         /educator/edslep.html

Publication Date: 1980 (Form 1), 1981 (Form 2), 1987 (Form 3)

Target Population: Secondary-level students in the United States whose
                         native language is not English

Cost: US$155 for 20 test booklets, 100 answer sheets,
                         manual, and audiotape

Test Purpose

The SLEP Test is a norm-referenced test designed to measure general ability
in understanding spoken and written English for international students in
U.S. secondary schools, although the test is also often used in postsecondary
schools within and outside the United States (Wilson, 1993b). Suggested
uses of SLEP Test scores include ESOL class assignment, placement in
mainstream English-medium courses, exemption from a bilingual program,
postprogram proficiency measurement, and program evaluation (ETS,
1997).

   The test's degree of impact depends on how the scores are used. ESOL
course placement and program exemption decisions can be considered
medium stakes, because they may affect students' academic timetables,
whereas the impact can be much broader when the test scores are used for
gatekeeping purposes for mainstream courses. If the SLEP Test is used for
ESOL program evaluation, its impact on curricula may be great (e.g., if low
gain scores lead to course redevelopment). Because the test is a norm-
referenced general proficiency test, however, it is probably not sensitive
enough for specific language program evaluation (Brown, 1995).

Test Methods

The SLEP Test includes a Listening part and a Reading part, each with 75
four-option multiple-choice items. The Listening part includes four sections.
The first contains photograph description items with single-sentence input
prompts, similar to items on the TOEFL. The next section has dictation
sentence-matching items, which appear to require listening and reading
skills. Next comes an innovative map section. For each item, examinees
identify which of four cars the speakers are riding in based on specific hints
on place and street names given in short, three-turn conversations. The final
Listening section is an extended conversation between secondary school

students and school staff members, divided into sections that are followed by comprehension questions.

The Reading part also includes four sections. In the first section, the examinee matches reactions (as might be seen in a thought bubble) to specific family members in a situation presented in a *Family Circus* comic strip. The next section consists of items with single-sentence descriptors, which must be matched to one of four line drawings. Most of the items in the first two Reading sections appear relatively easy. In the next section are three short passages with embedded multiple-choice cloze items, each followed by additional comprehension questions. The final Reading section includes comprehension items for a longer, literary reading passage.

When the SLEP Test is used for U.S. secondary school students, the authenticity level of the extended conversation and the cloze and literary reading passage sections is high, because the conversation content deals with experiences typical of U.S. student life, the student roles are read by adolescents, and the reading passages are adapted from U.S. secondary school texts.

The test is hand-scored by the institution administering it using the two-ply answer sheets provided, which make counting correct responses quick and easy. The number of correct responses is then transformed into a scaled score in the range of 10–35 for Listening and Reading or 20–70 for a single SLEP Test score.

Justifying Test Use

The *SLEP Test Manual* (ETS, 1997) gives the results of two studies as evidence for the justification of using SLEP Test scores to measure general ESOL proficiency. One study shows that native English speakers score higher on the test (average scores of 29–32) than do ESOL students (15–23), and the other shows that the longer students are exposed to or study English, the higher their SLEP Test scores are, with moderate correlations of .21–.40 with the variables *years of English study, time in this school,* and *time in U.S.A.* (see also Stansfield, 1984). Reliability estimates of the SLEP Test for foreign students entering U.S. Grades 7–11 were quite high, with K-R 20 estimates of .94 for the Listening test and .93 for the Reading test. Two other studies with postsecondary school participants in the United States also report high K-R 21 reliability estimates, one with adult immigrant students (Listening = .90, Reading = .88) reported by Ilyin, Spurling, and Seymour (1987), and one with community college ESL students, using a shortened, 100-item form of the test (Listening = .92, Reading = .90) reported by Wilson and Tillberg (1994). Two studies in Japan with college students report weaker reliability estimates: K-R 20 = .81 for the full test (Culligan & Gorsuch, 1999), and subsection reliability estimates (Rulon's formula, length set at k = 40) of .55 (*Family Circus* comic) to .77 (cloze passages) (K. M. Wilson, personal communication, November 27, 2001).

Correlations between the SLEP Test and the TOEFL provide sound concurrent validity evidence for the SLEP Test Listening section, the photograph and extended-conversation sections in particular, but raise questions concerning the Reading items. Three of the four item types in that section are more strongly correlated with each of the three TOEFL Listening item types (statements, dialogues, and minitalks) than they are with the TOEFL reading comprehension items, making it difficult to interpret the meaning of SLEP Test Reading scores. In addition, the study by Ilyin et al. (1987) reveals no difference in degree of correlation between SLEP Test Reading scores and CELT Listening section scores and CELT Structure (reading) section scores. Furthermore, Gillie (2002) has shown that the MAC II Listening Test is more strongly correlated with the SLEP Test Reading section than with the SLEP Test Listening section. These studies suggest that the SLEP Test Reading section may not be an accurate measure of reading ability.

It is the responsibility of test users to judge the appropriateness of the SLEP Test for their own situations. This includes estimating the test's reliability for their specific examinees and gathering evidence to help determine the validity of any decision made using SLEP Test scores.

Test of English as a Foreign Language Computer-Based Test (TOEFL CBT)

Reviewed by Jayanti Banerjee and Caroline Clapham

Publisher: Educational Testing Service, PO Box 6155, Princeton, NJ 08541-6155 USA; telephone 609-771-7100; fax 609-771-7500; toefl@ets.org; http://www.ets.org/toefl/

Publication Date: July 1998

Target Population: Mainly nonnative-English-speaking students who wish to study at institutions of higher learning where the language of instruction is English

Cost: US$110

Test Purpose

The TOEFL CBT is a proficiency test designed to provide evidence of the English language proficiency of nonnative-English-speaking applicants to higher education institutions where English is the language of instruction. Scores on the test are also used by U.S. government agencies, scholarship programs, and licensing and certification agencies. Individual institutions and academic departments determine the minimum level of English required; therefore, some institutions will require higher TOEFL scores than others.

The TOEFL is a high-stakes test because students' future lives may be affected by their test scores. The test has a great impact on language learning, and many language schools throughout the world offer TOEFL preparation classes.

Test Methods

The computerized version of the TOEFL draws on many of the item types used in the paper version. For example, the Structure and Writing sections contain tasks identical to those in the paper version, and the Listening and Reading sections contain many item types that are similar. However, the CBT has a wider range of item types, so that, for example, the Reading section has some text insertion tasks as well as multiple-choice questions. In addition, the Listening section, unlike its paper counterpart, includes pictures for candidates to view while listening to each test item. These pictures either set the scene of a conversation or give information that the speaker wants to convey.

The CBT consists of four sections: Listening, Structure, Reading, and Writing. All four are delivered via the computer, though students are given the choice of composing an essay straight onto the computer or writing it by hand. The Structure and Listening sections are computer adaptive, meaning that scores are based on test takers' language proficiency. For example, if one test item is too easy for a test taker, the next item is likely to be more difficult; more credit is given for answering hard questions correctly than for answering easy ones. Computer-adaptive tests have many advantages; for example, most items are of a suitable level of difficulty for individual candidates, and candidates should not have to answer as many questions as they might in a non-computer-adaptive test.

The Writing section is independently rated by two readers according to a 7-point scale (0–6). Each point on the scale has descriptors of the communicative features that characterize writers at that level. The final Writing score is an average of the two raters' judgments. This average score is then weighted and accounts for approximately half of the composite Structure/Writing score (0–30). The Listening and Reading sections are reported separately (each on a scale of 0–30). The total test score reported is the average of a test taker's scores on the three sections multiplied by 10 (0–300). The CBT result is valid for 2 years.

Because the test is taken on the computer, the scores on the machine-marked sections can be immediately reported. Candidates can therefore learn their scores for the Listening and Reading sections before leaving the test site. Because the scores for Structure and Writing are reported together, and because the composition is hand-scored after the testing session is over, candidates can initially be given only estimates of their Structure/Writing score and their total score. The total score, together with a separate Writing score, the composite Structure/Writing score, and separate Listening and Reading scores, is mailed to the student a few weeks after the test. The TOEFL CBT test battery does not assess speaking ability.

Test instructions are presented only on-screen. A tutorial at the start of each of the sections familiarizes test takers with the item types and gives candidates an opportunity to practice answering some items. In addition, two software-based practice tests are available (POWERPREP, 2003). Candidates may change their answers before confirming a response, but once they have confirmed an answer in the two adaptive sections of the test (Listening and Structure), they can make no further changes. The sections are timed (Listening, 40–60 minutes; Structure, 15–20 minutes; Reading, 70–90 minutes; Writing, 30 minutes), but the time limits are so generous that most candidates will have no trouble finishing. The entire test, including tutorials, takes approximately 4 hours.

Listening. The Listening section has two parts, the first consisting of a number of one- or two-turn dialogues or casual conversations, and the second, of a series of minilectures or group discussions. The material is presented only once. Test takers are not allowed to take notes. The items are usually multiple-choice questions in a written or a visual form; sometimes there are matching items. Candidates answer 30–50 questions, depending on the number of items that are being pretested.

All the input materials are in the academic domain; some items consist of social or interactive situations, for example, short interactions about academic-related issues such as borrowing a book from the library. Others are longer monologues or exchanges and are related to academic listening situations, in which the test taker has to listen to a minilecture or a discussion on a nonspecialist topic. In the minilectures, the texts are expository, with the lecturers presenting a body of information. As the test takers listen, context (e.g., a teacher standing in front of a blackboard) or content (e.g., a diagram) visuals are presented onscreen. (See Ginther, 2002, for an account of research into the visual aspect of the Listening test.)

The Listening questions require test takers to identify main ideas, supporting ideas, or important details or to infer the meaning of one or both of the speakers. These inferences can include the pragmatic implications of what one of the speakers has said and, apart from testing knowledge of specific vocabulary, can draw on the test takers' understanding of idiomatic expressions and grammatical constructions. The group discussions, which typically take the form of seminar discussions or note-reconstruction sessions, allow for more argumentative text types, but the two practice tests contain no samples of this kind of item (see Buck, 2001, for a more complete discussion of the TOEFL Listening test).

Test takers see the test questions only after they have listened to the text, so they have to depend heavily on memory when answering the questions.

Reading. The Reading section is not adaptive, so students can return to previously answered items and make changes. Test takers read four or five passages, each of 250–350 words, and answer 11 questions per text. In addition to the more standard multiple-choice items, this section contains items that ask test takers to decide where best to insert an additional sentence, or to click on sentences in the text that correspond to a particular item of vocabulary or identify a structural feature of the passage.

The reading passages, though nonspecialist, are varied in topic (e.g., human and social geography, sciences, and art history). Although some consist of argumentative texts, most are expository. Test takers are obliged to read (or at least scroll through) a whole passage before answering any questions. The questions test not only understanding of the gist but also the ability to make inferences, read for detail, understand the principles of discourse structure and textual cohesion, and show a knowledge of specific vocabulary items.

The Reading section comprises reading comprehension and vocabulary items, but the items testing the two skills are very different. The reading comprehension questions make use of the computer format and consist of an interesting range of question types. The reading passages themselves are well presented in an easy-to-read typeface, and test takers can scroll up and down the text while the appropriate test item remains opposite. The reading comprehension tasks seem to test many of the underlying factors of reading in a reader-friendly way. On the other hand, almost all the vocabulary items (which are multiple choice), although supposedly context based, are answerable without reading the texts in which the words appear.

Structure. In the Structure section, test takers answer 20–25 questions depending on the adaptivity algorithm. The prompts are all single sentences and are of two types: completion of incomplete sentences by choosing from a list of options and identification of the error from among four possibilities underlined in the sentence. The items are designed to check whether test takers can recognize appropriate standard written English, and they assess structural features such as plural forms, tense selection, and word order.

Unfortunately, the range of structures tested is not wide, and students may score at a level that gains them entrance to a college or university without being able to write accurate prose. However, students write an essay in the Writing section, and because structure is included in the marking criteria for that section, severe weaknesses in a grammatical production may lower a student's Writing score.

Writing. The Writing section consists of a single prompt from a published bank of essay questions (see ETS, 2001b), and the test taker has 30 minutes in which to write an essay on the required topic. There is no word limit. Paper is provided for (optional, unmarked) notes.

The content domain of the writing tasks is academic, and the tasks are argumentative. The scoring criteria indicate that test takers are expected to demonstrate an ability to organize their ideas logically, use a variety of syntactic forms available in standard written English, and select appropriate formal vocabulary.

The level of challenge presented by the writing topic can vary rather widely. For example, one topic asks candidates to reflect on a course that they have particularly enjoyed, and another asks them to discuss the relative merits and demerits of barter trade and trade using money. The former topic is less conceptually complex than the latter and might not stretch the candidate's language as much.

Another possible disadvantage is that candidates are allowed to write their essays by hand or on the computer, but there has as yet been no research into whether the two methods of writing produce similar results. Until that is known, test users cannot know for certain whether the TOEFL CBT is reliably assessing students' writing skills.

Justifying Test Use

ETS answers most of the questions a test taker or user might have in the TOEFL Technical Report Series, the TOEFL Research Report Series, and the TOEFL Monograph Series (see http://www.ets.org/). Papers about the validity of the test are available. Before the CBT was published, ETS produced a test manual every year that provided such figures as reliability estimates and *SEMs*. However, now, probably because of the adaptivity element, these data are no longer reported.

Since the paper version of the test was launched in 1965, teaching and testing theories have changed. With the emergence of the communicative movement, tests are required to be more authentic than they were (see, e.g., Wu & Stansfield, 2001) and to fit more closely the purpose for which they are designed. Although parts of the TOEFL have been changed, some sections remain noncommunicative.

Two of the major concerns about the validity of the TOEFL CBT relate to test construct. First, the TOEFL (although basing some sections on tertiary college domains) does not test academic language, and although recent versions of the TOEFL have attempted to be more communicative, the test is still heavily dependent on multiple-choice questions. The second major concern relates to what the scores on the TOEFL CBT actually say about students' levels of English. No large-scale research has investigated the effect of taking a test on the computer rather than taking that same test using paper and pencil, and until such research has been carried out, test users cannot know whether the two tests test the same constructs. A limited number of studies have examined aspects of this issue (see Russell, 1999).

Unfortunately, therefore, results on the paper-based TOEFL and the CBT cannot be matched, as the tests may test different skills. The computer test may be testing different language abilities and therefore be providing different scores, the CBT's Reading and Listening tests are different from the paper-based ones, and the CBT includes an essay task whereas the paper version does not. Test users therefore cannot know what scores on the TOEFL CBT actually mean.

Test of English for International Communication (TOEIC)

Reviewed by Diane Schmitt

Publisher: TOEIC Service International, TOEIC Testing Program, Educational Testing Service, Rosedale Road, Princeton, NJ 08541 USA; telephone 609-683-2866; fax 609-683-2022; toeic@ets.org; http://www.ets.org/toeic/

Publication Date: 1979

Target Population: People working in an international environment

Cost: Varies by location; contact area representative for current price.

Test Purpose

The TOEIC is a norm-referenced test designed to be a direct measure of real-life reading and listening ability. Subsequent research has shown it to be an indirect measure of writing and speaking ability. Originally commissioned by the Japanese Ministry of International Trade and Industry to promote an improvement in the level of English of workers in Japanese industry, the test continues to be used widely in Japan and Korea. In 2001, more than 2.5 million persons took the test worldwide, the vast majority from Japan and Korea. However, the number of TOEIC takers is growing in Europe, North and South America, Africa, and other parts of Asia.

By design, the TOEIC is a high-stakes test intended to provide general language proficiency evidence to international organizations for use in making employment decisions, such as initial selection, overseas postings, and promotion. Other uses of the test by language schools for placement and progress testing result in medium- to low-stakes decision making. Use by universities for evaluation prior to graduation is a new high-stakes use of the test.

A *can-do* guide based on self-report data from Japanese examinees contains a comprehensive list of basic job and daily life activities that test takers within particular Listening Comprehension and Reading score ranges can be expected to be able to perform. The mean scores of test takers across all regions where the test is given roughly correspond to the middle range of scores (230–350 per section). Such a test taker can be expected to read storefronts with ease and perform various other tasks with difficulty (e.g., understand explanations about how to perform a routine job-related task, read and understand an agenda for a meeting, write a memo to a supervisor describing progress on a project). The examinee handbook (ETS, 1998b) links scores in this range to the following jobs or functions: hotel head or assistant waiter, support staff in a business meeting with duties that may include taking notes, receptionist, and ability to take an overseas business trip with an assistant.

A mini–publishing industry has grown up around TOEIC preparation materials despite a clear emphasis in publicity materials on the value of activities promoting general language improvement over specific courses of study for the test. Two research studies carried out in Japan looked at the effects of different types of teaching on TOEIC scores. Robb and Ercanbrack (1999) generally found no significant difference in gain scores for university students following courses focused on general English, business English, or TOEIC preparation materials. Boldt and Ross (1998) found that a combination of specifically trained instructors, medium-sized classes, and the use of video materials resulted in more test takers achieving predetermined score targets, particularly at higher levels. One may conclude from these studies that any classroom change that results in teaching directly to the test is misguided. (See ETS, 2004a, for additional research reports.)

Test Methods

The test consists of 200 multiple-choice items equally divided between Listening (45 minutes) and Reading (75 minutes). The Listening section is delivered by audiotape. The first part has 20 picture prompts each followed by four single-sentence statements, one of which best describes the picture. Part 2 consists of 30 single-sentence questions or statements followed by three single-sentence response choices. Part 3 consists of 30 three-part exchanges between two speakers followed by a question requiring test takers to make an inference based on the content of the exchange. The 20 items in Part 4 consist of a series of 15- to 20-second monologues each followed by two or more factual or inference questions related to the talk. Part 5 consists of 40 single-sentence fill-in-the-gap items, which focus test takers' attention on grammar and lexis. Part 6 has a similar focus but uses 22 sentence-length error identification items. Part 7 consists of 38 items based on reading materials ranging from notices and letters to magazine articles, each approximately 50–200 words in length. The items require test takers to give attention to main ideas, details, and the drawing of inferences.

In sum, all responses are structured; test takers' responsibility is limited to selecting the correct answer. Raw scores for each section are converted to a scale range of 5–495 and combined for a total score range of 10–990. Scores are reported in profile and as a total score. The machine-scored, multiple-choice format is key to the high reliability and cost-effectiveness of the test.

Justifying Test Use

The Chauncey Group conducted a series of studies (Boldt & Ross, 1998; Dudley-Evans & St. John, 1996; ETS, 1998a; Wilson, 1993a; Woodford, 1982) on the TOEIC in order to equate new test forms, identify the relationship between the TOEIC and oral proficiency, link scores to *can-do* statements, and monitor the effects of instruction on score gains. However, a weakness in much of this research is that it has been carried out primarily with Japanese and Korean examinees. The publisher indicated that a number of score interpretation studies were being conducted using samples of test takers drawn from other first languages in Europe, Latin America, and other parts of Asia (personal communication, August 26, 2002). This research is urgently needed in order to confirm the robustness of score interpretation with examinees of other nationalities. The reported difference in mean scores between Japanese (451) and Korean (480) test takers and European (633) test takers suggests that the two groups are distinct and therefore that test users must be very cautious about applying score interpretations based on one group to the other. The *TOEIC Technical Manual* (ETS, 1998c) gives information for organizations wishing to conduct local benchmarking studies for interpreting test scores, and local TOEIC representatives are available to assist test users in interpreting TOEIC scores.

Test of Spoken English (TSE)

Reviewed by April Ginther

Publisher:	TSE Program Office, Educational Testing Service, PO Box 6157, Princeton, NJ 08451-6157 USA; telephone 609-771-7100; fax 609-771-7500; http://www.ets.org/tse/
Publication Date:	1980; revised 1995
Target Population:	Adult nonnative speakers of English working in an academic or professional environment in North America
Cost:	US$125

Test Purpose

The TSE is a high-stakes test of oral English proficiency that is used widely by institutions in North America to make decisions about an examinee's ability to communicate effectively in an academic or professional environment. The test is intended for decision-making purposes by institutions with respect to the performance of two very broad target populations: examinees who are being considered for positions as international teaching assistants or examinees being considered for positions in any other professional context.

As the test is designed as a general measure of oral language ability, the TSE is argued to be appropriate for "examinees regardless of native language, type of educational training, or field of employment" (ETS, 2000, p. 4). Between July 1995 and January 2000, the TSE was administered to 36,747 examinees who indicated they were taking the test for academic purposes and 46,121 examinees who indicated they were taking the test for professional purposes.

The original version of the TSE, developed in the late 1970s, underwent a revision that began in 1992, and the revised TSE became operational in 1995. A major part of the revision involved clarifying the relationship among current conceptualizations of communicative language ability, test specifications, and the rating scale (see Douglas & Smith, 1997). The current rating scale and its explication represent a move away from the structuralist assumptions that were prevalent when the test was first designed and include consideration of coherence, organization, audience awareness, and functional competence along with the more traditional focus on form.

Test Methods

The TSE is a semidirect test; that is, examinees respond orally to a variety of text-based and audio prompts. The actual test is presented on audiotape, and examinees' responses are recorded on audiotapes. Responses are monologic, not interactive, but the format and administration of the TSE allow for maintenance of standardized conditions. The response times allowed for individual items range from 30 to 90 seconds, and completion of the test's 12 items requires approximately 20 minutes.

The test is divided into four sections. The first, which is not scored, presents a series of warm-up questions that allow examinees to become familiar with taping their responses; the remaining items require the examinee to construct responses that demonstrate facility with a variety of language functions. For example, individual items may require an examinee to offer an apology, persuade, complain, give directions, express an opinion, give a definition, and interpret a graph. Although the test items do not appear to directly reflect the communicative requirements of any particular context, they elicit a variety of responses in a very short time under standardized conditions.

The completed audiotapes are rated by two independent raters who provide holistic scores for each item. Item scores are then averaged, and the final score is based on the average of the two raters. A third rater is assigned if the raters disagree by more than one score level. Final scores are reported in increments of 5 and range between 20 (no effective communication) and 60 (communication almost always effective). Based on the scores of the 64,701 examinees who took the TSE between July 1995 and January 2000, interrater reliability is reported as .92, test form reliability as .98, test score reliability as .89, and the *SEM* as 2.24 (ETS, 2000).

Justifying Test Use

ETS provides evidence in support of the validity of the TSE in the form of research reports, technical reports, and monographs (see ETS, 2004b). Given the strengths of ETS, the majority of these reports involve examinations of the psychometric characteristics of TSE scores; however, others examine the validity of the TSE in relation to conceptualizations of communicative success, the validity of the revisions to the TSE with respect to their relationship to theoretical discussions of communicative language use, and the validity of the TSE with respect to the similarity of discourse characteristics of native and nonnative speakers in response to TSE items. What ETS does not provide, and cannot be expected to provide, is evidence for the validity of local decisions based on TSE scores. Such studies, which are the responsibility of local institutions, are seldom undertaken, but should be in the interest of more comprehensive validation of the test's use.

In this light, because the scores are based on a short sample of speech, which is given in response to limited and generic tasks, test users must use caution in interpreting score levels. The fact that the test is not linked to any particular instructional or professional context ensures its applicability for widespread use but, at the same time, results in a situation in which inferences about the speaker's ability in relation to any particular context are problematic.

The TSE is clearly most suitable for use when examinees are not present at the local institution and are unavailable for assessments that might fit more closely with local needs and standards. The TSE's provision of a very general measure of language ability is its greatest strength but also its greatest weakness.

Woodcock-Muñoz Language Survey (WMLS)

Reviewed by Margaret E. Malone

Publisher: Riverside Publishing Co., 425 Spring Lake Drive, Itasca,
                    IL 60143-2079 USA; telephone 800-323-9540, 630-
                    467-7000 (outside the United States); fax 630-467-
                    7192; http://www.riverpub.com/

Publication Date: 1993; normative update 2001

Target Population: Pre-K (age 4) to adult ESOL students

Cost: $257 for normative update package plus test books and
                    25 test records in English or Spanish

Test Purpose

The WMLS measures Spanish and English cognitive language proficiency as
defined according to Cummins (1984). In short, the test predicts an
examinee's ability to survive in the target language (English or Spanish) in
an academic environment. According to the test manual (Woodcock &
Muñoz-Sandoval, 1993), the WMLS can be used to determine English and
Spanish proficiency, determine eligibility for Spanish bilingual services,
provide diagnostic information for teachers, determine student readiness for
transition into English-only instruction, monitor and evaluate program
effectiveness, and conduct research.

The test asks examinees to perform a number of entirely reactive tasks.
Examinees identify pictures of increasing cognitive difficulty; perform
language analogies; identify letters and words; and form drawings, letters,
and words dictated to them by the test administrator.

Based on the purposes listed in the test manual (Woodcock & Muñoz-
Sandoval, 1993), a number of decisions, ranging from relatively low to
critically high stakes, can be made on the basis of test results. As an
example of a relatively low-stakes purpose, teachers can use the test for
diagnosis to help improve or better structure classroom activities to meet
the needs of students. The test can also be used in program monitoring and
evaluation; depending on the role of the test relative to other instruments or
evaluation procedures, the test can be used for medium- to high-stakes
purposes. Finally, the test can be used to determine eligibility for entry to or
exit from a program. Under such circumstances, the test becomes high
stakes, because examinees' academic future may rest on the appropriateness
of the language program in which they are placed or from which they exit.

Depending on how the test is used, it may have great impact. It may
have positive washback by affirming the importance of cognitive language
ability in Spanish and English, and the very act of testing Spanish cognitive
language proficiency is encouraging. However, the test methods, described
below, may have positive and negative washback.

Test Methods

The test provides a variety of input to the examinee on a mini-easel propped up between the test taker and test administrator, and through instructions and aural input given by the administrator. Test visuals include colored pictures, numbers, and letters, and aural input includes numbers and words. The test does not include input on a videotape, audiotape, or CD-ROM; it includes only static input and not interactive input. Nor does the test provide standardized input from the test administrator, as would be the case if there were an accompanying tape or CD-ROM.

The test taker's role is responsive and not proactive or interactive. The test taker responds to structured items and is scored on a 2-point scale; 1 indicates correct, and 0 indicates incorrect. The test taker does not initiate any part of the test and produces minimal writing. The raw score is computed entirely by the test administrator, although the scaled scores can be computed according to a scoring program (included) or by hand.

Justifying Test Use

The test manual (Woodcock & Muñoz-Sandoval, 1993) gives ample information on applying scores to a variety of purposes. For example, the manual suggests ways to interpret the results for monolingual instructional programs as well as for age and grade equivalents. In addition, the manual suggests other approaches to interpreting the scores on each part of the test (oral and reading-writing) by examining how student performance on specific items or clusters of items might indicate areas needing attention from teachers. This information is particularly helpful because it explains, to a certain degree, possible reasons for student performance on specific items or parts of the test.

To determine test reliability, the developer employed a split-half method, and correlations ranged from as low as .77 for one age group on the picture tests to as high as .99 for another age group on the broad English ability cluster of the battery. Although such reliabilities are generally acceptable, interrater reliability is not reported, and possible differences between raters in either their scoring procedures or their consistency in administering the test are not accounted for.

The test manual (Woodcock & Muñoz-Sandoval, 1993) reports on three types of validity: content, concurrent, and construct. Although the information presented on content validity is generally adequate, it does not address one concern, which is how well the test actually measures cognitive language proficiency, at least as conceptualized by Cummins (1984). Although the test is well grounded in a number of theoretical constructs, to which it refers consistently, it is unclear how the content of the test actually reflects high-level cognitive tasks in speaking, reading, and writing outside the specific parameters of the researchers mentioned. The test has been designed as an indirect assessment of speaking, reading, and writing ability, yet it never asks the test taker to speak, read, or write very much, at least not in terms of the language that characterizes academic programs. Such a limited definition of cognitive language proficiency is a concern.

Woodcock and Muñoz-Sandoval (1993) also report on concurrent validity. Test taker performance was compared within the test batteries as well as with outside test batteries, ranging from oral language tests such as the PRE-Language Assessment Scales to the Stanford-Binet Intelligence Scales. The test developers sampled fairly thoroughly across age and grade levels. Their norming sample included a total of 6,359 subjects who ranged in age from 24 months to more than 90 years. The developers established norms for subjects in Spanish by equating levels of Spanish performance with equivalent English performance using 2,000 Spanish language subjects from Argentina, Costa Rica, Mexico, Peru, Puerto Rico, Spain, and the United States. More information about the limited English proficient students in the norming study would have been helpful.

Construct validity was determined, again, through correlations between the survey and other test measures. The manual is quite responsible in indicating the limitations of interpretations of this test.

The greatest concern arising from this test is that of administrator training. Although the manual provides more extensive information on test administration than many manuals (see Woodcock & Muñoz-Sandoval, 1993, chapter 8, for examiner training guidelines and practice exercises), how adequately users are trained is still unknown. The test manual suggests practicing on one's family members and suggests a variety of behaviors, such as lack of cooperation by preschoolers, that the administrator may encounter. Although such suggestions are helpful, this limited and variable training may affect interrater reliability. How might results differ if an experienced interviewer and a new one each administer the test? If undesirable interviewer behaviors are introduced into test administration, will they produce biased and unintended results? How much time is recommended for interviewer training, and how might the amount and quality of the time affect the results? Addressing these questions would likely lead to more accurate assessments of test takers' abilities.

Chapter 3

Using the Test Manual to Learn More About a Test

Any serious consideration of a test involves a careful examination of the test and the user's manual. *Standards for Educational and Psychological Testing* (Joint Committee on Standards for Educational & Psychological Testing, 1999)—the most authoritative source of professional standards in testing—emphasizes that test developers and users share responsibility for test practices. Developers should provide users with information on (a) what the target audience for the test is, (b) which abilities or skills it is designed to assess, (c) how to administer and accurately score the test, and (d) how to interpret and use scores appropriately. The *Standards* also indicates that developers are expected to present evidence that the scores obtained on the test are reliable and the interpretations based on them are justified (valid) given the intended use of the test. Test users, for their part, are expected to learn as much as possible about a test before using it, and this includes examining the manual and determining whether developers have fulfilled their professional responsibilities.

In this chapter we review the contents of the user manuals distributed by publishers of large-scale commercial language tests, drawing in particular from the manuals of tests reviewed in chapter 2, and conclude with guidelines for evaluating the contents of those manuals. Our premise is that test practices are enhanced when developers and users embrace the same professional standards. Adopting those advocated in the 1999 *Standards* will lead to improved test practices that benefit test takers and the entire educational community.

Contents of Test Manuals

Table 3.1 lists the major components of and information commonly found in manuals, although the relative emphasis placed on a component and the location of the information within the manual vary considerably. In addition, professional standards evolve over time as new knowledge and insights about testing emerge. Because it takes time for recent developments to be translated into established testing practices, the contents of manuals and professional standards may not always be congruent.

The component in the last row of Table 3.1 illustrates an inconsistency between testing standards and practices that has to do with the evolution of the notion of validity. The term has been widely used to describe different types or forms of validity, such as construct, concurrent, and content. In fact, the Joint Committee's 1974 edition of the *Standards* referred to these

Table 3.1. Major Components of Test Manuals and Their Contents

Component	Contents
Specifications	Purpose Target population Item formats Norming data Language ability assessed Task(s) Theoretical assumptions
Administration	Instructions Materials Administrator training
Scoring	Reporting Computation Interpretation
Reliability evidence	Internal consistency of test items Rater Test-retest Alternate (equivalent, equated, parallel) forms
Validity evidence	Construct validity Concurrent validity Criterion validity Content validity Face validity

types of validity, and many test manuals continue to refer to different types or forms of validity as opposed to sources of validity evidence as advocated by the Joint Committee's 1999 edition.

Over the past few decades, testing specialists have increasingly viewed validity as the process of marshaling the available evidence and theoretical support needed to present a compelling argument that the interpretation of test scores for a particular purpose is justified. Test users are now advised to examine all the relevant evidence in a manual in order to determine whether the interpretation of test scores for a specific test purpose is warranted (Joint Committee, 1999). The ability to make such a determination is predicated on an understanding of what test manuals contain, and that is the impetus for this chapter.

Test Specifications

Developing a test is a complex process that is enhanced by establishing and following a set of systematic procedures. The phrase *test specifications* is generally used to describe the various activities associated with planning and developing a test, including describing the test's purpose, writing test items, piloting the test, obtaining a norming sample, analyzing the performance of test items, and producing reliability and validity evidence that justifies use of the test in certain circumstances (Alderson, Clapham, & Wall, 1995).

Users can learn a great deal about a test by reviewing what publishers have to say about its development, and test specifications are an important component of the development process. (For a thorough treatment of language test specifications, consult *Testcraft: A Teacher's Guide to Writing and Using Test Specifications,* Davidson & Lynch, 2002.) Typically, publishers include statements about what the test measures (i.e., its purpose), who it is designed to be used with (i.e., the target population), how a sample population performed on the test (i.e., norming data), which language abilities or skills are assessed, what test takers will experience on the test, what kind of test items are used (i.e., item format), and what theoretical assumptions underlie the test.

Purpose and Target Population

Publishers often indicate the purpose and target population of their test in the first few pages of the manual. The first section of the manual for the Woodcock-Muñoz Language Survey (WMLS) (Woodcock & Muñoz-Sandoval, 1993), for example, is only four pages long, yet it briefly addresses aspects of test specifications, administration, and scoring. It begins with a two-sentence statement of the test purpose, describes the different parts of the test, and notes the aspects of language ability assessed by each part of the test. It also identifies the materials necessary to support administration, including the easel test book, test results sheet, test manual, and software. The last page of the first section indicates how results can be used to make particular assessment decisions.

The two IDEA Proficiency Test (IPT) technical manuals illustrate how publishers sometimes reorganize the information contained in manuals. The *IPT II Oral Grades 7–12 Technical Manual* (Amori & Dalton, 1998b) begins with a summary of theoretical considerations in language acquisition and the assessment of oral proficiency followed by a description of the test. The first two paragraphs of the *IPT I Oral Grades K–6 Technical Manual* (Ballard, Dalton, & Tighe, 2001b), however, address the fact that the 2001 version of the test has been updated and renormed, and the third paragraph describes the test purpose. The remainder of the initial section of the new manual is devoted to summarizing the redevelopment and history of the test.

Where the publisher locates information in the manual and how much emphasis it receives depends on the importance the publisher places on the information as well as on how important it is thought to be to test users. In the case of the IPT, the publisher begins the manual (Ballard, Dalton, & Tighe, 2001b) by stating that the current version of the test was revised and field tested on a new group of test takers, and subsequent paragraphs detail the redevelopment activities. Most test developers are engaged in collecting information on the performance of their tests and incorporating advances in language testing into the development of their products. Test publishers want to communicate any improvements in their measures to test users, and manuals become a primary way of doing so.

Item Format

The publisher of the Combined English Language Skills Assessment in a Reading Context (CELSA) indicates that test developers needed to construct a measure to assist program administrators and teachers in placing and monitoring the progress of more than 10,000 adult ESOL learners served by ESOL programs in San Francisco (Ilyin, 1993).

The manual goes on to present a rationale for the test-item formats selected by the developers (i.e., a multiple-choice cloze that utilized a reading context and had a conversational pattern) and asserts that the cloze is a more holistic measure of language ability. Moreover, when combined with the use of a conversational pattern, the developers argue, it better reflects the target population's everyday experiences with English. The manual submits that using a multiple-choice design facilitates large-scale test administration and scoring, something that an essay format, for example, would not accomplish as efficiently. It also describes how developers revised and integrated multiple versions of other, similar assessments into a new 75-item CELSA that emerged in a five-step process.

Additionally, the manual documents the developer's efforts to limit bias in the test and presents an extensive (eight-page) description of the norm group and field trials of the test items. Test bias, the unintended effects of the test on test takers, may be due to test takers' characteristics (e.g., ethnicity, native language, gender, age), test methods, administration procedures, or other factors. Developers strive to identify and, when possible, to limit the bias in their tests.

Norming Data

A *norm group* is defined in chapter 1 as the group the test was administered to in order to develop performance statistics or norms. Information on the performance of the norm group generally constitutes most of the reliability evidence that appears in test manuals. Unfortunately, although reliability evidence is some of the most important information in the manual, many users find it the least comprehensible because it involves the use of statistical procedures.

Publishers usually begin the presentation of norming data by summarizing the norm group's general performance on the test. Table 2 in the Test of Spoken English (TSE) manual (Educational Testing Service [ETS], 2001a), for example, lists the mean (arithmetic average) of all the scores in the norm group and the standard deviation (SD) for the group (see Appendix 3A). Both numbers reveal useful information about the performance of the group. The mean gives test users one estimate of the middle of the group's performance, around which scores tend to be clustered if they are distributed in a normal pattern. The standard deviation estimates how scores are distributed around this point by calculating the average distance of scores from the mean. Scores may be widely or narrowly dispersed around the mean, and the average relative distance is summarized in the value of the standard deviation. The larger the standard deviation, the greater the dispersion of scores around the mean. Table 2 of the manual (see Appendix 3A) also reports the distribution of test takers' scores by indicating the percentile rank of a particular score based on the range of scores on the test.

In the case of the TSE, test takers can obtain a score of 20–60. In addition to summaries of the norm group as a whole, manuals commonly include a set of summaries (again, in the form of tables) that report the performance of various subgroups within the norm group. Table 3 of the TSE manual (ETS, 2001a; see Appendix 3A) includes the mean, standard deviation, and percentile ranks of test takers who declared they were taking the test in order to demonstrate their suitability for university academic assistantships in research or teaching. This group is subdivided further, and data are presented on the performance of test takers from four language groups (native speakers of Chinese, Korean, Tagalog, and Hindi). The smallest of these subgroups contained 1,530 individuals, and the largest had 12,093.

Test users should take into account the size of the norm group and any subgroups when making inferences about the performances of test takers. Although there are no hard-and-fast rules governing group sizes, most publishers prefer to use norm groups that are larger than 1,000 and are reluctant to report the results of analyses on subgroups that contain fewer

than 30 subjects. The statistical inferences made about test takers' performances are based on the assumption that the scores reflect the pattern found
in a normal distribution (or what is popularly referred to as the *bell curve*),
in which the majority of scores cluster near the middle of the measure and
taper toward the ends. This distribution is less likely to be realized if the
number of scores in a set is especially small (fewer than 30) or the range of
scores is restricted for any reason.

The section of the Michigan English Language Assessment Battery
(MELAB) manual (Briggs & Dobson, 1994) titled "MELAB Statistics"
includes the range of scores obtained by the norm group (4,811 persons
who took the test between 1991 and 1993, p. 17). Table 2.1 in the manual
(see Appendix 3B) reports the range of scores for each part of the test and
the range of total scores. It also includes the mean, standard deviation, and
median for each part and the total score on the test. The median is another
useful estimate of the middle in a set of scores; it represents the point at
which half the scores in the set are above and half below it. Tables 2.3–2.6
of the MELAB manual (see Appendix 3B) summarize how scores in the
norm group were distributed in terms of the different parts of the test and
the total test. The tables display frequency distributions and contain the
number of test takers (represented by N in the tables) who obtained a
particular score, the percent of test takers who obtained the score, and the
percent of the total who obtained the score (cumulative percentage). Such
data give users an overview of how the norm group performed on separate
parts of the test and on the test as a whole.

Additionally, the MELAB manual (Briggs & Dobson, 1994) divides the
performance of the norm group into four subgroups based on the test
takers' reason for taking the test, native language, gender, and age. The
manual reports means and standard deviations for each subgroup's performance on each part as well as on the test as a whole. Although it is helpful to
know how test takers who shared particular characteristics (subgroups)
performed on the test, their performance may not be representative of the
larger population of all possible test takers. Hence, users should scrutinize
the summary data in manuals and determine how well the characteristics of
the norm group match those of the target population for the test. Generally,
the larger the norm group and the more it has in common with the target
population for the test, the greater the likelihood that intended test takers'
performances will be similar.

Tables A–G in the *IPT I Oral Grades K–6 Technical Manual* (Ballard et al.,
2001b) report summary data for two forms (E and F) of the test, including
the number of subjects in the norm group that were drawn from each
school, district, and state and their percentage of the entire group (Table A,
pp. 10–11; see Appendix 3C). Tables B–G (pp. 11–15) of the manual
present subgroup data (i.e., the number of subjects and their percentage of
the norm group) by age, gender, grade level, ethnicity, primary language,
and country of origin for each form as well as for the combined forms

(E and F). As stated in the manual, the target population for this measure is English language learners in Grades K–6, and the norming sample contained 891 children aged 6–14 from 50 different schools in 12 states.

Because most claims made in test manuals are based on the performance of the norm group, users should examine and evaluate the characteristics of this group of test takers. Two fundamental questions are whether the sample includes enough subjects and whether it contains sufficient diversity. For example, the TSE manual (ETS, 2001a) reports a norm group of 82,868 subjects, and the WMLS (Woodcock & Muñoz-Sandoval, 1993), a group of 6,359. In general, the larger the norm group, the greater the likelihood that it will adequately sample all potential test takers. Large norm groups permit test developers to analyze the performance of subgroups within the sample and perform statistical procedures on these groups. It is common practice to divide the norm group by characteristics such as gender, first language, grade level, age, country of origin, and geographical location. Because the power of some statistical procedures is related to the size of the sample, test users should be wary of analyses performed on subgroups of fewer than 30 subjects.

Field trials that employ large, diverse, balanced norm groups permit test developers to draw inferences—albeit cautiously—about test takers' performance on the test and allow test users to make modest generalizations about potential test takers' performance on it. Yet, even when the size and diversity of a norm group is impressive, users should consider how closely it resembles local test takers. If local test takers differ in important ways from the norm group, their performances may differ, too.

The examiner's and technical manuals for the IPT I and II—Oral English (Amori & Dalton, 1998a, 1998b; Ballard et al., 2001a, 2001b) describe the development history of this collection of assessments. The publisher reports that test users' reactions to earlier versions of the IPT I and II led to changes in two existing forms of the test and the construction of two new forms. Selected characteristics of the norm group (geographical regions from which subjects were drawn and the total number of subjects from each region) appear in these manuals, but users receive somewhat less detail regarding test development and specifications than is included in the other manuals described in this chapter.

When a test changes in any significant way, it is important to determine how a subsequent sample group of test takers performs on it. Hence, any revised test is piloted on a group of test takers, and the results are analyzed to produce reliability and validity evidence. The revisions to the IPT I entailed modifying, reordering, and deleting test items as well as examining test instructions and prompts and making changes to improve the comprehensibility of test items. The revised assessment was field tested on 1,500 test takers who ranged in age from 6 to 14 years, and new norms were developed based on the results. The publisher of the Maculaitis Assessment of Competencies Test of English Language Proficiency II (MAC II) reports that the revised assessment was normed on a population of more than 10,500 school children (Grades K–12) in 19 states and 36 different school districts (Maculaitis, 2001b). The IPT I—Oral and the MAC II were field tested on norm groups that reflect the target populations for the respective test.

Language Abilities Assessed

Manuals are generally quite clear about what language abilities or skills the test assesses because tests can be designed to assess a single language skill, multiple language skills, or general language proficiency. For instance, the MAC II is a measure of general language proficiency that assesses the speaking, listening, reading, and writing skills of nonnative speakers of English in Grades K–12. The TSE, on the other hand, is designed to assess the oral communication skills of nonnative speakers of English who expect to attend North American postsecondary institutions. Other tests reviewed in chapter 2 have been constructed to measure the functional literacy skills of adult ESOL learners, the academic listening skills of postsecondary ESOL learners, and the ability to use English for vocational purposes in international contexts. Manuals often include a detailed discussion of exactly how the test measures particular skills or abilities, and this typically involves descriptions of the kinds of test items included to elicit the language use from which judgments about test performance are made.

Tasks

As noted in chapter 1, the terms *test item* and *test task* are frequently used interchangeably to refer to what test takers are asked to do during the test. Do they read a short passage and select the correct answer from four possible choices? Do they listen to brief conversational exchanges and construct appropriate responses or listen to short lectures and take notes? Do they read and respond to a written prompt? One of the test tasks in the WMLS requires test takers to examine visual representations (pictures) of different objects and to name them. A task in Section 3 of the MELAB requires test takers to read a passage and respond to questions based on it. Manuals should contain adequate descriptions of the test tasks, and users should consider how consistent the tasks are with the stated test purpose.

Theoretical Assumptions

Developers of well-constructed tests seek to incorporate into the design of their measures what is known or thought to be true about second language acquisition and language testing. Hence, test manuals refer to the theoretical assumptions that underlie their tests. The MAC II manual (Maculaitis, 2001b) states that "the orientation of the MAC II is most closely aligned with the Communicative Competence Theories of language proficiency (Savignon, 1977)" (p. 2) and is consistent with the theoretical distinctions Cummins (1984) posits between interpersonal and academic language ability. The IPT I—Oral manual (Ballard et al., 2001a) devotes several pages to the theoretical assumptions its developers believe underlie the test. These assumptions include the claim that the test measures aspects of grammatical and sociolinguistic competence as conceptualized in Canale and Swain's (1980) theoretical representation of what contributes to competence in communicative language ability. The developers also claim that the IPT I measures two aspects (language competence and strategic competence) of Bachman's (1990) theoretical representation of communicative language ability.

Administration

Administration procedures affect test results. As a result, publishers take extraordinary steps to ensure that their test is administered under comparable conditions. This is necessary in order to reduce the potential measurement error that may occur when users fail to follow the developer's administration protocols. Not following the administration procedures limits the value of the scores obtained with the test and is likely to compromise reliability evidence reported in the manual.

Instructions

One way for test developers to standardize the administration of a test is to include very explicit instructions on how to organize the immediate test environment, what to communicate to test takers before and during the test, and how to record and manipulate test results. To increase the likelihood that all test takers receive the same test input, developers include written instructions in test booklets and may resort to written scripts for test administrators or audiorecordings of instructions to make them more uniform.

Materials

Successful test administration depends on a variety of materials. In the case of large-scale, standardized tests, materials typically include test booklets, answer sheets, audio or visual media, writing prompts, scripts, scoring templates or software, and user manuals. Effective administration of a test assumes that users have examined all the materials, thoroughly understand them, and follow the procedures outlined in the manual. Poorly prepared test materials that contain ambiguous instructions or procedures threaten the accuracy of the measure.

Administrator Training

In assessments that utilize a one-on-one oral interview format, such as that used in the Basic English Skills Test (BEST), it is essential for examiners to have participated in training and to be extremely familiar with the administration and scoring procedures of the test. Some publishers are so concerned with the consequences of inconsistent administration that they require purchasers to complete training programs or demonstrate the ability to administer the assessment properly as a condition of sale. Most publishers, however, respond by providing test users with detailed instructions, often accompanied by examples and practice materials.

Given the potential bias that can be introduced through administration procedures, users have a responsibility to review instructions and to be completely familiar with how to administer a particular assessment before attempting to use it. Additionally, users should evaluate the administration procedures described in manuals and determine if they effectively limit the unintended consequences of inconsistent test administration.

Scoring

Chapter 2 includes several tests that must be scored or rated by the publisher. The MELAB and the TSE cannot be scored or rated locally, and test takers' results are invalid unless sent directly from the publisher to the examinee or school. The manuals for these tests (Briggs & Dobson, 1994; ETS, 2001a) include information on how the tests are scored and how performance is divided across components (subscales) of the test.

In the case of the MELAB, each of the three parts (Composition, Listening, and Grammar/Cloze/Vocabulary/Reading) is reported on a numerical scale with a total score that represents the average of the scores for each of the three parts. Test subscores give users valuable information that is otherwise lost when only a total score is reported. Two test takers may obtain the same total score on the MELAB but have very different subscores on the Composition or Listening sections of the test. Subscores permit users to compare test takers' language abilities across skills and gain additional insights into individuals' relative strengths and limitations in the target language.

Reporting

As mentioned in the discussion of norming data, a publisher usually reports the mean score obtained by the norm group on the test and lists the corresponding percentile rank of each score to illustrate how the scores are distributed within the norm group. For example, based on a norm group of 82,868 examinees tested between July 1995 and January 2000, a TSE score of 55 places a test taker in the group at the 90th percentile, or among the top 10% of test takers (ETS, 2001a). Percentile ranking allows users to compare a test taker's performance relative to the others in a group. Knowing that a score of 55 places someone in the top 10% may be helpful in making certain decisions based on test performance.

Yet, as mentioned in chapter 1, no test is perfectly precise. The concept of the standard error of measurement (*SEM*) is a way to express the imprecision in a test and to estimate the range within which a test taker's true score lies. The *SEM* for the TSE is 2.24, which means that an examinee who has a reported score of 55 will likely have a true score of 52.76–57.24 (68% of the time). Doubling the *SEM* has the effect of extending the range within which a test taker's true score is likely to lie and thereby increases the probability of capturing it. Thus, doubling the *SEM* for the TSE assures the user that a test taker's true score lies within a range of 50.52–59.48 approximately 95% of the time. These probabilities are based on the assumption that the performance of test takers in the norm group conforms to the pattern observed in a normal distribution of scores.

Users want to know the *SEM* for a test because it is a concrete way of expressing reliability. Taking the *SEM* into consideration, especially when making high-stakes decisions, reduces the likelihood of setting cut scores that ignore the imprecision in an instrument. Test users are responsible for knowing the *SEM* of widely used, high-stakes tests such as the TSE and the Test of English as a Foreign Language (TOEFL).

Computation

The majority of tests reviewed in chapter 2 can be hand-scored following the instructions in the manual, although the scoring procedures vary depending on the nature of the particular task and test item format. Clearly, the simplest procedure involves totaling the number of correct or incorrect responses and calculating a score for each component of the test. Most procedures produce what is referred to as a *raw score* (e.g., the number of correct or incorrect responses subtracted from the total). A raw score is converted to a scaled score using a conversion table included with the test materials, and the scaled score is based on the results of the norming group's performance on the different forms of the test.

In the case of the WMLS, the examiner enters the data recorded on the test sheet into a computer software program that automatically converts raw scores to scaled scores and produces a *SEM* estimate for each individual score rather than the more widely used practice of reporting an average *SEM* estimate for the norming group. Among other things, scaled scores permit users to make inferences about test takers' performances regardless of which form of the test was administered.

Fixed item-response types, such as the multiple-choice items in the CELSA, use an objective scoring procedure that requires little time and training. Tests can be scored by hand using a template, with a scanner, or with computer software. In contrast, the BEST utilizes a more open-ended response format that requires the examiner to rate test takers' responses to interview questions using several different scales. To score test takers' performances consistently, raters must be given sufficient instructions, be trained adequately, and have ample practice. The BEST manual (Kenyon & Stansfield, 1989) devotes 40 pages to administering and scoring the instrument, including practice exercises for scoring every test item. Such detailed coverage of the administration and scoring procedures is intended to enhance the consistency of raters' assessments of test takers' performance. This level of detail is especially important when the test taker assumes partial or complete responsibility for constructing responses to test items and when performance is scored on the basis of rater judgments. In such cases, manuals must provide comprehensive instructions, and users must thoroughly understand and practice the scoring procedures.

Interpretation

We emphasize throughout this volume that test results may be used to make a range of decisions, from high-stakes selection decisions to determinations of placement or progress. In every case, users should use test results wisely and should not use them to make decisions that are inconsistent with the purpose of the test, which usually appears near the front of the manual. Some tests are designed to fulfill multiple purposes. For example, the BEST manual (Kenyon & Stansfield, 1989) indicates that the results may be used to place learners, monitor their progress, diagnose their relative ability to perform basic language use tasks, identify candidates, and evaluate programs. In a set of tables, scaled BEST scores are linked to eight performance levels that represent functional language ability. By comparing scores with performance descriptions, users can use test scores to make a variety of inferences about test takers' basic communication and literacy skills.

As noted in the section on reporting, TSE results may be used to gauge one test taker's performance relative to another, to the norm group, or to a predetermined criterion score. This information is especially useful in making high-stakes selection and certification decisions. The manual (ETS, 2001a) states that the aim of the TSE is to determine nonnative speakers' ability to communicate orally in North American academic and professional settings. Test takers complete a set of 12 timed speech tasks that are recorded on an audiotape and rated by at least two trained ETS examiners using a scale that ranges from 20 to 60 points. Scores are reported in 5-point increments and correspond to five communicative performance levels; a table lists the nine possible scores together with the accompanying performance description. The complete TSE scale—including performance descriptors—appears in an appendix. The tables and appendix provide test users with the means to interpret scores and compare them across test takers.

Reliability Evidence

Test manuals typically contain multiple estimates of the reliability of test scores. Some of the most widely used approaches to estimating reliability include demonstrating that scores are consistent across test items (internal consistency), stable across time (stability of scores and ratings by assessors), and comparable across forms (equivalence of multiple forms). Developers use statistics to compute the estimates. The results are organized into and displayed in manuals as reliability tables.

No test is perfect. Even very good tests contain a degree of measurement error, and developers try to account for and minimize it. Bachman (1990) has identified three principal sources of error that affect test taker performance. He refers to the first source as "test method facets" (p. 164). This source occurs as a result of the physical context in which the test is administered, its organization and administration procedures, the "input" and "responses" test takers receive and produce, and the "relationship between input and response" (p. 119). The second source occurs as a result of individual characteristics and includes the test takers' mental orientation; knowledge of the content being tested; and individual attributes such as gender, ethnicity, and first language. Both sources contribute to systematic variation in a test taker's performance on a test. The third source of error consists of random factors, or unanticipated and inconsistent error that may result from environmental events (e.g., a fire drill during the test), administration procedures (e.g., a low-quality audiorecording), or various test taker factors (e.g., fatigue, insufficient motivation, or anxiety) (pp. 164–165). Such "threats to reliability," as Henning (1987) refers to them, contribute to "fluctuations" (p. 75) in test scores, and developers strive to limit them. The reliability estimates reported in manuals are based solely on the performance of the norm group; thus all predications and any inferences about other test takers' performances on the test must take this into account.

Reliability estimates are determined by computing a reliability coefficient, a statistical calculation that ranges from 0 to 1 and represents the amount of measurement error in a test score. For example, the WMLS manual (Woodcock & Muñoz-Sandoval, 1993) reports an internal consistency reliability coefficient of .815 for 4-year-olds on the Picture Vocabulary section (Table 7-4, p. 53). This reliability coefficient indicates that scores from the norm group for this age sample on this section of the test are 81.5% consistent, and 18.5% of the variance in the score is due to measurement error. According to the 1985 edition of the *Standards* (American Educational Research Association, American Psychological Association, & National Council on Measurement in Education, 1985), a reliability coefficient of at least .90 for any total score and .80 for any subscores on a test is considered adequate. Therefore, the coefficient reported in Table 7-4 of the WMLS manual demonstrates sufficient reliability, at least for this component (the Picture Vocabulary section) of the test and for this segment of the norm group (test takers at the age 4 level).

Establishing the Internal Consistency of Test Items

One of the most widely reported forms of reliability evidence presented in manuals is internal consistency. It refers to how consistent scores on one part of a test are with scores on other parts of the test or to consistency among individual test items. In a well-constructed test, items that measure the same trait would be expected to produce consistent scores.

Several procedures can be used to estimate the internal consistency of a test, but one of the most convenient methods is *split-half*. It entails dividing a single form of the test into two equal parts, often by selecting all odd-numbered items for one data set and all even-numbered items for the other. A correlation coefficient is calculated for the two halves, and an adjustment is made to compensate for the fact that the results represent only half the test. A frequently used adjustment procedure is the Spearman–Brown prophecy formula (Brown, 1996).

Other procedures for estimating internal consistency reliability include Cronbach's alpha and Kuder–Richardson (K-R) formulas 20 and 21. The Spearman–Brown and K-R formulas assume that test items are equivalent in terms of difficulty and independence. In the case of cloze or dictation tests, these two assumptions may not be met, so the test developer should choose another approach to estimating reliability—such as the test-retest or alternate forms method (Bachman, 1990).

The developers of the WMLS used the split-half method for calculating the internal consistency of items in their test and applied the Spearman–Brown adjustment to the obtained results to achieve the reliability estimates reported in Table 7-4 of the manual (Woodcock & Muñoz-Sandoval, 1993, p. 53). In selecting the Spearman–Brown formula, the developers assumed test takers' scores on one half of the test were not related to performance on the other half and that the two halves were, in effect, equal tests. The MELAB manual (Briggs & Dobson, 1994) makes use of two other ways of calculating internal consistency reliability estimates, K-R 21 and Cronbach's alpha. One reason developers elect these two alternatives is that they produce similar results and are easier to compute than a split-half method using the Spearman–Brown formula (Brown, 1996).

Establishing the Consistency of Raters

Numerous language tests assign scores based on the ratings of assessors. Among the test manuals discussed in this chapter, four include rater assessments of test takers' language performance.

Intrarater Reliability. Raters need to be consistent in their judgments of a test taker's performance, or error is introduced into the evaluation process and the results become less reliable. One technique for determining whether an individual rater's judgments are consistent is to have the rater rerate a test taker's performance after an adequate time interval. The two ratings are usually assumed to represent equivalent forms of the same test, and a correlation coefficient is calculated, most often using the Spearman rank-order procedure. Some developers, however, may use other procedures to estimate reliability, including Cronbach's alpha. The developers of the MELAB report that intrarater reliability estimates for the composition section of their test ranged from .87 to .92 (Briggs & Dobson, 1994, p. 27, Table 3.3) for a 1986 study of three raters who scored the same 50 compositions twice.

Interrater Reliability. Test developers need to demonstrate that the same rater consistently rates a test taker's performance, but they also want to show that different raters consistently assess test takers' performance in the same or very nearly the same way. The TSE is rated by two ETS-certified assessors who must independently score the test taker's performance using the same rating scale. The final score reflects the average of the two assessors' scores unless they exceed established parameters, in which case a third rater assesses the performance and the two closest ratings are averaged to determine the test taker's final score.

The TSE score user guide (ETS, 2001a) reports interrater reliability estimates of .92 based on 64,701 test takers who took various forms of the test between July 1995 and January 2000 (p. 9, Table 1; see Appendix 3A). These estimates are evidence of a high degree of consistency between raters who are scoring the same test taker's performance. No details are offered regarding the specific procedures employed in the reported reliability estimates; however, the publisher lists several research reports (Bejar, 1985; Boldt, 1992) in the guide (p. 23) that may explain the statistical procedures that were used to obtain the results displayed in Table 1.

The same procedures described for estimating intrarater reliability may be used in establishing interrater reliability evidence; however, Bachman (1990) recommends using Cronbach's alpha procedure. In this approach, each rater's scores are totaled, and a coefficient alpha is calculated based on the summed ratings. Table 3.2 in the MELAB manual (Briggs & Dobson, 1994, p. 26; see Appendix 3B) reports using the Spearman–Brown prophecy formula and the Pearson product–moment formula to produce interrater reliability estimates.

Establishing the Stability of Test Performance

Test-Retest Reliability. One widely used method for developing reliability evidence related to a test involves administering it to the same group of test takers twice within a reasonable interval, typically 2 weeks. The CELSA manual (Ilyin, 1993) reports obtaining a test-retest reliability coefficient of .93 based on giving one version of the test (CELSA 1) twice in a 2-week period and computing an estimated reliability coefficient between the scores for the two administrations. Several test-retest administrations occurred using different versions of the CELSA with different groups, and in every case the reliability estimates ranged from .93 to .96. Correlations of this magnitude represent a high degree of stability in the scores of test takers, and developers will present it as one example of evidence that performance on the test is reliable. For this reliability evidence to be compelling, the interval between administrations cannot be long enough for changes in the test takers' abilities to occur or short enough for test takers to recall the contents of the test.

Alternate (Equivalent or Parallel) Forms Reliability. Test users need multiple equated forms of a test when planning to administer it to the same test takers or use it repeatedly. Most publishers, therefore, develop several forms of a test to use interchangeably. The development of comparable forms usually entails administering at least two forms to the same group and determining how test takers perform on each. Correlating the scores obtained for the two forms permits developers to make claims about the extent to which the forms are comparable. Highly correlated forms are assumed to be equivalent and reliable.

However, developing multiple forms of a test that yield the same results despite including different test items is a daunting task. For this reason, some developers make a distinction between *equated* forms (which are easier to construct) and *equivalent* forms. The latter require the developer to demonstrate that the forms have no significant differences between their means, variances, and correlations with other tests. When manuals contain conversion tables that permit scores on one form to be converted and compared with scores on other forms, the developers have produced equated forms (Henning, 1987).

This section has reviewed a number of widely used estimates of reliability. Test users should review the reliability evidence reported in manuals to determine if it is sufficiently compelling. Additionally, they should marshal all the relevant available evidence and ascertain whether the test is carefully constructed, utilizes appropriate administration and scoring procedures, and generally offers adequate reliability evidence. Users must remember that any reliability estimates reported in manuals pertain to the performance of the test takers in the norm group, and any claims about their applicability to other groups are justified only to the extent the two groups are the same.

Validity Evidence

The collection of reliability evidence is only part of the complex task of validating a test; users should also expect to find ample validity evidence reported in a manual. As highlighted in Table 3.1 above, construct, concurrent, criterion, and content are some of the most frequently cited forms of validity evidence in manuals.

Construct Validity Evidence

In the simplest terms, construct validity is the representation and measurement of an unobservable ability by inferences drawn from language test performance. An ability can be represented by conceptual models, for example, Bachman's (1990) notion of *communicative language ability* or

Cummins' (1984) notion of *cognitive academic language proficiency* (CALP), in which the nature of the ability is hypothesized and usually supported by studies that reveal the relationship between the construct the test is intended to measure and the test. The WMLS manual (Woodcock & Muñoz-Sandoval, 1993) avers that the test measures the CALP construct and presents intercorrelations of the three proficiency scales in the test (i.e., Oral Language, Reading-Writing, and Broad English) and the four discrete scales (i.e., Picture Vocabulary, Verbal Analogies, Letter-Word Identification, and Dictation) as evidence that the test measures the abilities required to do well in school. Lower correlations between separate scales are said to be due to the fact that they measure different but complementary aspects of what constitutes cognitive-academic language ability, and higher correlations are posited to result from the fact that two or more scales are measuring similar aspects of the same general ability (i.e., CALP).

The MELAB manual (Briggs & Dobson, 1994) draws on two models of language ability—communicative competence (Canale, 1983) and Bachman's (1990) model of communicative language ability—to support the publisher's contention that sections of the MELAB measure selected aspects of language ability. The manual offers users additional construct validity evidence in the form of the results of a factor analysis procedure that was applied to Part 2 (Listening), Part 3 (Grammar/Cloze/Vocabulary/Reading), and the combined parts (2, 3, and 1, the Composition section) of the test. Factor analysis is a statistical procedure used to reduce a large number of variables (e.g., those in a test or questionnaire) to a smaller number that are hypothesized to represent certain underlying abilities. In the case of the MELAB, these underlying abilities are assumed to reflect current conceptions of language ability as represented in the communicative language ability and communicative competence models. The derived factors are assumed to be highly correlated, and indeed they were in this case.

Some test developers believe construct validity subsumes all other forms of validity evidence. Thus, they submit that the validation process requires developers to present a sound theoretical rationale and convincing empirical evidence that the test credibly measures what it is intended to measure.

Concurrent Validity Evidence

One common form of empirical evidence in manuals is concurrent validity. Concurrent validity is established when there are strong positive correlations between two tests or between the test and a criterion that assesses the same construct. This form of validity is also referred to in some manuals as *criterion-related validity*.

Such evidence takes a variety of forms. For example, the developers of the MELAB compared the performance of a group of test takers on the TOEFL with their performance on the MELAB. By computing the correlation coefficient between test takers' performance on the two measures, developers can determine how closely performance on one is related to performance on the other. The higher the correlation between the two tests, the stronger the relationship is assumed to be. Correlations may be positive or negative and do not reflect a cause-effect relationship but rather the strength of the association between the two variables. Few variables are perfectly related and hence capable of producing validity coefficients of 1.0 or −1.0. So, for test development purposes, correlations greater than .70 are considered fairly strong.

The MELAB manual (Briggs & Dobson, 1994) presents concurrent validity evidence by reporting a correlation of .704 between the total scores of the MELAB and TOEFL. The magnitude of this coefficient suggests that the two tests are closely related; they are probably measuring the same language abilities. Concurrent validity evidence is most persuasive when both tests purport to measure the same thing and when the criterion test is recognized as a credible measure. It is possible for two tests to be strongly correlated and to be equally poor at assessing what they are intended to measure. Users must determine whether the concurrent validity evidence presented in a manual is compelling.

Criterion Validity Evidence

Validity evidence can also be established by comparing scores on the test to some criterion other than another test. In the *IPT II Oral Grades 7–12 Technical Manual* (Amori & Dalton, 1998b), the publisher maintains that the test has demonstrated criterion-related validity evidence by correlating teachers' predictions of their students' IPT II placement level with students' scores on the test. The obtained coefficient of .78 reported in Table GG (p. 41) between teachers' predictions and students' test scores is said to be evidence of a strong, positive, statistically significant relationship between the ability of the test to measure students' language ability and teachers' perceptions of the students' proficiency.

The correlation was obtained by means of a statistical procedure referred to as Pearson product–moment correlation, a formula that permits developers to compute the strength of the relationship between two sets of interval data. According to the notation below Table GG (Amori & Dalton, 1998b, p. 41), the possibility of obtaining such a result by chance in this case was considerably less than 1 in 100 (i.e., $p < .001$). In other words, the developers can be 99.9% certain that their results are due to factors other than chance. In this case, however, the teacher judgments (i.e., predictions) of student abilities—as reflected in placements into the six IPT II—Oral skill levels—have been treated as interval data, and some statisticians do not consider them such (Bailey, 1998).

Another example of criterion-related validity evidence is found in the BEST manual (Kenyon & Stansfield, 1989), in which the developers report the correlation coefficients they obtained between the four subscales of the test and the total score for the oral interview section. The manual indicates that each subscale correlates highly with the total score, as is expected, and at a somewhat lower level with each of the other subscales. Because each subscale is intended to measure a related but separate aspect of functional language ability, these lower correlations are evidence of the complementary nature of the subscales and represent another form of criterion-related validity evidence reported in test manuals.

Content Validity Evidence

The first type of validity evidence presented in the *IPT II Oral Grades 7–12 Technical Manual* (Amori & Dalton, 1998b) addresses the content of Forms C and D of the test. The publisher asserts that the test has content validity because each of the test items for each form of the test adequately samples the six linguistic domains (syntax, lexicon, phonology, morphology, comprehension, and oral expression) purportedly measured by the assessment. Content-related validity can refer to the adequacy of the sample of language being tested or to the judgment by an expert that the focus of the test items matches the developer's claims about what is measured by the test. The publisher of the IPT II—Oral expects users to accept that a single test item is capable of measuring multiple aspects of language ability, and the manual displays a set of tables (CC–FF) indicating the aspects of language ability measured by each item. Although one assumes test items were reviewed by experts and judged to be appropriate, the manual does not state this explicitly.

In contrast, the CELSA manual (Ilyin, 1993) does not refer to content validity per se but notes that course instructors (experts) believed the test items reflected a representative sample of what was taught in their courses. This constitutes an example of content validity evidence, although the reader must infer it.

Face Validity Evidence

Some manuals refer to *face validity* when discussing test takers' and users' perceptions of a test. Most testing specialists consider such perceptions essentially intuitive and impressionistic and therefore of limited value in developing a validity argument. When this form of validity evidence includes considerations of the authenticity of test items and tasks, it could be viewed as an aspect of content-related validity evidence.

The *Standards* (Joint Committee, 1999) state that "no type of evidence is inherently preferable to others; rather, the quality and relevance of the evidence to the intended test use determines the value of a particular kind of evidence" (p. 17). In short, every form of validity evidence reported in a manual contributes to the user's ability to make judgments about the test. Rather than considering each as a different form of evidence, the language testing profession is increasingly conceptualizing validity as a unitary notion—one that considers all the available evidence in support of inferences made from the scores of a particular test. Bachman (1990) advises that no single form of validity evidence is sufficient in and of itself, but taken together, multiple forms of validity evidence may demonstrate the appropriateness of making certain inferences based on the scores of a test. He goes on to say that the process of validating a test is really about validating "the way we interpret or use the information gathered through the testing procedure" (p. 238).

Reviewing Test Manuals

This chapter opened by relating the current professional standards for test development and use. The process of justifying the use of a test for a particular test purpose is the joint responsibility of developers and users. Test publishers must produce manuals that adequately describe their tests and present the information so that it is comprehensible to the average test user. Users must examine test manuals carefully, evaluate the contents critically, and establish local norms based on local administrations and the characteristics of their own test takers. Ensuring high professional standards in the development and use of language tests requires collaboration. Developers, publishers, and users must share a commitment to creating well-designed measures and using them responsibly.

Table 3.2 presents a set of questions based on the professional standards advocated in the Joint Committee's (1999) *Standards*. As users review the activities and claims of test developers, they should consider how well the contents of a manual reflect current trends and accepted practices in language testing. Determining the answers to the questions in Table 3.2 should guide and assist users in completing their appraisals of test manuals.

Table 3.2. Questions to Consider in Reviewing the Contents of Test Manuals

Component	Questions
Specifications	• Is the purpose of the test stated? • Is the target population specified? • Is the norming population described in adequate detail, and is it sufficiently diverse? • What language abilities or skills are purported to be assessed by the test? • What types of tasks do test takers complete? • What types of test items are included? Are they authentic and sufficient in number to provide a reasonable sample of the ability the test is intended to measure? What theoretical assumptions about language are reflected either explicitly or implicitly in the test?

Table 3.2. *Continued*

Component	Questions
Administration	• Is there an adequate description of the test environment and organization? • Are the test administration procedures standardized and clear? • Are instructions unambiguous and practice materials adequate? • Are training materials and procedures (if applicable) thorough?
Scoring	• Is there a clear description of how to calculate test performance? • Are data on test takers' performances complete, including their performances on the total test as well as any of its parts? • Is sufficient information included to interpret the meaning of a particular score?
Reliability evidence	• What types of reliability evidence are presented? • Is there evidence that the items of the test and raters' assessment of performances on the test are consistent? • Are the reported reliability estimates convincing? • Are there multiple forms of the test, and, if so, is there evidence that they are comparable?
Validity evidence	• What types of validity evidence are presented? • Is there evidence that performance on the test is closely related to performance on another credible measure of the same language ability or skill? • Is there evidence that the content of the test is representative of the domain it is intended to measure? • Would a panel of experts (and test takers) be likely to deem the test an assessment of what it purports to measure? • On the whole, has the developer presented a compelling validation argument (i.e., presented the test user sufficient evidence, both empirical and theoretical, that the interpretations and use of the scores for a particular test purpose are justified)?

Appendix 3A. Norming Data From *TSE and SPEAK Score User Guide* (ETS, 2001a)

Table 1. Average TSE Reliabilities and Standard Errors of Measurement (SEM) — Total Group and Subgroups

(Based on 64,701 examinees who took primary TSE and SPEAK forms between July 1995 and January 2000.)

	Total (N = 64,701)	Academic (N = 29,254)	Professional (N = 35,447)
Interrater Reliability	0.92	0.91	0.92
Test Form Reliability	0.98	0.97	0.98
Test Score Reliability	0.89	0.89	0.90
SEM	2.24	2.26	2.22

Table 2. Percentile Ranks for TSE Scores — Total Group

(Based on 82,868 examinees who took TSE between July 1995 and January 2000.)

TSE Score	Percentile Rank
60	97
55	90
50	75
45	51
40	24
35	6
30	1
25	<1
20	<1
Score Mean	45.27
S.D.	6.77

Table 3. Percentile Ranks for TSE Scores — Academic Examinees*

TSE Score	Academic Total (36,747)	Chinese (12,093)	Korean (3,608)	Tagalog (2,778)	Hindi (1,530)
60	98	>99	99	98	97
55	91	98	97	91	84
50	76	91	93	73	53
45	53	72	81	41	22
40	25	36	49	12	5
35	6	7	15	1	<1
30	1	1	3	0	<1
25	<1	<1	<1	0	0
20	0	0	<1	0	0
Score Mean	45.04	42.27	40.60	46.64	49.46
S.D.	6.65	5.17	5.67	5.37	5.28

*Based on examinees who, on their TSE answer sheets, indicated that they were teaching or research assistant applicants, or undergraduate or graduate school applicants, to an academic institution between July 1995 and January 2000.

Appendix 3B. Norming Data From *MELAB Technical Manual* (Briggs & Dobson, 1994)

Table 2.1 Score Descriptives for 4,811 First-Time MELABs Administered 1991-1993

	Part 1 (Composition)	Part 2 (Listening)	Part 3 (GCVR)	Final MELAB
Minimum Scaled Score	53	33	25	38
Maximum Scaled Score	97	100	100	99
Median Scaled Score	75	79	77	77
Mean Scaled Score	75.42	77.40	74.69	75.84
Standard Deviation	7.90	12.13	14.87	10.40
Reliability[1]	.90	.89	.94	.91
SEM[2]	2.50	4.02	3.64	3.12

[1] Reliability figures were calculated using the mean interrater correlation for Part 1 (see Section 3.1; note that the set of compositions used to calculate this coefficient is not identical to the set summarized in Table 2.1) and from KR 21 applied to raw scores for Part 2 and Part 3. The reliability estimate for the Final MELAB Score is the mean of these estimates for Part 1, Part 2, and Part 3.

[2] Standard error of measurement

Table 2.3 Frequency Distribution of Final MELAB Scores
(Based on 4,811 first-time MELABs administered 1991-1993)

Final MELAB Score	N	Percent with the Score	Cumulative Percent	Final MELAB Score	N	Percent with the Score	Cumulative Percent
99	3	0.1	100.0	71	139	2.9	32.4
98	7	0.1	99.9	70	123	2.6	29.5
97	14	0.3	99.8	69	126	2.6	27.0
96	22	0.5	99.5	68	126	2.6	24.3
95	22	0.5	99.0	67	103	2.1	21.7
94	39	0.8	98.6	66	85	1.8	19.6
93	48	1.0	97.8	65	103	2.1	17.8
92	76	1.6	96.8	64	96	2.0	18.7
91	80	1.7	95.2	63	102	2.1	13.7
90	95	2.0	93.5	62	83	1.7	11.6
89	99	2.1	91.6	61	64	1.3	9.8
88	128	2.7	89.5	60	46	1.0	8.5
87	137	2.8	86.8	59	39	0.8	7.5
86	154	3.2	84.0	58	37	0.8	6.7
85	118	2.5	80.8	57	62	1.3	6.0
84	157	3.3	78.3	56	50	1.0	4.7
83	196	4.1	75.1	55	42	0.9	3.6
82	165	3.4	71.0	54	21	0.4	2.8
81	181	3.8	67.6	53	23	0.5	2.3
80	207	4.3	63.8	52	31	0.6	1.8
79	173	3.6	59.5	51	16	0.3	1.2
78	191	4.0	55.9	50	11	0.2	0.9
77	176	3.7	51.9	49	10	0.2	0.6
76	168	3.5	48.3	48	7	0.1	0.4
75	142	3.0	44.8	47	5	0.1	0.3
74	166	3.5	41.8	46	3	0.1	0.2
73	138	2.9	38.4	44	5	0.1	0.1
72	150	3.1	35.5	38	1	0.0	0.0

Table 2.4 Frequency Distribution of MELAB Part 1 (Composition) Scores
(Based on 4,811 first-time MELABs administered 1991-1993)

MELAB Part 1 Score	N	Percent with the Score	Cumulative Percent
97	18	0.4	100.0
95	46	1.0	99.6
93	101	2.1	98.7
90	135	2.8	96.6
87	191	4.0	93.8
85	254	5.3	89.8
83	334	6.9	84.5
80	393	8.2	77.6
77	586	12.2	69.4
75	600	12.5	57.2
73	692	14.4	44.8
70	482	10.0	30.4
67	468	9.7	20.3
65	207	4.3	10.6
63	199	4.1	6.3
60	59	1.2	2.2
57	24	0.5	1.0
55	14	0.3	0.5
53	8	0.2	0.2

Table 2.5 Frequency Distribution of MELAB Part 2 (Listening) Scaled Scores
(Based on 4,811 first-time MELABs administered 1991-1993)

MELAB Part 2 Score	N	Percent with the Score	Cumulative Percent	MELAB Part 2 Score	N	Percent with the Score	Cumulative Percent
100	18	0.4	100.0	69	78	1.6	23.1
98	71	1.5	99.6	68	61	1.3	21.5
96	54	1.1	98.2	67	100	2.1	20.2
95	22	0.5	97.0	66	64	1.3	18.2
94	67	1.4	96.6	65	61	1.3	16.8
93	43	0.9	95.2	64	51	1.1	15.6
92	132	2.7	94.3	63	52	1.1	14.5
91	112	2.3	91.5	62	51	1.1	13.4
90	159	3.3	89.2	61	60	1.2	12.4
89	198	4.1	85.9	60	53	1.1	11.1
88	103	2.1	81.8	59	63	1.3	10.0
87	203	4.2	79.7	58	51	1.1	8.7
86	209	4.3	75.4	57	22	0.5	7.6
85	180	3.7	71.1	56	70	1.5	7.2
84	200	4.2	67.3	55	22	0.5	5.7
83	146	3.0	63.2	54	48	1.0	5.3
82	224	4.7	60.2	53	28	0.6	4.3
81	124	2.6	55.5	52	37	0.8	3.7
80	131	2.7	52.9	50	29	0.6	2.9
79	150	3.1	50.2	49	15	0.3	2.3
78	121	2.5	47.1	47	19	0.4	2.0
77	167	3.5	44.6	46	20	0.4	1.6
76	195	4.1	41.1	45	4	0.1	1.2
75	165	3.4	37.0	43	9	0.2	1.1
74	122	2.5	33.6	42	4	0.1	0.9
73	81	1.7	31.1	40	19	0.4	0.9
72	134	2.8	29.4	37	10	0.2	0.5
71	43	0.9	26.6	35	8	0.2	0.2
70	124	2.6	25.7	33	4	0.1	0.1

Table 2.6 Frequency Distribution of MELAB Part 3 (GCVR) Scaled Scores
(Based on 4,811 first-time MELABs administered 1991-1993)

MELAB Part 3 Score	N	Percent with the Score	Cumulative Percent	MELAB Part 3 Score	N	Percent with the Score	Cumulative Percent
100	18	0.4	100.0	65	114	2.4	25.6
99	36	0.7	99.6	64	55	1.1	23.2
98	42	0.9	98.9	63	85	1.8	22.1
97	59	1.2	98.0	62	74	1.5	20.3
96	69	1.4	96.8	61	64	1.3	18.8
95	83	1.7	95.3	60	37	0.8	17.4
94	91	1.9	93.6	59	62	1.3	16.7
93	92	1.9	91.7	58	18	0.4	15.4
92	106	2.2	89.8	57	53	1.1	15.0
91	129	2.7	87.6	56	48	1.0	13.9
90	66	1.4	84.9	55	73	1.5	12.9
89	106	2.2	83.6	54	42	0.9	11.4
88	115	2.4	81.4	53	48	1.0	10.5
87	169	3.5	79.0	52	16	0.3	9.5
86	124	2.6	75.5	51	43	0.9	9.2
85	141	2.9	72.9	50	33	0.7	8.3
84	177	3.7	69.9	49	31	0.6	7.6
83	109	2.3	66.3	48	51	1.1	7.0
82	119	2.5	64.0	47	25	0.5	5.9
81	122	2.5	61.5	46	29	0.6	5.4
80	134	2.8	59.0	45	34	0.7	4.8
79	137	2.8	56.2	44	42	0.9	4.1
78	129	2.7	53.4	43	59	1.2	3.2
77	102	2.1	50.7	40	25	0.5	2.0
76	106	2.2	48.6	39	17	0.4	1.5
75	115	2.4	46.4	38	12	0.2	1.1
74	81	1.7	44.0	37	5	0.1	0.9
73	88	1.8	42.3	36	18	0.4	0.7
72	88	1.8	40.4	35	2	0.0	0.4
71	107	2.2	38.6	34	6	0.1	0.3
70	105	2.2	36.4	33	2	0.0	0.2
69	82	1.7	34.2	32	3	0.1	0.2
68	89	1.8	32.5	31	3	0.1	0.1
67	139	2.9	30.7	30	1	0.0	0.0
66	105	2.2	27.8	25	1	0.0	0.0

133

Table 3.2 MELAB Part 1 Interrater Reliability

Dates	N of Comps	Mean of Comp Scores	SD of Comp. Scores	N of Pairs of Raters	Range r^1	Mean r	Median r
12/90 - 4/92	4020	75.56	6.99	31	.52[4] to .92	.82	.83
12/92 - 11/93	2304	74.19	7.90	23	.68 to .90	.82	.83

Dates	N of Comps	Range Adjusted r^2	Mean Adjusted r	Median Adjusted r	SEM[3]
12/90 - 4/92	4020	.68[4] to .96	.90	.90	2.21
12/92 - 11/93	2304	.81 to .94	.90	.90	2.50

[1] r is the Pearson product-moment correlation coefficient.

[2] Adjusted r is an estimate of the reliability of the final composition scores (MELAB Part 1 scores) based on two raters per composition. It is obtained using the Spearman-Brown prophecy formula.

[3] SEM is the standard error of measurement of the composition scores.

[4] The minimum value in the range is very atypical. The next lowest r was .69, the second lowest adjusted r .82.

Appendix 3C. Norming Data From *IPT I Oral Grades K–6 Technical Manual* (Ballard, Dalton, & Tighe, 2001b)

TABLE A
LIST OF PARTICIPATING DISTRICTS
FORMS E AND F
Spring 2000

STATE	DISTRICT	SCHOOL	N	%
Arizona	Alhambra	Granada East	16	1.8
		Granada Primary	24	2.7
	Tucson	Cavett Elementary	9	1.0
		Reynolds Elementary	7	0.8
		Richey Elementary	10	1.1
		Roskruge Elementary	8	0.9
		VanBuskirk Elementary	11	1.2
California	Bishop Union	Elm Street	14	1.6
		Pine Street	18	2.0
	North Monterey County	Castroville Elementary	41	4.6
	Pomona	Lexington Elementary	42	4.7
	Saddleback Valley	Gate Elementary	14	1.6
	San Diego	Bethune Elementary	23	2.6
		Bird Rock Elementary	29	3.3
Colorado	Cherry Creek	Polton Elementary	3	0.3
Delaware	Red Clay Consolidated	Baltz Elementary	3	0.3
		Richie Elementary	1	0.1
		William C. Lewis Elementary	2	0.2
Florida	Seminole County	Bear Lake Elementary	71	8.0
		Casselberry Elementary	10	1.1
Kansas	Garden City	Alta Brown Elementary	6	0.7
		Bernadine Sitts Elementary	12	1.3
		Buffalo Jones Elementary	6	0.7
		Charles O. Stones Elementary	10	1.1
		Jennie Wilson Elementary	6	0.7
Michigan	Berkley	Avery Elementary	60	6.7

STATE	DISTRICT	SCHOOL	N	%
New Jersey	River Edge	Cherry Hill	12	1.3
		Roosevelt	2	0.2
New Mexico	Moriarty Municipal	Moriarty Elementary	44	4.9
		Mountainview Elementary	12	1.3
	Santa Fe	Agua Fria Elementary	38	4.3
North Carolina	Clinton City Schools	Butler Avenue School	12	1.3
		L.C. Kerr Elementary	12	1.3
		Sampson Middle School	4	0.5
Texas	Como-Pickton	Como-Pickton Elementary	18	2.0
	Corpus Christi	Martin Middle	8	0.9
		Menger Elementary	35	3.9
	Katy	Alexander Elementary	12	1.3
		Hutsell Elementary	24	2.7
		Mayde Creek Elementary	24	2.7
		Nottingham Elementary	27	3.0
	Kilgore	Kilgore Heights Elementary	30	3.4
	New Braunfels	Carl Schurz Elementary	7	0.8
		Lamar Primary	1	0.1
		Memorial Intermediate	4	0.5
		Memorial Primary	1	0.1
		Seele Elementary	11	1.2
	Olney	Olney Elementary	15	1.7
Utah	Provo	Franklin Elementary	14	1.6
		Timpanogos Elementary	68	7.6
		TOTAL	**891**	**100.0***

Chapter 4

Evaluating the Usefulness of Tests

The information in testing manuals is an essential part of test evaluation, but when teachers and administrators consider a test for a particular purpose, they need to examine the available information along with the test itself in view of the situation in which they might use it. Potential test users need to consider, for example, the Kuder–Richardson 20 reliability of a test for the reported sample, but ultimately the question of whether or not to adopt a test hinges not on any one of the statistics reported in the test manual but instead on an overall evaluation of the usefulness of a test for a certain testing situation.

This chapter describes how the types of information typically found in published test manuals can become part of a more comprehensive evaluation of test usefulness. The idea of test usefulness is related to the discussion of validity in chapter 1, and we therefore begin with a brief discussion of how validation theory from educational measurement motivates examination of test usefulness by outlining how the theory falls short of what ESOL practitioners need. We then introduce methods that have been developed for conducting a *test usefulness analysis* (Bachman & Palmer, 1996), demonstrate how the information in a test manual can be used in such an analysis, and summarize the basic procedure that you can use in conducting your own usefulness analyses.

The Limitations of Validation Theory

In chapter 1, we defined validity as the justification for test interpretation and use and introduced the idea of a validity argument, which is a way of expressing evidence pertaining to validity. For example, if teachers in a program are developing end-of-course achievement tests, they might want to include in the validity argument for these tests (a) judgments from teachers that the tests reflect what was taught, (b) evidence that students who took the course score higher on the tests than do similar students who did not take the course, and (c) an indication that knowledge of the test prompted students to study in a productive way. Validation theory suggests that these three pieces of evidence should support the use of a test, and therefore, to the extent that those considering use of the test are working within validation theory, such evidence should help support the validity of the test use.

The validation theory introduced in chapter 1 is important because it grounds discussion of language assessment within current thinking in educational measurement. At the same time, language professionals engaged in assessment, and particularly language test users, need to find their way through the broader concerns, which are summarized in *Standards for Psychological and Educational Testing* (Joint Committee on Standards for Educational & Psychological Testing, 1999). Although forming a basis for practice, validation theory is limited as a means for providing language teachers with a way of evaluating assessments in the ways outlined in Table 4.1.

At first, one might think that validation theory is too theoretical because it was written by and for educational measurement specialists. However, even measurement specialists see validation theory as a means for conceptualizing validity in testing rather than as a procedure for deciding whether or not a particular test use is sufficiently valid (e.g., Kane, 2001). Validation theory is distanced even further from language assessment practitioners by the divide that exists between the knowledge of people who test and those who teach. Although it is hoped that improved training through in-service and preservice programs and the increased availability of resources directed to practitioners will narrow this divide, teachers are unlikely to gain significant expertise in measurement theory anytime soon. What is needed, then, is a practice-oriented heuristic for considering the information provided in testing manuals in a manner that is consistent with current theoretical perspectives.

Such a heuristic also needs to address the related problem that validation theory is too open-ended. If validity is considered as an argument that can draw on a wide range of evidence, how much evidence does one need to justify test use? The validation theory developed by educational measure-

Table 4.1. Limitations of Applying Validation Theory to Language Testing Practice

Limitation	Explanation	Possible Solution
Too theoretical	Validation theory offers a means for conceptualizing validity in testing rather than a procedure for deciding whether or not a particular test use is sufficiently valid.	Develop heuristics for analysis of validity.
Too open-ended	Validation theory encompasses a wide range of concerns that most people would not be able to address without specifying any practical boundaries.	Develop a finite set of questions that potential test users should consider in assessing the validity of a test use.
Too general in purpose	Validation theory is intended to offer principles for assessment across a range of subject areas in education in addition to psychological testing.	Identify validity principles that take into consideration applied linguists' perspectives and ideals for language assessment.
Too group oriented	Validation theory conceptualizes validity from the perspective of the test users investigating test use for a group even though it acknowledges that differential performance by individuals poses a threat to validity.	Add to validation theory as it is currently conceived the concept of fairness, which could be considered from the perspective of the test taker.

ment specialists is so far-reaching that, as Shepard (1993) pointed out, one might get the idea that validation is a totally unrealistic and unreachable goal. If so, validation theory becomes irrelevant for testing practice, in which tests must be chosen or developed and used within real time constraints. Moreover, teachers, who may not be in a position to conduct validation research, must make decisions about assessments on the basis of the information available in the manuals and examination of the test itself.

A third problem with validation theory for language assessment is that it is too general in purpose, failing to consider applied linguists' perspectives and ideals for language assessment. As TESOL professionals, we believe that language teaching and assessment is best driven by some field-specific knowledge about language, language learning and teaching, and language assessment. The many graduate courses, reference books, journal articles, and conferences on language assessment do not mirror the precise issues and practices appearing in courses, books, papers, and conferences on educational measurement. Validation theory needs to be adapted rather than adopted in order to work for language assessment practice.

The fourth limitation of validation theory is that it conceptualizes validity from the perspective of the test users who think of test interpretation and use in terms of how a group of test takers performs on a test. This perspective takes the individual into account only insofar as evidence for test bias against an individual is considered to pose a threat to validity. Test bias is studied through the study of group test performance. This group perspective needs to be augmented by an individual perspective focused on test fairness—how the use of a test affects individual test takers.

An Approach to Test Usefulness in Practice

Language testing practice needs to address these four limitations while maintaining the foundations provided by validation theory. A number of language testing textbooks are helpful in explaining the key concepts in measurement for practitioners. In particular, we have found valuable Bachman and Palmer's (1996) outline of heuristics for considering the usefulness of a test for a particular purpose. Their approach is to outline the qualities that applied linguists see as critical for language assessments. These qualities include concepts from educational measurement, such as construct validity, but also those that applied linguists would value, such as authenticity.

Bachman and Palmer (1996) have applied the general principles of validity inquiry to second language testing by defining the specific types of arguments that they believe should be considered in language test development, revision, and evaluation. We have found that this approach addresses the first three limitations of validation theory. Addressing the fourth limitation requires a different perspective on the testing situation—one that considers the individual test taker. We discuss this issue from the perspective of test fairness.

Language Test Qualities

The six qualities of test usefulness are outlined and defined briefly in Table 4.2. Bachman and Palmer (1996) supply specific questions to use in a detailed analysis, particularly during test development. For example, one of the questions to ask in the analysis of reliability is "To what extent do characteristics of the test rubric vary in an unmotivated way from one part of the test to another, or on different forms of the test?" (p. 280). The

**Table 4.2. Qualities of Test Usefulness
(Bachman & Palmer, 1996, chapter 2)**

Reliability	The consistency of the performance reflected in scores
Construct validity	The appropriateness of the inferences made on the basis of test scores
Authenticity	The correspondence of characteristics of the test tasks to characteristics of relevant nontest contexts where language is used
Interactiveness	The expected extent of involvement of test takers' knowledge and interest and of their communicative language strategies in accomplishing a test task
Impact	The positive consequences that a test can have for society and educational systems and for the individuals within the systems (i.e., learners and teachers)
Practicality	The adequacy of the available resources for the design, development, use, and evaluation of the test

response to this question during test development might point to a revision that would improve the test instructions. Our discussion of these six qualities, in contrast, focuses on how to use the questions to evaluate the information offered in test manuals as it applies to a particular testing situation.

Reliability

We discussed reliability in chapters 1 and 3 as the consistency reflected in test scores or as the absence of error in test scores. Accordingly, Bachman and Palmer (1996) define reliability as the absence of unmotivated variation in test scores, which expresses the idea that one person's error might be another person's construct of interest.

For example, consider an oral interview in which test takers are asked to respond appropriately to a formal introduction in a role play but fail to do so because they do not realize that the prompt in the role play is a formal introduction. Their informal response earns them a low score on that task. Across the whole group of examinees, some recognize the prompt and others do not, which contributes to their scores. Does the prompt used to elicit the informal introduction decrease the overall reliability obtained from the test scores? It depends. If the test is intended to measure production of formal responses to introductions (and other responses), the prompt that was unclear to some test takers might be thought of as contributing unmotivated variation to the test scores. If the test is intended to measure interactive communicative language ability, test users would want scores to be influenced by how well test takers understood and took cues for producing formal responses, so the prompt would not be considered as a contributor to unmotivated variation in test scores. In short, interpretation of reliability is closely tied to the construct that the test is intended to measure.

We have noted that reliability is typically reported in test manuals but that the reliability coefficient reported can be derived in a number of different ways. For example, the Woodcock-Muñoz Language Survey manual (Woodcock & Muñoz-Sandoval, 1993) reports a split-half reliability of .815 on one part of the test, the Michigan English Language Assessment Battery manual (Briggs & Dobson, 1994) reports intrarater reliabilities of .87 to .92 for scores on the composition section of their test, and the Combined English Language Skills Assessment in a Reading Context manual (Ilyin, 1993) reports a test-retest reliability of .93. As described in chapter 3, each of these methods of calculating reliability has a different meaning, but in interpreting this information for a particular test usefulness analysis, the test user needs to remember that reliability is a characteristic of test scores, not tests. Therefore, users need to interpret the statistics reported in the manual in view of the particular test takers whose scores were used to make the reliability estimates. The question is, How similar is the group for whom reliability was reported to the group of test takers for whom the test is being investigated? Because each of the methods for calculating reliability is useful for estimating a particular type of error, the potential test user also needs to consider the extent to which the estimate speaks to the error that may exist in the test scores in the setting of interest.

Construct Validity

The usefulness analysis requires the potential test user to estimate the extent to which inferences made on the basis of test scores are likely to be appropriate for the use of those scores. The inferences refer to the conclusions that will be drawn about the test takers' language ability. Test manuals contain some important information that helps make such a judgment under the headings of content validity and concurrent validity, some of which pertains to construct validity as explained in chapter 3. The potential test user should examine the manual for any evidence about what the test developers intend the test to measure. Clues might be found in the names of the sections of the test, a description of the test purpose, or descriptions of test content. The question for the usefulness analysis is how well the constructs measured by the test fit the purpose for the test in the particular test setting.

Authenticity

Because of the value that applied linguists place on authentic language use and the importance of the language on the test for eliciting what is measured, Bachman and Palmer (1996) suggest including authenticity as an important consideration in evaluation of test usefulness. The general idea of authenticity has been cited as an ideal for tests in other subject areas (e.g., Linn, Baker, & Dunbar, 1991; Wiggins, 1993), but Bachman and Palmer give specific criteria for analyzing important characteristics of the target language use (TLU) domain. These criteria provide analytic categories for evaluating the degree of correspondence of the language test with the language of the setting of interest to score users.

This principle is most easily seen in tests of language for specific purposes. If you are testing examinees' ability to interact with customers who are checking in and out of a hotel, you will want the language on the test to include oral and written exchanges about the cost of rooms, dates, polite greetings, and so on. The same principle holds even when the range of linguistic registers is wider, although the larger the range of registers, the more challenging the authenticity demand becomes. The idea is that register is important and that test users are interested in test takers' performances in a range of registers.

Interactiveness

Interactiveness is defined as the expected extent of involvement of test takers' knowledge and interest and of their communicative language strategies in accomplishing a test task. Some people (e.g., Douglas, 2000) might consider interactiveness within the concept of authenticity because it refers to how the learner's language knowledge is engaged in constructing meaning during language use—which is typically what happens during language use outside the language classroom. But in terms of analysis, in which authenticity refers to an analysis of the observable setting and language and interaction of the test and nontest setting, interactiveness refers to the hypothesized and intended engagement of the test taker in language performance during test taking. Because language use requires engagement of language users' linguistic and nonlinguistic knowledge, strategies, and affect, so should language test taking.

Research on the strategies that test takers use in some tests (i.e., those that fail on the interactiveness criterion) has shown that they can be more like problem-solving strategies than communication strategies (Cohen, 1998). Thus, the analysis requires the potential test user to hypothesize the full range of abilities that the test taker may draw on during the test.

Impact

Analysis of potential test impact requires consideration of how test use might affect the people who are directly and indirectly involved with the test. Impact, also called *washback* or *consequences* (Bailey, 1996; Shepard, 1997; Wall, 1997), includes factors directly related to the outcomes of testing, such as accurate placement into classes or informative diagnosis for students. It also includes the test's potential effects on students, such as their attending to what they need to study because they know they will have a test, or the effects it might have on teachers, such as their planning to cover certain points in their teaching.

Impact can extend beyond the classroom and even into the community, when, for example, parents feel that their children are being tested fairly as a way of ensuring that they obtain the most appropriate instruction. Virtually all specialists in language assessment consider impact to be important for selecting a test even though the investigation of impact has not shown clear and direct relationships between tests and teaching or learning (Alderson & Hamp-Lyons, 1996; Alderson & Wall, 1993).

Practicality

Exactly as the term suggests, *practicality* refers to the adequacy of the available resources for the design, development, use, and evaluation of the test. Examination of the testing manual or inquiries to the publisher will reveal the test's monetary cost, but the potential test user also needs to consider the personnel and equipment necessary for delivering the test, scoring it, and communicating the results to the relevant people. In addition, most testing requires keeping records of results and doing some form of analysis, such as calculating reliability estimates. All of the testing needs should be considered in view of the actual resources available or obtainable for testing. In our experience, ESOL testing programs require resources beyond what anyone considers before the testing program exists or when testing is conducted haphazardly, so potential test users should be prepared to calculate expenses and obtain the required funding.

Test Fairness

Consideration of the qualities of language tests is intended to help test users evaluate and improve testing with the aim of making tests as useful as possible. Some researchers argue, however, that test use should also be evaluated in terms of its fairness for individual test takers. Kunnan's (1997) definition of *fairness* resembles the broad validation theory discussed above because it incorporates principles for fair test development, use, and evaluation:

> Fairness in language assessment refers to 1) the use of fair means (both in test content and in test method) for assessing language abilities, 2) the fair use of test scores obtained from tests, 3) ethics, accountability and test standards that promote fairness in general, and 4) research on assessment procedures and practices that acknowledges and engages otherness and difference. (pp. 93–94)

The breadth of these fairness concerns reflects the discussion of fairness in chapter 7 of the *Standards* (Joint Committee, 1999), which presents several different views of fairness, including lack of bias (i.e., items that function differently for members of subgroups of test takers), equitable treatment in the testing process, equality in the outcomes of testing, and opportunity to learn (e.g., achievement testing across a region in which some students were taught what is tested and others were not). Consideration of test fairness has clear implications for the use of scores from tests other than ESOL tests to evaluate ESOL learners' achievement, progress, and aptitude in all school subjects. In these cases, ESOL test takers are a subgroup of the overall population that may be disadvantaged through this practice. However, the fairness issues are less clear-cut in ESOL testing, so test users should consider the role of fairness in the overall evaluation of a test by whatever means they see fit as they attempt to engage in ethical testing practices.

A Sample Test Usefulness Analysis

To demonstrate how to apply the test usefulness analysis for evaluating a test for a particular situation, we draw on an example of a testing situation that we are familiar with: the adoption of a test for a program that currently administers one that was developed by the teachers who work in the program. The evaluation will consider the six qualities of usefulness in addition to fairness and draw a conclusion about adopting the test.

Testing Context: Iowa State University ESL Program

This testing context at Iowa State University, in the United States, is familiar to many U.S. ESOL professionals in higher education. International students have applied to the university, submitting acceptable scores on the Test of English as a Foreign Language (TOEFL), and are therefore accepted into academic programs. Based on years of experience with such students and TOEFL scores, faculty across the campus recognize that individual variation exists in the English proficiency of students who have submitted acceptable TOEFL scores. Some of these students need to take additional English classes, so the Department of English offers courses in academic English: two levels with emphasis on grammar and writing, one level emphasizing reading and vocabulary, and one level for listening.

The ESOL students and courses are only one aspect of this program, which is administered through a multifaceted English department, and ESL is one of many programs that compete for attention and resources. Despite limited personnel and financial resources, the present ESL testing program succeeds in testing and placing hundreds of new students during the week before classes begin each semester. The people responsible for the program are interested in exploring alternatives that might improve the quality of the placements and the efficiency of the process. In this setting, the testers are interested in the possibility of adopting a computer-delivered test if it is judged to be appropriate.

Analysis of the ACT ESL Placement Test

The ACT ESL Placement Test, reviewed in chapter 2, was developed for placement at a variety of institutions, including universities. The manual (ACT, 2000b), the *Research and Data Report* (ACT, 2000a), and the sample items from ACT offer a lot of information about the quality of the test. The analysis of test usefulness incorporates this information along with an analysis of the needs of the testing context (see Table 4.3).

Reliability and Construct Validity

The first two areas, reliability and construct validity, rely on information obtained from ACT documents about the test and from an examination of the test. Examination of the test tasks and instructions does not raise concerns about introduction of unmotivated variation. The ACT documents do not report a reliability estimate for the test but show the spread of scores across its five levels. Based on knowledge of how reliability is estimated, one would expect good internal consistency reliability from this spread of scores. At the same time, however, the sample from which the scores are obtained is much larger and more diverse than the intended group of test takers. As a consequence, test users cannot assume an equivalent spread of scores in the Iowa State setting. This information reveals a drawback because it is likely to lower the reliability of the expected scores on the test.

Positive aspects with respect to construct validity include the clear definition of what the test is intended to measure, some evidence that the test measures the intended constructs, and the similarity of these constructs to those of interest in the Iowa State program. Negative aspects include the lack of stronger evidence concerning the constructs measured and the lack of a measure of writing ability, which is an important construct for place-ment in the classes of interest.

Authenticity and Interactiveness

Examination of the testing materials reveals some match between the academic language of interest to test users and the language on the test, at least at the higher levels. Accordingly, these texts would be expected to engage test takers' knowledge and communicative strategies. On the negative side, the selected-response format used throughout the test does not match the linguistic production required of test takers in their academic language use or their ESOL writing classes.

Impact and Practicality

Potentially positive factors related to impact and practicality include appropriate placement, staff experience with a computer-based test, and the availability of the computer labs for testing. On the negative side are the computer problems that might occur during testing, and the cost of buying testing materials and paying staff to monitor administration. If 2 hours are

Table 4.3. Summary of Usefulness Analysis for the ACT ESL Placement Test at Iowa State University

Quality	Positive Attributes	Negative Attributes
Reliability	• The test was designed to elicit only variation motivated by the ability of interest for the learners of interest. • Instructions and response types are unlikely to contribute unmotivated variance to test scores. • Based on sample sizes of over 5,000 examinees for each test, the test obtains a wide range of scores; this range would contribute to high reliability for this group.	• The test was designed to discriminate among a broader range of language abilities than those that will be represented in the Iowa State candidature.
Construct validity	• The constructs of reading, listening, and grammar/usage are relevant for the intended use. • The construct definitions are reflected in the proficiency descriptors, which include aspects of the constructs of interest in the Iowa State context. • ACT offers guidance for setting valid cut scores. • Case-study example shows good matches between test placements based on listening scores and faculty judgments.	• The construct of interest at Iowa State, writing, is not represented well by selected-response items. • No correlational evidence indicates a relationship with other measures.
Authenticity	• Students complete many assignments at Iowa State online, so taking the test online would be authentic relative to many of their experiences in the target language use domain. • The texts and listening materials at the high level were designed to be as authentic as possible relative to natural native-speaker oral and spoken texts, some from academic materials. • The tasks at the advanced level require examinees to engage in the cognitively complex language analysis that they will do in academic classes.	• The future language use context is tied to specific academic areas whereas the test appears to be less specific. • The low-level texts are simpler than those learners are likely to encounter outside the classroom. • The online test tasks are not the same as many tasks that learners will perform in other contexts.

(continued on p. 148)

Table 4.3. Continued

Quality	Positive Attributes	Negative Attributes
Interactiveness	• Some of the language input appears within texts consisting of more than one sentence and therefore would require activation of topical knowledge.	• Some of the language input consists of short segments of language that may not require activation of topical knowledge, affect, or communicative strategies.
Impact	• The test content appears interesting for test takers. • Test takers may have some flexibility in the time at which they can take the test. • Test results may help in placing examinees accurately, thereby improving instruction. • Staff gain experience in working with a computer-based test.	• We do not know if the test takers will experience anxiety from taking the test online. • We do not know if the equipment and software will work properly.
Practicality	• Students could take the test in one of the English department's computer labs, which would be available when the testing is done (the week before classes start). • Automatic scoring and score reporting would work well in this setting, where scores are needed quickly.	• The 28-seat computer lab would have to be monitored for long periods of time while all students cycle through. • The estimated annual cost would be approximately US$4,000 (based on information obtained from the publisher).

reserved for each group of 28 students to take the test, it will take at least 2 days for all students to take the test during fall semester, if all goes well. Alternatively, if more labs are engaged and the number of staff monitors is increased, the time period could be cut. In the Iowa State setting, none of the negatives is insurmountable, but they are the factors likely to be raised in response to a proposed adoption of the ACT ESL Placement Test.

It is no accident that the analysis ends with recognition of the factors that will be noted by the potential critics of test adoption. The analysis of manuals, tests, and test settings is not complete without considering the potentially most salient forces in the ultimate decision. Validation theory conceptualizes the potential critics or those who need to be convinced by a validity argument as the *audience* for the argument. The notion of audience captures in a satisfying way the idea that any test analysis or validity argument consists of discourse that attempts to convince someone about the test. What it takes to convince people depends in large part on who they are, what they know, and what they are willing to believe (Cherryholmes, 1988). Taken to its extreme, the notion of an audience for a validity argument suggests that teachers preparing an analysis of an ESOL test for school administrators might narrow their argument only to meet the concerns of the administrator, who is genuinely interested in the quality of the test but might be unaware of how to conceptualize what that means. The potential relativity of this approach can be anchored to some extent in the usefulness analysis, which systematizes the concerns and knowledge of the profession to guide the range of considerations (Chapelle, Jamieson, & Hegelheimer, 2003) even if in the end decision makers give some considerations greater weight.

We have described this analysis of test usefulness—including a final note about the audience for the analysis—without any mention of the test takers' perspectives. This is precisely the point proponents of test fairness make when they argue that fairness must include more than the concerns of test users. In terms of the Iowa State ESL test, the fairness issue would involve whether the administration of a test by computer would be unfair to students who have had little experience in using computers, whether the way the constructs were measured would be fair to all examinees, and whether it is fair to test students immediately on arrival on campus. Openness to evidence that the testing process and test use may have treated some individuals unfairly is more important than any speculation about fairness issues.

Your Usefulness Analysis

Table 4.4 summarizes the process used to analyze the usefulness of the ACT ESL Placement Test for the ESL program at Iowa State University. The manual and the test itself provide input for the analysis of reliability and construct validity, but this analysis needs to be conducted in view of the test takers and test purpose in the test setting. Authenticity and interactiveness are analyzed through an examination of the test and consideration of the target language use context and the test takers. Analysis of impact and practicality depends primarily on the factors in the testing context. The questions provided in Table 4.4 are intended to guide analysis, but they are not the only questions that might be asked in each area. Not included in the table is the overarching concern of fairness, which should be considered throughout test selection and use.

Table 4.4. Questions for Analysis of Usefulness Based on Information From the Test Manual, the Test, and the Test Situation

What to Do	What to Keep in Mind	What to Ask
Examine the test manual and test.	Reliability	• Do the test instructions and test tasks minimize unmotivated variation? • Does the test manual indicate appropriate reliability estimates for your purpose? • Is the group on which reliability estimates were calculated similar enough to yours? • Are there factors in your testing situation that would negatively affect reliability, other than those considered by the test developer?
	Construct validity	• Are the constructs and content measured by the test similar to what you are interested in testing? • How strong is the evidence that the test measures the construct that the manual says it measures?
Analyze the test content.	Authenticity	• To what extent do the language and the items on the test correspond to those that are relevant to your students?
	Interactiveness	• To what extent do the test tasks engage the test takers' language knowledge and strategies?
Consider your test setting.	Impact	• To what extent will use of the test positively affect the students, teachers, and program? • Are there any negative consequences that the test might have in your situation?
	Practicality	• Do you have the resources required to use the test successfully?

Conclusion

Throughout this chapter, we have been concerned with linking theory to practice, and principles to concrete, day-to-day practices in English language classrooms and programs. Some of the problems with validation theory for practice in ESOL assessment are that it is too theoretical, too open-ended, too general purpose, and too group oriented. A valuable approach is Bachman and Palmer's (1996) usefulness analysis along with the consideration of test fairness. The Iowa State example shows how those considerations would be used to conduct a usefulness analysis of a particular test for ESL placement and reveals how information from the test manual, the test, and the test setting come into play in the analysis. The summary in Table 4.4 provides an outline of the usefulness questions that a potential test user might rely on in conducting a usefulness analysis.

Chapter 5

Deciding to Develop a Test

In this chapter we consider a situation that ESOL teachers often face: The tests they have examined do not pass the usefulness analysis or are judged to be unfair to prospective test takers. We describe a number of instances when teachers might want to consider developing their own tests and outline how they would do so, mentioning the resources available to teachers for test development. Our intent is not to give comprehensive instructions for developing tests but rather to give an overview of key aspects of the process and suggestions on where to obtain additional help.

Why Tests Sometimes Fail

Even though professional test developers have produced and conducted research on a number of excellent tests, these tests cannot possibly meet all the assessment needs of teachers. We have frequently been asked to recommend tests for situations in which the ideal test did not exist and the teachers would likely have to develop their own. The following scenarios illustrate four such cases.

Scenario 1: No Suitable Oral Language Placement Test Exists

The first scenario comes from an intensive language program in the United States in which teachers have worked hard together to develop a curriculum that they feel effectively concentrates on oral language. The teachers have revised the curriculum by carefully analyzing the linguistic needs of their students, and even though these needs vary considerably, the teachers have identified the content and language that students find relevant and useful.

Teachers need an appropriate placement test that, like the curriculum, concentrates on oral language. They have looked at the published placement tests that they could find, but none passes the usefulness analysis, in particular because the tests have limited construct validity and insufficient authenticity. A placement test that assesses constructs other than the oral language ability of learners will lead to misplacements. Most of the students come from contexts where English is not the primary language, and after years of study of written English, their development of written and oral language proficiency has been uneven. The placement test for this program needs to assess ability in oral language, and the teachers need to develop such a test.

Scenario 2: Unit Test Items Are Inauthentic

The second scenario is a situation that teachers face regularly in their classrooms: A teacher needs a unit test that assesses what she has taught from a course textbook and her own materials. Although some textbooks are accompanied by unit tests, the teacher needs to judge to what extent they pass the usefulness analysis because they accurately measure what she wants to assess.

In this scenario, the tests in the book fail in part because they consist solely of selected-response items. After all the oral and written productive practice that the teacher has carefully included in the teaching, she sees multiple-choice and matching questions as too inauthentic and lacking in construct validity. She needs to write her own test.

Scenario 3: Assessment Procedures Do Not Match the Curriculum

The third scenario comes from a public school setting in the United States, where a federal government mandate requires that English language learners be tested to determine whether they need ESOL instruction. This school enrolls a large number of English language learners and has therefore developed a strong curriculum in ESOL over time. In fact, the curriculum, consisting of many classes in which students can study language through content, far exceeds what is covered by the test that has been used for many years.

The teachers are developing students' language ability through content-based instruction, and they believe the test used to determine whether the learners need the course should also test language through content. The inauthenticity of the existing test for this otherwise model program represents a poor match between the assessment procedures and the curriculum that the teachers have worked so hard to create. They need to develop a suitable test.

Scenario 4: Learners Need a Completely Oral Test

The fourth scenario involves teachers working in a program that teaches oral English to immigrants. The large majority of the teaching focuses on speaking and listening, with the goal of helping the learners be able to negotiate everyday life and acquire basic life skills during their first year and, it is hoped, get to a level at which they may be able to go on to a more comprehensive ESOL program.

In this program, in which most of the learners lack literacy in their own language as well as in English, the introduction of written language on a test would seem unfair to the learners. Particularly for diagnosing program participants' English abilities and assessing their progress, the teachers need tests that are conducted completely through oral language, so they need to develop their own.

In each of these situations, none of the tests described in chapter 2 fits the testing need and would likely be judged to lack construct validity for the particular test purpose. Teachers in Scenario 1 would note that the Comprehensive English Language Test (CELT) and the Michigan English Language Assessment Battery (MELAB) assess reading and writing but not oral language ability. None of the tests reviewed in chapter 2 is designed to assess what is taught in a single course based on a particular textbook and supplemental, teacher-developed materials. In Scenario 3, teachers would find that the Bilingual Syntax Measures I and II, the Maculaitis Assessment of Competencies Test of English Language Proficiency II (MAC II), the Secondary Level English Proficiency (SLEP) Test, the IDEA Proficiency Test (IPT) I—Oral, and the Woodcock-Muñoz Language Survey (WMLS) are unsuitable because they are intended to be general measures of language proficiency learners have acquired in the curriculum. Finally, in Scenario 4, the Combined English Language Skills Assessment in a Reading Context (CELSA) would be inappropriate because it requires literacy skills in English. The Basic English Skills Test (BEST) is a possibility if the literacy component is not administered, but program staff want to be able to assess progress and therefore decide to develop assessments more finely tuned to the learners' levels and the course content.

Developing a Passing Test

A number of books are available for practitioners who are developing tests. One publication that speaks especially well to teachers is *Testcraft: A Teacher's Guide to Writing and Using Language Test Specifications* (Davidson & Lynch, 2002). Another title that focuses on the types of tests most often constructed by teachers is *Criterion-Referenced Language Testing* (Brown & Hudson, 2002). Cambridge University Press's Cambridge Language Assessment Series is devoted to the assessment of language ability. Titles include *Assessing Reading* (Alderson, 2000), *Assessing Writing* (Weigle, 2002), *Assessing Listening* (Buck, 2001), *Assessing Speaking* (Luoma, 2004), *Assessing Vocabulary* (Read, 2000), and *Assessing Grammar* (Purpura, 2004), as well as titles that address the use of statistics to analyze language assessments (Bachman, 2004) and the assessment of English for specific purposes (Douglas, 2000). Most of these sources contain examples of teacher-constructed assessments.

In addition to offering examples of how to develop and evaluate a placement and an achievement test, Hughes' (2003) *Testing for Language Teachers* contains a 10-step process for developing teacher-constructed assessments. Bachman and Palmer's (1996) *Language Testing in Practice,* which has been cited repeatedly in this book, includes a three-stage framework for evaluating test usefulness as well as 10 examples of assessments constructed for a variety of assessment purposes. All of these resources have been designed for practicing teachers, who will find the contents accessible and useful in constructing their own language assessments.

Based on the advice presented in these sources, it is clear that the test development process involves several key elements. Our summary of these elements draws on concepts presented by Davidson and Lynch (2002). They describe their approach in terms that are accessible to most ESOL teachers:

> Our approach to test development is intended to be inclusive, open, and reflective. We promote tests that are crafted by a group of invested individuals, and we especially promote the inclusion in that group of individuals not normally invited into test development discussions. (p. 2)

Drawing on the test development principles and processes described by Davidson and Lynch, we submit that there are four important aspects of test development: interested individuals, the test specification, ideas from experts, and the table of specifications.

Interested Individuals

In the scenarios above, we described the testing needs from the perspective of the teacher or teachers, but other interested individuals may want or need to be involved. In test development, it is important to identify these persons because their input often affects the test development process.

Davidson and Lynch (2002) refer to "the mandate" as the "combination of forces which help decide what will be tested and to shape the actual content of the test" (p. 77). The mandate, which is the starting point for test development, arises because some people are interested in having a test when none existed; developing a better test to replace an insufficient one; or changing a test to keep up with the changing learners, theories, or curricula. Individuals interested in encouraging test development might be close to the test setting, such as course teachers, or they may be outside the class and language program, such as members of a committee at a university charged with overseeing English language issues. In any case, the individuals who help shape the mandate are a key element in the process. Davidson and Lynch indicate that most test development occurs in a group, so the typical types of group dynamics issues, such as personalities, personal agendas and beliefs, and power relationships, come into play. Their study of group test development suggests that a group of approximately three to five members may be ideal, but the size of the group depends on the size of the project. Our experience suggests that clear and strong leadership is important for good progress but that teamwork is also essential.

The Test Specification

Davidson and Lynch (2002) place the test specification, or "test spec" (p. 4), as they call it, at the center of the test development process. Drawing on the contributions of renowned measurement experts, they define the test spec as consisting of five parts: (a) a general description of what is to be tested, (b) the prompt attributes, (c) the response attributes, (d) a sample item, and (e) the specification supplement. See Davidson and Lynch's text for an extensive discussion of the test spec; here we simply point out that the test spec consists of pieces that are well within the teacher's capability to conceptualize.

By keeping the test development process as concrete as possible and focusing on the specification, Davidson and Lynch capitalize on what teachers know rather than beginning with assessment concepts that may be unfamiliar and less tangible. Typically, teachers can begin the process by saying, "I think we need to measure how well the students can write an essay," which becomes the first iteration of the general description. In the second part, the prompt attribute, teachers specify what they will ask learners to do to show that they can write an essay, and the response attribute describes how the test taker responds and what constitutes a quality response. A sample item in this case becomes an example of one of the prompts that members of the test development team deem appropriate to assess how well the students can write an essay. The specification supplement consists of any additional specification required to implement the item appropriately. For example, the prompt for the essay may require test takers to read something in addition to the prompt before beginning to compose or to examine and consider certain data, such as a chart or graph, before writing about them.

Each of the five parts of the test spec should be developed within the context of a group that takes multiple perspectives into account. Such a process results in dynamic consideration of alternatives and, as Davidson and Lynch (2002) indicate, consideration of each part of the test spec leads to reconsideration of other parts. In the aforementioned case of developing a writing prompt, the test developers' discussion would inevitably return to the general description and the prompt attribute. This is a desirable characteristic of the process, they argue, because the goal is to produce the most consistent, defensible test spec possible based on a consensus rather than to adopt a linear process that proceeds from the development of the general description through the explication of the specification supplement.

From Specs to a Table of Specifications

A test spec is conceived as a building block for a test. Because a test is typically constructed through the combination of test specs, part of the test development process consists of constructing a plan indicating which test specs should form the basis for the test and the percentage of weight to be given to each spec. For example, the test spec for *ability to write an essay* might form one part of an overall achievement test in an academic writing course. Although the test development team might agree that this test spec should be given considerable weight on the test, members should also be concerned about the potential problems when a test consists of a single writing prompt (e.g., the potential of topic bias, which negatively affects construct validity). Moreover, the test developers would likely agree that writing essays in a global sense was not the only ability taught in the course; nor should learners be expected to have acquired complete competence in academic writing by the end of the course. Instead, the course is designed, more realistically, to teach strategies of academic writing (e.g., outlining, editing, and using a concordancer), and as a consequence, these skills would be reasonable to consider as additional test specs.

Ultimately, however, when the test developers are satisfied with the variety of draft test specs, they need to define how the specs are to be combined into a complete test. This step in the process can be difficult because teachers typically think in terms of determining relative degrees of emphasis rather than applying specific percentages of weight to the various aspects of the abilities they are assessing. Developing a table of specifications or a blueprint for the test can involve a significant shift in perspective for teachers. For this reason, as well as to obtain a variety of ideas, we recommend consulting the work of researchers in language assessment for guidance and suggestions on how to work through this stage of the process.

Ideas From the Experts

Davidson and Lynch (2002) take a grassroots approach to test development, drawing primarily on the teachers' expertise in analyzing what and how language might be assessed. This approach is completely justified because, as we argue in chapter 1, teachers know a lot about what should be assessed and what constitutes a fair assessment task. As we also noted in chapter 1, the field of language assessment is deep and rich enough that teachers can gain important benefits by becoming more familiar with its substantial knowledge base. Therefore, we encourage teachers to consult the books named in Developing a Passing Test above as well as those in the annotated bibliography. Taken together, they address every aspect of assessing language ability and are excellent sources of ideas on developing each aspect of the test specification.

The general description for a placement test in an intensive language program might include a test spec concerning vocabulary taught at various levels of the program. If the curriculum selects and targets particular words for each level of the program, teachers may want to use these words as one means of determining the level in which to place test takers in the program. However, in any discussion of vocabulary, members of the team will object to assessment of decontextualized vocabulary. How can the general description be phrased to preclude decontextualized vocabulary assessment? What kind of test items can be used to assess vocabulary in context? Can such items constitute a valid assessment of vocabulary in context? The development team will have to address these issues in the General Description of the test spec, where the statement about assessing vocabulary will have to be framed so as to take account of the desire to assess vocabulary in context. The discussion of this issue will benefit significantly by considering the contents of Read's (2000) *Assessing Vocabulary,* which begins with a discussion of three key dimensions of vocabulary assessment: discrete versus embedded, selective versus comprehensive, and context independent versus context dependent. These dimensions provide the concepts that teachers would need to draw on to begin to discuss vocabulary assessment in more depth than can be achieved based on a commonsense definition of vocabulary.

Test developers will prepare better prompt attributes for the test spec if they have examined and discussed a number of alternatives that they can choose from. Each of the books in the Cambridge Language Assessment Series contains many examples of items that can serve as data for discussion of the attributes. Moreover, each of the books discusses the attributes at an abstract or generalizable level by considering test task characteristics, such as the test setting, rubric, and input to the test taker.

The response attribute includes the behavior and language product requested of the test taker and the way that this production will be assessed. All test developers are interested in having tests that require examinees to produce language, but the expertise required to evaluate such production is an important issue to consider. Turner and Upshur (2002) and Papajohn (2002) illustrate the complexity inherent in the development and use of such scales. Considerable research in this area has helped clarify at least some of the issues and provide some options for test developers. Any discussion of scoring procedures for a writing assessment should include careful consideration of chapter 6 of Weigle's (2002) *Assessing Writing,* which discusses the three types of scales that test developers would most likely consider (i.e., primary trait, holistic, and analytic). The definition of these three types of scales along with the numerous examples of scoring scales and discussion of their use should stimulate discussions among test developers regarding the options for the response attribute section of the test spec.

One of the notes that should be placed in the specification supplement of an online reading test is whether or not the test takers should be able to look at the text while they are answering the comprehension questions. A computer-based test can be designed to present the text on one screen and the questions on a subsequent screen that does not allow the test taker to return to the text. Alternatively, the learner can have access to the text by clicking the *Back* arrow or scrolling up to the text. Members of the test development team will want to discuss these options before making a decision. The team may also find it useful to consult Alderson's (2000) *Assessing Reading,* which considers some of the research on this issue:

> If one is interested in knowing whether candidates can answer relatively low-level, linguistically oriented, explicit questions, then they should be allowed to refer to the text. If, on the other hand, one is interested in knowing whether candidates can understand the main idea of the text, it might be better to remove the text before allowing them to answer the question. (p. 108)

Like the perspectives presented in the other books in the Cambridge Language Assessment Series, this perspective does not resolve the issue of whether or not the text should be accessible to students as they answer questions. Instead, it offers additional information for the test developers' discussion.

Test development appropriately starts with interested individuals and draws on their collective vision and expertise in setting a mandate, but as test development progresses, the discussion of possibilities need not be limited by the collective knowledge in the room. We would therefore suggest consulting a number of books that deal with how to describe what is tested and what to include in a prompt and in response attributes, as well as a large variety of attributes and lots of sample items. Reviews of relevant published tests, including those in chapter 2, can serve as a source of useful examples and spark ideas that advance the discussion.

Other sources of practical information on test design and evaluation are journals such as *Language Testing* and *Language Assessment Quarterly*, as well as occasional papers in *ELT Journal, Foreign Language Annals*, and *TESOL Quarterly* (see especially Boyd & Davies, 2002; Laufer & Nation, 1999; Lynch, 2001; Manley, 1995; McNamara, 2001; Papajohn, 2002; Read & Chapelle, 2001; Shohamy, 1997, 2001a; Turner & Upshur, 2002; Upshur & Turner, 1995; Wall, Clapham, & Alderson, 1994). Laufer and Nation describe how they developed a vocabulary test to diagnose, place, and design ESOL curricula, and Read and Chapelle lay out a framework for conceptualizing comparative features of different vocabulary assessments. Laufer and Nation present test specifications and the test analyses they performed in order to construct multiple forms of the assessment, whereas Read and Chapelle consider their particular type of assessment relative to other approaches to measuring vocabulary ability. In short, serial publications offer access to the latest developments in assessment practices and can inform practitioners' efforts to develop their own language assessments.

Evaluating and Improving Your Test

In chapter 4, we presented a conceptualization for evaluating published tests intended for a particular testing situation. Would these same criteria apply to teacher-developed tests? In the four scenarios outlined at the beginning of this chapter, we described the problems of adopting published tests in terms of their construct validity and authenticity, notions presented in chapter 4. Does this mean that any new test must be judged against the full list of usefulness qualities, that is, reliability, construct validity, authenticity, interactiveness, impact, and practicality?

This question is at the center of a current debate concerning exactly what standards to apply and methods to adopt in evaluating teacher-developed assessments. Some language testers (Bachman, 2000; Brown & Hudson, 2002) advocate applying the same process and procedures to validating all assessments regardless of their purpose, context, or type. Others (Lynch, 2001; McNamara, 2001; Shohamy, 2001a) question whether it is possible or appropriate to try to validate teacher-developed assessments—in particular those referred to as alternatives to traditional standardized tests—using traditional methods because many alternative types of assessment emerge from what Lynch describes as another culture represented by a fundamentally different orientation to assessment than the culture of language testers. This debate is unlikely to be resolved soon; nor should it keep teachers from using advances in language testing to respond more effectively to the assessment challenges of language teaching and learning. Clearly, language testers and teachers are beginning to cross cultures, to the benefit of both, so rather than take a strong position concerning the best approach for evaluating teacher-developed assessments, we simply mention some of the options discussed in the current language assessment literature.

Regardless of the methods adopted, evaluating teacher-constructed tests begins by considering the purpose, stakes, impact, and type of assessment, and systematically collecting and analyzing information about the test and the development process from multiple sources. Typically, the evaluation process proceeds by comparing various kinds of collected evidence with test specifications and using it to analyze the test and make improvements. The sources of information can include analysis of performance data, discourse analyses, narratives describing test development activities, discussions with stakeholders, and critical appraisals of all of these types of data.

Analyzing Performance on the Test

As discussed in chapter 3, internal consistency and item discrimination are two common procedures for analyzing how test takers perform on test items. The same ideas can be applied to analysis of teacher-developed assessments, but the specifics may be different depending on factors such as how big the group of test takers is, whether the test is high stakes or low stakes, and whether it is intended to make norm-referenced or criterion-referenced decisions. The different considerations and different procedures are described by Brown (1996) and Bachman (2004).

Item analysis can lead to decisions about eliminating poor test items to improve the quality of an assessment and collecting good items used to develop alternate forms of a moderate- to high-stakes test that must be administered frequently, for example, every semester. Such procedures also are involved in establishing cut scores for making important decisions based on test performance, such as whether an ESOL student in a K–12 school has acquired enough English proficiency to be placed in mainstream classes or whether a learner has mastered the curriculum content of an intensive English program and is ready to advance to the next level of instruction.

Collecting and analyzing this kind of information can lead to improvements in the quality of the test and the decisions based on the results. Brown and Hudson (2002) describe in detail exactly how to conduct these item analyses on teacher-developed assessments. Published accounts of test developers' efforts to evaluate their assessments are also useful reading. For instance, Wall et al. (1994) describe their response to the challenge of evaluating a placement test they developed for an intensive English program. They report how they used item analyses and other sources of information to develop and improve their test.

Statistical analyses of performance on the assessment can be complemented by qualitative analyses of the discourse test takers construct in response to various test tasks. By applying discourse analysis or conversation analysis procedures to language use to examine the structural, functional, and rhetorical features exhibited by test takers, developers gain important insights into how their assessments operate. Lazaraton (2002) describes the use of conversational analysis to explore test takers' oral performances on a university-level ESOL placement test and the Cambridge Assessment of Spoken English. These assessments and the rating scales used to judge the quality of test takers' responses were designed based on theoretical frameworks of what is thought to contribute to communicative language ability. When the results of discourse analyses are compared with and found to be consistent with theoretical explanations of language ability, they may become powerful empirical evidence of the credibility of the teacher-developed assessment.

Analyzing Raters' Assessments and Test Developers' Rationales

In Scenario 4 above, teachers are rating the speaking ability of test takers. In such cases, test developers need to know how consistent the teachers in the program are in rating students. Intra- and interrater reliability estimates can be calculated and used to determine the degree of consistency in these ratings. This information, in turn, can be used to improve the assessment (i.e., the rating scale) and help train assessors. Again, Brown and Hudson (2002) provide an excellent description of how to calculate these kinds of reliability estimates. For suggestions on how to construct and avoid common problems with rating scales, refer to Upshur and Turner (1995). They report on the process they followed to develop and evaluate an oral rating scale used to evaluate second language (L2) performance on a story-retelling task. Manley (1995) details how a large, urban K–12 school district developed an oral language assessment for foreign language ability using a collaborative process that included many interested individuals (stakeholders). The appendixes of the article contain examples of the scoring rubric and rating guidelines developed by the team.

Narrative descriptions of test development activities and pertinent discussions can form another source of information about the assessment because they contain the rationales for the decisions that test developers make as they, for example, include two writing prompts on a test, do not allow test takers access to the text while they respond to comprehension questions, or include vocabulary on a placement test. These types of test design decisions typically have to be justified to individuals who were not part of the design process but who ultimately need to be convinced of the soundness of the test design. Written records can be compared against test specifications and used as additional evidence of test takers' performance on the assessment and its broader impact (Davidson & Lynch, 2002).

Considering Fairness, Test Consequences, and Codes

Because of the significant consequences that tests can have for individuals and society, evaluation of tests includes a consideration of fairness and the effects of testing on teaching and learning. On the one hand, these large issues seem most relevant to the high-stakes testing that is typically the domain of test publishers. On the other hand, would any teacher want to be a part of a test design process that resulted in a test that was unfair or that negatively affected the test takers? In fact, the point of embarking on a test development project is often precisely to produce a fair test.

Fairness concerns include how much an assessment favors particular individuals or groups of test takers and the societal impact of an assessment on test takers' access to educational, vocational, economic, or other personal opportunities. *Standards for Educational and Psychological Testing* (Joint Committee on Standards for Educational & Psychological Testing, 1999) addresses these and several other fairness issues and emphasizes that test developers should treat test takers justly throughout the assessment process and should consider whether they have developed an appropriate test for the appropriate test takers, delivered it under appropriate conditions, and used the scores to make appropriate decisions. Additionally, the *Standards* specifies that test developers and users should consider how ethno-linguistically different test takers perform on a given assessment. L2 tests—whether the standardized variety like the TOEFL or teacher-constructed ones—affect teaching and learning.

Evaluating the impact of tests on the instructional process has been a topic of interest for a number of years. What is new is the inclusion of teacher-developed assessments in the discussion and the consideration of what is assessed, how it is assessed, and what evidence is needed to validate their use (McNamara, 2001). Codifying and disseminating the ethical principles and standards of practice endorsed by a profession is a wide-spread approach to promoting more ethical actions on the part of individuals (Stoynoff, 1993). It is a tack that could improve assessments and assessment practices. The International Language Testing Association has developed a code of ethics (Boyd & Davies, 2002), as have several other language testing organizations, and the *Standards* (Joint Committee, 1999) contains the practices deemed essential for those who use or develop tests.

Applying Critical Perspectives

The term *critical perspective* has been used in applied linguistics to refer to analytic perspectives linking professional practices to social, political, and cultural concerns with the aim of promoting changes that lead to greater social justice and equality. Critical perspectives view language teaching within a social context, where it is affected by shared values and jointly constructed meanings. Accordingly, critical voices point out the inherent power of tests and the potential for their misuse. Shohamy (1997, 2001a, 2001b), one of several prominent voices advocating the inclusion of a critical perspective in language assessment, encourages developers and users of assessments to consider their impact and to strive to create ones that are "educational, democratic, ethical, and, at the same time, valid" (2001a, p. 390). According to Shohamy (2001a), a principled approach

> to democratic assessment practices implies the following:
>
> 1. the need to apply critical language testing (CLT) [a set of principles developed by the author; for a description, see Shohamy, 2001b; Lynch, 2001] to monitor the uses of tests as instruments of power, to challenge their assumptions, and to examine their consequences;
>
> 2. the need to conduct and administer testing in collaboration and in cooperation with those tested;
>
> 3. the need for those involved in the testing act to assume responsibility for the tests and their uses;
>
> 4. the need to consider and include the knowledge of different groups in designing tests;
>
> 5. the need to protect the rights of test-takers. (p. 376)

Proponents of critical perspectives argue that one cannot ignore the disparities in power and authority that exist between individuals who develop tests and those who take them. The fact is that tests are used for purposes they were not intended to fulfill, and test developers, test takers, parents, educators, and government agencies have the right and arguably the responsibility to question the ethicality and fairness of an assessment and to justify its use.

Developing appropriate methods for evaluation of testing practices, like developing the test itself, is an ongoing process that will depend on the interested individuals and the audience for the evaluation. The professional literature in language assessment offers a wealth of resources for learning about the issues and options as well as for drawing on the knowledge and perspective of authorities in the field.

Conclusion

Throughout this book, you, the reader, have been in the position of the judicious consumer, examining the testing products developed, researched, and advocated by others. In this chapter, the tables have been turned, and we have challenged you to consider when and how to develop your own test. We have outlined some basic ideas and presented references that will help with test development, but developing a test is only half of the story. In the tradition of reflective practice, test developers become testing researchers as they improve and justify the use of the test. Having studied the tests, testing manuals, and test qualities in chapters 2, 3, and 4, respectively, you should feel much more confident than before in assuming responsibility for selecting, using, and, when necessary, constructing language assessments. Additionally, experience in developing a test with a group together with access to the books on language testing described in this chapter and the annotated bibliography dramatically increase the chances that you will end up with tests that are useful for test users and appropriate for test takers.

Annotated Bibliography

Alderson, J. C. (2000). *Assessing reading* (Cambridge Language Assessment Series). Cambridge: Cambridge University Press.

The book provides a valuable overview of the nature of reading, related research, and implications for assessing second language (L2) reading ability. The author introduces Bachman and Palmer's (1996) test development framework and illustrates how to apply it to creating reading assessments for various professional purposes and contexts. ESOL teachers will find the various procedures for assessing reading ability that are presented in chapters 7 and 9 especially useful in developing their own classroom assessments.

Alderson, J. C., Clapham, C., & Wall, D. (1995). *Language test construction and evaluation.* Cambridge: Cambridge University Press.

Although the book is intended to serve as a resource for program administrators and teachers responsible for constructing or selecting language tests—particularly tests used to place learners in language programs or to evaluate their achievement at crucial points—it is also an excellent introductory resource for classroom teachers who wish to acquire basic information regarding testing principles and practices. The authors present complex constructs using clear, comprehensible language that does not presume any previous knowledge of testing terminology or statistics.

Alderson, C., Krahnke, K., & Stansfield, C. (Eds.). (1987). *Reviews of English language proficiency tests.* Washington, DC: TESOL.

Despite being dated, this volume is the most comprehensive archive of tests (46) of English language ability available in a single source. For tests that have not been revised or replaced by others, the reviews are likely to remain relevant and useful to readers. Even when a test has been revised, readers may benefit from consulting this resource and considering whether the revised version of the test adequately addresses any reported weaknesses in the previous version.

Bachman, L. F. (1990). *Fundamental considerations in language testing.* **Oxford: Oxford University Press.**

This excellent resource covers the essential issues in test development and the use of language test results. Authored by one of the preeminent figures in language testing research, the book offers readers an introduction to such considerations as measurement, test methods, reliability, and validity, and it includes one of the most comprehensive theoretical frameworks available for exploring the nature of communicative language ability.

Bachman, L. F., & Palmer, A. S. (1996). *Language testing in practice.* **Oxford: Oxford University Press.**

This volume builds on the framework articulated in *Fundamental Considerations in Language Testing* (Bachman, 1990) and applies it to the practical challenge of developing particular tests of English language ability for a variety of contexts. Following a discussion of test usefulness and language ability, the authors present the phases and procedures associated with the test development process. The final section of the book includes descriptions of 10 different test development projects that illustrate how the process and considerations described in the previous sections may be applied in professional contexts.

Bailey, K. M. (1998). *Learning about language assessment: Dilemmas, decisions, and directions.* **Boston: Heinle & Heinle.**

Characterized by a personal and inviting style, this resource represents a novel approach to introducing essential concepts and procedures associated with teacher-developed assessments. It permits readers with no previous knowledge of testing to learn and apply the content of the text to the assessment of reading, writing, speaking, and listening ability in English. Each chapter reflects the same tripartite format: The author relates a teacher's personal experience to the theme of the chapter; presents key terms and concepts related to the topic from the perspective of the language testing expert; and, finally, presents tasks through which readers consolidate their learning by applying what is covered in the chapter. The book offers a balance between promoting reflection on assessment practices and promoting more informed use of tests and test results. The treatment of statistical procedures is especially effective and nontechnical.

Brown, J. D. (1996). *Testing in language programs.* **Upper Saddle River, NJ: Prentice Hall Regents.**

Program administrators and classroom teachers will find this book a useful resource. It includes a review of different types of tests, test development procedures and related considerations, statistical concepts and computations, and the function of tests within language programs. Some readers may find the extensive attention devoted to statistics daunting and unhelpful. However, for those who wish to increase their understanding of these tools and their relationship to test development, Brown offers a comprehensible and quite thorough introduction. Chapter 2 includes a checklist that may be useful in evaluating specific language tests.

Brown, J. D. (Ed.). (1998). *New ways of classroom assessment* **(New Ways in TESOL Series). Alexandria, VA: TESOL.**

The volume consists of various teacher-developed assessments organized around a common presentation format that introduces the assessment (approximately 100 words), describes how to implement it, discusses feedback and scoring or rating of performances, notes special considerations and alternatives, and in most cases includes several references. A matrix located at the back of the book categorizes assessments by language skill, test method (e.g., portfolio, journal, conference, self-assessment), and location in the volume, which permits readers to find a particular type of assessment quickly. The contents of this book represent the range of everyday assessment activities classroom teachers employ to determine the efficacy of their teaching and the extent of students' learning.

Brown, J. D., & Hudson, T. (2002). *Criterion-referenced language testing.* **Cambridge: Cambridge University Press.**

Practitioners who must construct their own assessments will find the first three chapters of this book especially helpful. The authors provide a good introduction to the differences between norm- and criterion-referenced testing followed by specific suggestions for improving the quality of teacher-developed assessments of learner achievement in ESOL courses and programs. Brown and Hudson discuss the use of traditional and alternative forms of assessment and explicate basic statistical concepts and procedures, reliability, and validity, with particular attention to their significance in constructing criterion-referenced tests. Chapter 7 includes useful advice on how to undertake a criterion-referenced test development project.

Buck, G. (2001). *Assessing listening* **(Cambridge Language Assessment Series). Cambridge: Cambridge University Press.**

There is a great deal of practical advice in *Assessing Listening,* and the volume represents an extremely accessible introduction to an aspect of language ability that tends to be underrepresented in the assessment literature. As is the pattern in other volumes in the series, the author presents an overview of what constitutes this particular language ability together with selected research on listening comprehension that draws on work in first and second language studies. Chapter 4 includes several useful frameworks for formulating conceptions of listening ability. Chapter 8 considers how listening ability is assessed in five different standardized tests. Teachers will find a great deal of practical advice on how to locate sample discourse, create listening tasks, and assess test takers' performances.

Cohen, A. D. (1994). *Assessing language ability in the classroom* **(2nd ed.). Boston: Heinle & Heinle.**

This resource offers a solid introduction to language testing and the procedures associated with formal and informal assessments of various language abilities (e.g., listening, speaking, reading, written expression). It is written in a clear, accessible style that requires no prerequisite knowledge. Essential terms and constructs are succinctly explicated, and numerous practical examples are presented together with suggestions on how to apply the content to typical professional challenges.

Council of Europe. (2001). *Common European framework of reference for languages: Learning, teaching, and assessment.* **Cambridge: Cambridge University Press.**

The volume provides a thorough introduction to the Common European Framework—a systematic method for considering, coordinating, and communicating about language learning and proficiency. In addition to describing a system for teaching and assessing communicative language ability, the book includes a review of essential concepts related to testing language proficiency (chapter 9) and a description of an innovative and ambitious computer-based language assessment system (Appendix C) called DIALANG. The latter initiative permits language users to engage in free, Internet-based self-assessments of their proficiency in any of the 14 different European languages that make up the DIALANG system.

Davidson, F., & Lynch, B. (2002). *Testcraft: A teacher's guide to writing and using language test specifications.* **New Haven, CT: Yale University Press.**

This extremely practical and accessible introduction to the design and construction of teacher-developed (criterion-referenced) tests assumes no prior knowledge of language testing or statistical procedures. The book presents a systematic process that practitioners may adopt; stages in the process include determining what to assess, preparing test specifications according to a rubric, writing test items, preparing and implementing the assessment on a trial basis, and finalizing the measure. (The authors' rubric consists of a General Description, Prompt Attribute, Response Attribute, Sample Item, and Specification Supplement.) Chapters 5–7 consider the context of test development activities, including the ways circumstances and people affect what emerges from the process, group dynamics, and professional responsibility.

Davies, A., Brown, A., Elder, C., Hill, K., Lumley, T., & McNamara, T. (1999). *Dictionary of language testing.* **Cambridge: Cambridge University Press.**

Although the primary audience for this book is the testing specialist, it represents an excellent reference for anyone who desires a concise, comprehensive guide to the vocabulary of language testing. Compiled by a team of leading experts at the University of Melbourne, in Australia, this resource offers readers over 600 specific entries and is enhanced by extensive and effective cross-referencing. The text for each entry ranges from several sentences to a page in length, which permits surprisingly detailed coverage of some entries.

Douglas, D. (2000). *Assessing languages for specific purposes* **(Cambridge Language Assessment Series). Cambridge: Cambridge University Press.**

The volume focuses on tests of specific language use, such as those that assess the use of English for various vocational purposes (e.g., business communication, medical practice, or teaching). It includes frameworks that consider the nature of specific-purpose language ability, the language use situation, and test task characteristics. Chapter 6 analyzes selected specific purpose tests that utilize listening and speaking abilities, and chapter 7 focuses on tests that emphasize reading and writing abilities. These chapters provide concrete and informative exemplars for anyone engaged in developing ESOL tests of specific language use.

Genesee, F., & Upshur, J. (1996). *Classroom-based evaluation in second language education.* **Cambridge: Cambridge University Press.**

In this clear and well-written book, Genesee and Upshur present a practical treatment of assessment that focuses on classroom evaluation. The authors assume that readers do not have prior knowledge of language testing or statistics and cover the range of evaluations that teachers use, including procedures associated with tests as well as those that are not (e.g., observations, portfolios, journals, surveys). Chapter 14 frames classroom assessment in terms of a set of diverse procedures that can be selected and used at different points in the instructional cycle (e.g., before teaching, during teaching, after teaching), depending on the decisions teachers must make and the type of information they need.

Henning, G. (1987). *A guide to language testing: Development, evaluation, research.* **Boston: Heinle & Heinle.**

Practitioners who develop tests and those who use the results will find the contents of this volume accessible, although the intended audience also includes researchers and preservice teachers in TESOL graduate programs. The book presents a basic introduction to the measurement of language ability and contains chapters that cover measurement scales and scoring, item analysis, common statistical procedures, reliability, validity, and technology-based testing practices. Notable features of the book are the inclusion of a glossary in Appendix C, the effective division of content into manageable units within each chapter, and the test evaluation checklist located at the end of chapter 1.

Hughes, A. (2003). *Testing for language teachers* **(2nd ed.). Cambridge: Cambridge University Press.**

This book represents an updated and expanded version of a practical resource designed for language teachers who want to improve their ability to develop tests of various language abilities. One notable improvement is the inclusion of a chapter that deals with developing tests for language learners who are under age 12. Other improvements include the expansion of Appendix 1 to include Internet resources as well as more discussion of selected statistical procedures related to test development activities. About half of the book covers basic considerations in language testing and principles of test construction, and the remainder of the volume is devoted to the assessment of specific language abilities (writing, speaking, reading, listening, grammar and vocabulary, and general proficiency). These latter chapters make generous use of authentic materials and therefore provide readers with tangible models for developing teacher-made classroom assessments for a range of ESOL learners.

Joint Committee on Standards for Educational & Psychological Testing. (1999).
Standards for educational and psychological testing. **Washington, DC: American Educational Research Association.**

This resource represents a collaborative effort by a consortium (the American Educational Research Association, the American Psychological Association, and the National Council on Measurement in Education) to codify the professional standards applied "to the evaluation of tests, testing practices, and the effects of test use" (p. 2). The volume is intended to benefit a diverse audience, including test developers, publishers, and consumers, and classroom teachers and program administrators will find the detailed descriptions of the 15 standards informative and useful in evaluating commercially available assessments. Although the text may be dense in places for readers who lack a background in measurement, there is a glossary, and the standards themselves are presented succinctly and in transparent prose. As might be expected, the most technical standards address aspects of test construction, evaluation, and documentation (Part I) and comprise Standards 1–6. Standards 9 (testing individuals of diverse linguistic backgrounds) and 11 (the responsibility of test users) are especially important for anyone responsible for administering, interpreting, and applying the results of standardized tests to nonnative speakers of English.

Luoma, S. (2004). *Assessing speaking* **(Cambridge Language Assessment Series). Cambridge: Cambridge University Press.**

Assessing speaking is a complex undertaking, and the issues surrounding the assessment of learners' speaking abilities are still emerging. This book provides conceptual and practical frameworks for developing speaking tests and assessments. It introduces the concept of speaking and presents research on speaking tasks and assessment scales. It provides teachers and test developers with practical guidelines for designing and developing suitable speaking tests and assessment tools for language learners.

McNamara, T. (2000). *Language testing* **(Introduction to Language Study Series). Oxford: Oxford University Press.**

This title shares the same basic organization and features of the other books in Oxford's Introduction to Language Study Series: survey, supplemental readings, annotated references, and a glossary of key terms. The survey section renders a succinct, uncomplicated overview of the primary issues and concepts in language testing. This section is a little more than 80 pages in length and highlights key terms in bold that are cross-referenced and defined in the glossary. The annotated references represent additional resources, and they are graded based on the perceived difficulty of the respective text. Supplemental readings correspond to and complement the chapters and contents in the survey section. In short, this volume provides a nontechnical introduction to the field of language testing, including treatment of test design and construction, measurement, reliability, validity, professional responsibility, and new perspectives.

Purpura, J. (2004). *Assessing grammar* (Cambridge Language Assessment Series). Cambridge: Cambridge University Press.

Despite movements to diminish the role of grammar in the L2 curriculum, *Assessing Grammar* views grammar as the fundamental linguistic resource for communicative language use. It therefore presumes that language educators need to know what the target grammar is, how to teach it, how it is learned, and how to assess students' acquisition of the forms and their associated meanings. In addition to reviewing the research in grammar teaching and learning, this volume presents an expanded framework of grammatical knowledge, accounting for both the form and the meaning dimensions, that can serve as a basis for test design, operationalization, interpretation, and validation. This book also provides practitioners and researchers with principles and procedures for constructing large-scale and classroom-based grammar assessments that could be used to make educational and research decisions. Finally, in a discussion on learning-oriented assessments, this book shows language educators how grammar assessments can be used to promote grammatical processing in classroom contexts.

Read, J. (2000). *Assessing vocabulary* (Cambridge Language Assessment Series). Cambridge: Cambridge University Press.

Read presents a framework for conceptualizing and categorizing vocabulary assessments that is applicable to teacher-developed and commercially produced large-scale measures of vocabulary ability. In addition to reviewing research on L2 vocabulary acquisition, the book examines the design of several standardized vocabulary measures (including the TOEFL) as well as those developed by practitioners and used to assess placement, progress, or achievement.

Weigle, S. (2002). *Assessing writing* (Cambridge Language Assessment Series). Cambridge: Cambridge University Press.

In keeping with the format adopted for the series, *Assessing Writing* begins with a consideration of the nature of writing, including a discussion of theory and research related to the topic. The book examines considerations in developing writing assessments and divides the process into three stages (test design, operationalization, and administration). Practitioners will find the chapters on rating procedures, portfolio assessment, and the application of technology to writing assessment especially informative. Chapter 7 reviews five standardized ESOL writing assessments and discusses each in light of the key points raised in earlier chapters.

References

ACT. (2000a). *ACT ESL Placement Test research and data report.* Iowa City, IA: Author.

ACT. (2000b). *COMPASS/ESL reference manual.* Iowa City, IA: ACT.

ACT. (2000c). *Welcome to ACT's ESL Placement Test.* Iowa City, IA: Author.

ACT. (2001). *ACT ESL Placement Test research and data report.* Iowa City, IA: Author.

Alderson, J. C. (2000). *Assessing reading* (Cambridge Language Assessment Series). Cambridge: Cambridge University Press.

Alderson, J. C., Clapham, C., & Wall, D. (1995). *Language test construction and evaluation.* Cambridge: Cambridge University Press.

Alderson, J. C., & Hamp-Lyons, L. (1996). TOEFL preparation courses: A study of washback. *Language Testing, 13,* 280–297.

Alderson, J. C., Krahnke, K., & Stansfield, C. (Eds.). (1987). *Reviews of English language proficiency tests.* Washington, DC: TESOL.

Alderson, J. C., & Wall, D. (1993). Does washback exist? *Applied Linguistics, 14,* 115–129.

Alderson, J. C., & Wall, D. (1996). Editorial. *Language Testing, 13,* 239–240.

American Educational Research Association, American Psychological Association, & National Council on Measurement in Education. (1985). *Standards for educational and psychological testing.* Washington, DC: American Psychological Association.

Amori, B., & Dalton, E. (1998a). *IPT II Oral grades 7–12 examiner's manual.* Brea, CA: Ballard & Tighe.

Amori, B., & Dalton, E. (1998b). *IPT II Oral grades 7–12 technical manual.* Brea, CA: Ballard & Tighe.

Association of Language Testers in Europe. (2004a). *The can-do statements: Overall general ability.* Retrieved September 27, 2004, from http://www.alte.org/can_do /general.cfm

Association of Language Testers in Europe. (2004b). *Framework and can-do. The can-do statements: Overall general ability.* Retrieved September 8, 2004, from http:// www.alte.org/can_do/framework/table.cfm

Bachman, L. F. (1990). *Fundamental considerations in language testing.* Oxford: Oxford University Press.

Bachman, L. F. (2000). Modern language testing at the turn of the century: Assuring that what we count counts. *Language Testing, 17,* 1–44.

Bachman, L. F. (2004). *Statistical analysis for language assessment.* Cambridge: Cambridge University Press.

Bachman, L. F., & Palmer, A. S. (1996). *Language testing in practice.* New York: Oxford University Press.

Bailey, K. M. (1996). Working for washback: A review of the washback concept in language testing. *Language Testing, 13,* 257–279.

Bailey, K. M. (1998). *Learning about language assessment: Dilemmas, decisions, and directions.* Boston: Heinle & Heinle.

Bailey, K. M. (1999). *Washback in language testing* (TOEFL Monograph Series No. MS-15). Princeton, NJ: Educational Testing Service.

Ballard, W., Dalton, E., & Tighe, P. (2001a). *IPT I Oral grades K–6 examiner's manual.* Brea, CA: Ballard & Tighe.

Ballard, W., Dalton, E., & Tighe, P. (2001b). *IPT I Oral grades K–6 technical manual.* Brea, CA: Ballard & Tighe.

Balliro, L. (1993). What *kind* of alternative? Examining alternative assessment. *TESOL Quarterly, 27,* 558–561.

Barton, P., & Coley, R. (1994). *Testing in America's schools.* Princeton, NJ: Educational Testing Service.

Beeston, S. (2000). The UCLES item banking system. *UCLES Research Notes, 2,* 8–9.

Bejar, I. I. (1985). *A preliminary study of raters for the Test of Spoken English* (TOEFL Research Report No. 18). Princeton, NJ: Educational Testing Service.

Boldt, R. F. (1992). *Reliability of the Test of Spoken English revisited* (TOEFL Research Report No. 40). Princeton, NJ: Educational Testing Service.

Boldt, R. F., & Ross, S. J. (1998). *The impact of training type and time on TOEIC scores* (TOEIC Research Summary No. 3). Princeton, NJ: Chauncey Group.

Boyd, K., & Davies, A. (2002). Doctors' orders for language testers: The origin and purpose of ethical codes. *Language Testing, 19,* 296–322.

Briggs, S., & Dobson, B. (1994). *MELAB technical manual.* Ann Arbor: University of Michigan.

Brindley, G. (1998). Outcomes-based assessment and reporting in language learning programmes: A review of the issues. *Language Testing, 15,* 45–85.

Brown, J. D. (1995). Developing norm-referenced language tests for program-level decision making. In J. D. Brown & S. O. Yamashita (Eds.), *Language testing in Japan* (pp. 40–47). Tokyo: Japan Association for Language Teaching.

Brown, J. D. (1996). *Testing in language programs.* Upper Saddle River, NJ: Prentice Hall Regents.

Brown, J. D., & Hudson, T. (1998). The alternatives in language assessment. *TESOL Quarterly, 32,* 653–675.

Brown, J. D., & Hudson, T. (2002). *Criterion-referenced language testing.* Cambridge: Cambridge University Press.

Buck, G. (2001). *Assessing listening* (Cambridge Language Assessment Series). Cambridge: Cambridge University Press.

Burt, M. K., & Dulay, H. C. (1978). *Bilingual Syntax Measure II manual* (English ed.).San Antonio, TX: Harcourt Brace Jovanovich.

Burt, M. K., Dulay, H. C., & Hernández Chávez, E. (1975). *Bilingual Syntax Measure manual* (English ed.). San Antonio, TX: Harcourt Brace Jovanovich.

Burt, M. K., Dulay, H. C., & Hernández Chávez, E. (1976). *Bilingual Syntax Measure technical handbook.* San Antonio, TX: Harcourt Brace Jovanovich.

Burt, M. K., Dulay, H. C., Hernández Chávez, E., & Taleporos, E. (1980). *Bilingual Syntax Measure II technical handbook.* San Antonio, TX: Harcourt Brace.

Business Language Testing Service. (2000a). *Candidate test report: BULATS English Speaking Test.* Cambridge: University of Cambridge Local Examination Syndicate.

Business Language Testing Service. (2000b). *Candidate test report: BULATS English Standard Test.* Cambridge: University of Cambridge Local Examination Syndicate.

Business Language Testing Service. (2000c). *Candidate test report: BULATS English Writing Test.* Cambridge: University of Cambridge Local Examination Syndicate.

Canale, M. (1983). On some dimensions of language proficiency. In J. Oller (Ed.), *Issues in language testing research* (pp. 333–342). Rowley, MA: Newbury House.

Canale, M. (1987). The measurement of communicative competence. *Annual Review of Applied Linguistics, 8,* 67–84.

Canale, M., & Swain, M. (1980). Theoretical bases of communicative approaches to second language teaching and testing. *Applied Linguistics, 1,* 1–47.

Chalhoub-Deville, M. (1997). Theoretical models, assessment frameworks and test construction. *Language Testing, 14,* 3–22.

Chapelle, C. (1998). Construct definition and validity inquiry in SLA research. In L. F. Bachman & A. D. Cohen (Eds.), *Second language acquisition and language testing interfaces* (pp. 32–70). Cambridge: Cambridge University Press.

Chapelle, C. (1999). Validity in language assessment. *Annual Review of Applied Linguistics, 19,* 254–272.

Chapelle, C. (2001). *Computer applications in second language acquisition: Foundations for teaching, testing, and research.* Cambridge: Cambridge University Press.

Chapelle, C. A., Jamieson, J., & Hegelheimer, V. (2003). Validation of a Web-based ESL test. *Language Testing, 20,* 409–439.

Cherryholmes, C. (1988). Construct validity and the discourses of research. In *Power and criticism: Poststructural investigations in education* (pp. 99–129). New York: Teachers College Press.

Clackamas Community College. (1993). *BEST Oral Interview short form: Training video.* Salem, OR: Office of Community College Services.

Cohen, A. D. (1994). *Assessing language ability in the classroom* (2nd ed.). Boston: Heinle & Heinle.

Cohen, A. D. (1998). Strategies and processes in test-taking and SLA. In L. F. Bachman & A. D. Cohen (Eds.), *Interfaces between second language acquisition and language testing research* (pp. 90–111). Cambridge: Cambridge University Press.

Comprehensive Adult Student Assessment System. (2000a). *Comprehensive Adult Student Assessment System (CASAS) ESL Appraisal, Form 20.* San Diego, CA: CASAS, Foundation for Educational Achievement.

Comprehensive Adult Student Assessment System. (2000b). *Test administration manual/Employability Competency System.* San Diego, CA: CASAS, Foundation for Educational Achievement.

Comprehensive Adult Student Assessment System. (2000c). *Test administration manual/Life Skills.* San Diego, CA: CASAS, Foundation for Educational Achievement.

Comprehensive Adult Student Assessment System. (2001). *Comprehensive Adult Student Assessment System (CASAS) technical manual.* San Diego, CA: CASAS, Foundation for Educational Achievement.

Conoley, J. C., & Impara, J. C. (Eds.). (1995). *The twelfth mental measurements yearbook.* Lincoln, NE: Buros Institute of Mental Measurements.

Cook, V. (1993). *Linguistics and second language acquisition.* London: Macmillan.

Council of Europe. (2001). *Common European framework of reference for languages: Learning, teaching, and assessment.* Cambridge: Cambridge University Press.

Culligan, B., & Gorsuch, G. (1999). Using a commercially produced proficiency test in a one-year core EFL curriculum in Japan for placement purposes. *JALT Journal, 21,* 7–25.

Cummins, J. (1979). Cognitive/academic language proficiency, linguistic interdependence, the optimum age question and some other matters. *Working Papers on Bilingualism, 19,* 121–129.

Cummins, J. (1984). *Bilingualism and special education: Issues in assessment and pedagogy.* Austin, TX: Pro-Ed.

Davidson, F., & Lynch, B. (2002). *Testcraft: A teacher's guide to writing and using language test specifications.* New Haven, CT: Yale University Press.

Davies, A. (1997). [Special issue on ethics in language testing]. *Language Testing, 14*(3).

Davies, A., Brown, A., Elder, C., Hill, K., Lumley, T., & McNamara, T. (1999). *Dictionary of language testing.* Cambridge: Cambridge University Press.

Del Vecchio, A., & Guerrero, M. (1995, December). *Handbook of English language proficiency tests.* Albuquerque, NM: New Mexico Highlands University, Evaluation Assistance Center—Western Region. Retrieved August 6, 2004, from http://www.ncela.gwu.edu/pubs/eacwest/elptests.htm

Douglas, D. (2000). *Assessing languages for specific purposes* (Cambridge Language Assessment Series). Cambridge: Cambridge University Press.

Douglas, D., & Chapelle, C. (Eds.). (1993). *A new decade of language testing research.* Alexandria, VA: TESOL.

Douglas, D., & Smith, L. (1997). *Theoretical underpinnings of the Test of Spoken English revision project* (TOEFL Monograph Series No. MS-9). Princeton, NJ: Educational Testing Service.

Dudley-Evans, T., & St. John, M. (1996). *Report on business English: A review of research and teaching materials* (TOEIC Research Summary No. 2). Princeton, NJ: Chauncey Group.

Dulay, H. C., & Burt, M. K. (1973). Should we teach children syntax? *Language Learning, 23,* 245–258.

Educational Testing Service. (1997). *SLEP Test manual.* Princeton, NJ: Author.

Educational Testing Service. (1998a). *TOEIC can-do guide: Linking TOEIC scores to activities performed using English.* Princeton, NJ: Author.

Educational Testing Service. (1998b). *TOEIC examinee handbook.* Princeton, NJ: Author.

Educational Testing Service. (1998c). *TOEIC technical manual.* Princeton, NJ: Author.

Educational Testing Service. (2000). *TSE and SPEAK score user guide.* Princeton, NJ: Author.

Educational Testing Service. (2001a). *TSE and SPEAK score user guide.* Princeton, NJ: Author.

Educational Testing Service. (2001b). *Writing topics.* Retrieved October 4, 2004, from http://ftp.ets.org/pub/toefl/989563wt.pdf

Educational Testing Service. (2004a). *TOEIC research.* Retrieved August 6, 2004, from http://www.ets.org/ell/research/toeic.html

Educational Testing Service. (2004b). *TSE research reports.* Retrieved August 22, 2004, from http://www.ets.org/ell/research/tse.html

English Language Institute, Testing & Certification Division. (1986). *English Language Institute Listening Comprehension Test manual.* Ann Arbor: University of Michigan.

English Language Institute, Testing & Certification Division. (1994, December). *Notice contrasting the Michigan English Language Assessment Battery with other ESL/EFL tests available from the publisher* [file name notice.doc 12/2/94]. Ann Arbor: University of Michigan.

English Language Institute, Testing & Certification Division. (1998, October). *ESL test publications.* Ann Arbor: University of Michigan.

Fox, J. (Ed.). (2000). *CAEL Assessment test score and users' guide.* Ottawa, Ontario, Canada: Carleton University, Language Assessment and Testing Research Unit.

Fox, J. (Ed.). (2002a). *CAEL Assessment test score and users' guide.* Ottawa, Ontario, Canada: Carleton University, Language Assessment and Testing Research Unit.

Fox, J. (2002b). *PreCAEL Academic Diagnostic and Placement Test (PreCAEL ADAPT)*. Ottawa, Ontario, Canada: Carleton University, Language Assessment and Testing Research Unit.

Fraser, W., & Brisson, M. (Eds.). (2003). *The CAEL Assessment test takers' preparation guide*. Manotick, Ontario, Canada: Penumbra Press & Northward Journal Communications.

Frederickson, N. (1984). The real test bias: Influences of testing on teaching and learning. *American Psychologist, 39*, 193–202.

Fulcher, G. (2004). *Resources in language testing page*. Retrieved October 20, 2004, from http://www.dundee.ac.uk/languagestudies/ltest/ltr.html

Gardner, D. (1996). Self-assessment for self-access learners. *TESOL Journal, 5*(3), 18–23.

Geranpayeh, A. (2001). CB BULATS: Examining the reliability of a computer based test using test-retest method. *UCLES Research Notes, 5*, 14–16.

Gillie, P. E. (2002). *English as a second language (ESL) class placement levels: Studies in proficiency tests, teacher accountability, and student participation*. Unpublished doctoral dissertation, Loyola University, Chicago.

Ginther, A. (2001). *Effects of the presence and absence of visuals on performance on TOEFL CBT listening-comprehensive stimuli* (TOEFL Research Report No. RR 66). Princeton, NJ: Educational Testing Service.

Ginther, A. (2002). Context and content visuals and performance on listening comprehension stimuli. *Language Testing, 19*, 133–167.

Goals 2000: Educate America Act, 20 U.S.C. § 5801 (1994).

Gottlieb, M. (1995). Nurturing student learning through portfolios. *TESOL Journal, 5*(1), 12–14.

Harris, D. P., & Palmer, L. A. (1986). *CELT examiner's instructions and technical manual*. New York: McGraw-Hill.

Henning, G. (1987). *A guide to language testing: Development, evaluation, research*. Boston: Heinle & Heinle.

Herman, J. L., Aschbacher, P. R., & Winters, L. (1992). *A practical guide to alternative assessment*. Alexandria, VA: Association for Supervision & Curriculum Development.

Huerta-Macías, A. (1995). Alternative assessment: Responses to commonly asked questions. *TESOL Journal, 5*(1), 8–11.

Hughes, A. (2003). *Testing for language teachers* (2nd ed.). Cambridge: Cambridge University Press.

Ilyin, D. (1993). *User's guide for CELSA: Combined English Language Skills Assessment in a Reading Context*. Montecito, CA: Association of Classroom Teacher Testers.

Ilyin, D., Spurling, S., & Seymour, S. (1987). Do learner variables affect cloze correlations? *System, 15*(2), 149–160.

Impara, J. C., & Plake, B. S. (Eds.). (1998). *The thirteenth mental measurements yearbook*. Lincoln, NE: Buros Institute of Mental Measurements.

International English Language Testing System. (2004). *Standards against which IELTS must be measured*. Retrieved November 8, 2004, from http://www.ielts.org /teachersandresearchers/standardsandconstructs/article147.aspx

Jennings, M., Fox, J., Graves, B., & Shohamy, E. (1999). The test-taker's choice: An investigation of the effect of topic on language test performance. *Language Testing, 16,* 426–456.

Joint Committee of the American Psychological Association, American Educational Research Association, and National Council on Measurement in Education. (1974). *Standards for educational and psychological tests*. Washington, DC: American Psychological Association.

Joint Committee on Standards for Educational & Psychological Testing. (1999). *Standards for educational and psychological testing*. Washington, DC: American Educational Research Association.

Jones, N. (2000). BULATS: A case study comparing computer based and paper-and-pencil tests. *UCLES Research Notes, 3,* 10–13.

Kane, M. T. (2001). Current concerns in validity theory. *Journal of Educational Measurement, 38,* 319–342.

Kenyon, D., & Stansfield, C. (1989). *Basic English Skills Test manual*. Washington, DC: Center for Applied Linguistics.

Keyser, D. J., & Sweetlands, R. C. (1994). *Test critiques: Vol. X*. Austin, TX: Pro-Ed.

Kramer, J. J., & Conoley, J. C. (Eds.). (1992). *The eleventh mental measurements yearbook*. Lincoln, NE: Buros Institute of Mental Measurements.

Kunnan, A. J. (1997). Connecting fairness with validation in language assessment. In A. Huhta, V. Kohonen, L. Kurki-Suonio, & S. Luoma (Eds.), *Current developments and alternatives in language assessment: Proceedings of LTRC 96* (pp. 85–105). Jyväskylä, Finland: University of Jyväskylä.

Language Assessment and Testing Research Unit. (n.d.). *CAEL-related research 1991–1999*. Ottawa, Ontario, Canada: Carleton University, School of Linguistics and Applied Language Studies.

Laufer, B., & Nation, P. (1999). A vocabulary-size test of controlled productive ability. *Language Testing, 16,* 33–51.

Lazaraton, A. (2002). *A qualitative approach to the validation of oral language tests*. Cambridge: Cambridge University Press.

Linn, R. L. (1994). Performance assessment: Policy promises and technical measurement standards. *Educational Researcher, 23*(9), 4–14.

Linn, R. L., Baker, E. L., & Dunbar, S. B. (1991). Complex, performance-based assessment: Expectations and validation criteria. *Educational Researcher, 20*(8), 15–21.

Lumley, T., & Qian, D. (2001, February). *Is speaking performance assessment based mainly on grammar?* Paper presented at the 23rd Language Testing Research Colloquium, Saint Louis, MO.

Luoma, S. (2004). *Assessing speaking* (Cambridge Language Assessment Series). Cambridge: Cambridge University Press.

Lynch, B. (2001). Rethinking assessment from a critical perspective. *Language Testing, 18,* 351–372.

Maculaitis, J. D. (2001a). *MAC II administrative manual.* Brewster, NY: Touchstone Applied Science Associates.

Maculaitis, J. D. (2001b). *MAC II handbook.* Brewster, NY: Touchstone Applied Science Associates.

Manley, J. (1995). Assessing students' oral language: One school district's response. *Foreign Language Annals, 28,* 93–102.

McCollum, P. A. (1983). The IDEA oral language proficiency test: A critical review. In S. S. Seidner (Ed.), *Issues of language assessment: Volume 2. Language assessment and curriculum planning* (pp. 85–93). Chicago: Illinois State Board of Education.

McNamara, M. J., & Deane, D. (1995). Self-assessment activities: Toward autonomy in language learning. *TESOL Journal, 5*(1), 17–21.

McNamara, T. (2001). Language assessment as social practice: Challenges for research. *Language Testing, 18,* 333–349.

Messick, S. (1989). Validity. In R. L. Linn (Ed.), *Educational measurement* (3rd ed., pp. 13–103). New York: Macmillan.

Messick, S. (1994). The interplay of evidence and consequences in the validation of performance assessments. *Educational Researcher, 23*(2), 13–23.

Moss, P. A. (1992). Shifting conceptions of validity in educational measurement: Implications for performance assessment. *Review of Educational Research, 62,* 229–258.

Murphy, T. (1995). Tests: Learning through negotiated interaction. *TESOL Journal, 4*(2), 12–16.

National Commission on Excellence in Education. (1983). *A nation at risk: The imperative for educational reform.* Washington, DC: U.S. Government Printing Office.

No Child Left Behind Act of 2001, 20 U.S.C. § 6301 (2002).

Notes on the test review feature. (1999). *Language Testing, 16,* 127.

Papajohn, D. (2002). Concept mapping for rater training, *TESOL Quarterly, 36,* 219–233.

POWERPREP Software: Preparation for the Computer-Based TOEFL Test (Version 1). (2003). Princeton, NJ: Educational Testing Service. Available from http://www.ets.org/ell/testpreparation/toefl/index.html

Powers, D., Schedl, M., Wilson-Leung, S., & Butler, F. (1999). *Validating the revised Test of Spoken English against a criterion of communicative success* (TOEFL Research Report No. RR 63). Princeton, NJ: Educational Testing Service.

Purpura, J. (2004). *Assessing grammar* (Cambridge Language Assessment Series). Cambridge: Cambridge University Press.

Read, J. (2000). *Assessing vocabulary* (Cambridge Language Assessment Series). Cambridge: Cambridge University Press.

Read, J., & Chapelle, C. (2001). A framework for second language vocabulary assessment. *Language Testing, 18,* 1–32.

Robb, T., & Ercanbrack, J. (1999). A study of the effect of direct test preparation on the TOEIC scores of Japanese university students. *TESL-EJ, 3*(4), 1–22.

Russell, M. (1999). Testing on computers: A follow-up study comparing performance on computer and on paper. *Education Policy Analysis Archives, 7*(20). Retrieved August 6, 2004, from http://epaa.asu.edu/epaa/v7n20/

Savignon, S. J. (1997). *Communicative competence: Theory and classroom practice* (2nd ed.). New York: McGraw-Hill.

Shaw, S. (2004.) IELTS Writing: Revising assessment criteria and scales (Phase 3). *Research Notes, 16,* 3–7.

Shepard, L. (1993). Evaluating test validity. *Review of Research in Education, 19,* 405–450.

Shepard, L. (1997). The centrality of test use and consequences for test validity. *Educational Measurement: Issues and Practice, 16*(2), 5–8, 13, 24.

Shohamy, E. (1997). Testing methods, testing consequences: Are they ethical? Are they fair? *Language Testing, 14,* 340–349.

Shohamy, E. (2001a). Democratic assessment as an alternative. *Language Testing, 18,* 373–391.

Shohamy, E. (2001b). *The power of tests: A critical perspective on the uses of language tests.* Harlow, England: Longman/Pearson.

Smolen, L., Newman, C., Wathen, T., & Lee, D. (1995). Developing student self-assessment strategies. *TESOL Journal, 5*(1), 22–27.

Spolsky, B. (1978). Introduction: Linguists and language testers. In B. Spolsky (Ed.), *Papers in applied linguistics* (Advances in Language Testing Series, No. 2, pp. v–x). Arlington, VA: Center for Applied Linguistics.

Spolsky, B. (1995). *Measured words.* New York: Oxford University Press.

Stansfield, C. (1984). Reliability and validity of the Secondary Level English Proficiency Test. *System, 12*(1), 1–12.

Stiggins, R. J. (1997). *Student-centered classroom assessment* (2nd ed.). Upper Saddle River, NJ: Prentice Hall.

Stoynoff, S. (1993). Ethics and intensive English programs. *TESOL Journal, 2*(3), 4–6.

Stoynoff, S. (1996). Resources in language testing and assessment. *TESOL Quarterly, 30,* 781–786.

Strong-Krause, D., Larsen, J., & Smith, K. (1999). *ESLCAPE.* Provo, UT: Brigham Young University.

Swain, M. (1993). Second language testing and second language acquisition: Is there a conflict with traditional psychometrics? *Language Testing, 10,* 193–207.

TESOL. (1997). *ESL standards for pre-K–12 students.* Alexandria, VA: Author.

Towards a European framework: ALTE, LangCred, and the Council of Europe together at EAIE. (1994). *ALTE News, 3*(2), 8.

Turner, C. E., & Upshur, J. A. (2002). Rating scales derived from student samples: Effects of the scale maker and the student sample on scale content and student scores. *TESOL Quarterly, 36,* 49–70.

University of Cambridge ESOL Examinations. (2003). *IELTS handbook.* Cambridge: Author. Retrieved November 8, 2004, from http://www.ielts.org/library /handbook_2003.pdf

Upshur, J., & Turner, C. (1995). Constructing rating scales. *ELT Journal, 49,* 3–12.

Wall, D. (1997). Impact and washback in language testing. In C. Clapham & D. Corson (Eds.), *Encyclopedia of language and education: Vol. 7. Language testing and assessment* (pp. 291–302). Dordrecht, Netherlands: Kluwer Academic.

Wall, D., Clapham, C., & Alderson, C. (1994). Evaluating a placement test. *Language Testing, 11,* 321–344.

Weigle, S. (2002). *Assessing writing* (Cambridge Language Assessment Series). Cambridge: Cambridge University Press.

Weir, C. J. (1990). *Communicative language testing.* Hertfordshire, England: Prentice Hall International.

Wiggins, G. P. (1993). *Assessing student performance: Exploring the purpose and limits of testing.* San Francisco: Jossey-Bass.

Wilson, K. M. (1993a). *Relating TOEIC scores to oral proficiency interview ratings* (TOEIC Research Summary). Princeton, NJ: Chauncey Group.

Wilson, K. M. (1993b). *Uses of the Secondary Level English Proficiency (SLEP) Test: A survey of current practice* (Research Report No. 43). Princeton, NJ: Educational Testing Service.

Wilson, K. M., & Tillberg, R. (1994). *An assessment of selected validity-related properties of a shortened version of the Secondary Level English Proficiency Test and locally developed writing tests in the LACCD context.* Princeton, NJ: Educational Testing Service.

Woodcock, R., & Muñoz-Sandoval, A. (1993). *Woodcock-Muñoz Language Survey comprehensive manual.* Itasca, IL: Riverside.

Woodford, P. (1982). *An introduction to TOEIC: The initial validity study* (TOEIC Research Summary). Princeton, NJ: Chauncey Group.

Wu, W., & Stansfield, C. (2001). Towards authenticity of task in test development. *Language Testing, 18,* 187–206.

Contributors

Stephen Stoynoff is a professor of English and director of the MA TESL program at Minnesota State University, Mankato, in the United States, where he teaches courses in research methods, language testing, and second language literacy. He was editor of *TESOL Journal* from 1998 through 2003 and serves on the Editorial Panel of *ELT Journal*.

Carol A. Chapelle is a professor of TESL/applied linguistics at Iowa State University, in the United States, where she teaches courses in second language acquisition, language assessment, computer-assisted language learning, ESL, and linguistics. She is the author of books on technology for language learning and was editor of *TESOL Quarterly* from 1999 to 2004.

Jayanti Banerjee's specialist areas are language testing and English for academic purposes (EAP). Her current research interests combine these areas. She is interested in the interpretation and use of EAP language proficiency test scores, the assessment of students in EAP courses, and questionnaire design and validation.

Lindsay Brooks is an experienced teacher and researcher in the area of language testing, regularly presenting on her current PhD research at international conferences. She is an instructor at the University of Toronto, in Canada, where she teaches in the TESL Certificate Program at Woodsworth College and the English Language Program.

Norman Brown is a graduate of St. Olaf College (BA), Central Seminary of Minneapolis (MRE, MDiv., ThM), and Minnesota State University, Mankato (MA in TESL). He taught Koine Greek at Pillsbury College for 14 years and currently teaches ESL at Owatonna High School, in the United States.

Micheline Chalhoub-Deville is a professor in the Foreign Language and ESL Education Program at the University of Iowa, in the United States. She has served as chair of the TOEFL Committee of Examiners and as a member of the TOEFL board. She serves on the Editorial Board of *Language Testing* and of *Language Assessment Quarterly*. She is the founder and first president of the Midwest Association of Language Testers.

Yeonsuk Cho earned a PhD in educational psychology at the University of Illinois at Urbana-Champaign, specializing in language testing. She currently works as an assessment specialist at Ballard & Tighe Publishers, in the United States. Her research interests include test development and validation, and writing assessment.

Caroline Clapham was validation officer for the International English Language Testing System until 2003, and previously taught language testing at Lancaster University, in England. She is editor of *Language Testing and Assessment* and Volume 7 of Kluwer Academic's *Encyclopedia of Language and Education* (1997), author of *The Development of IELTS* (Cambridge University Press, 1996), and coauthor (with Alderson and Wall) of *Language Test Construction and Evaluation* (Cambridge University Press, 1995).

Tina Scott Edstam is the grant coordinator for a Title III teacher development project focusing on long-term collaborative processes for serving English language learners; she is an adjunct faculty member at the University of Minnesota, in the United States. Her interests include teacher professionalism and ESL practices and policies in the public schools.

April Ginther is an associate professor of ESL and director of the Oral English Proficiency Program at Purdue University, in the United States. Using a locally developed computer-based, semidirect test, the program screens approximately 500 prospective international teaching assistants for oral English proficiency each academic year.

Jeff S. Johnson received his EdD from Temple University and is currently the MELAB Program director in the Testing and Certification Division of the English Language Institute at the University of Michigan, in the United States. His professional interests include language test validation research and composition rater reliability.

Sari Luoma holds a PhD in applied linguistics from the University of Jyväskylä. She has held research and development positions related to initial development and maintenance of language testing systems at the University of Jyväskylä and at the Defense Language Institute. She is author of *Assessing Speaking* (Cambridge University Press, 2004). Currently, she is assessment director at Ballard & Tighe Publishers, in the United States.

Margaret E. Malone holds a PhD in applied linguistics from Georgetown University. She is senior testing associate in the Language Testing Division at the Center for Applied Linguistics, in the United States. Previously, she directed language testing for

Peace Corps—Worldwide, designed and delivered technical assistance to language programs in six states, and taught graduate-level courses at Georgetown and American universities.

Keith Morrow was involved in the development of communicative language testing in the United Kingdom. He was chief examiner for the Royal Society of Arts examinations in the Communicative Use of EFL, and later for the Cambridge Certificates in Communicative Skills in English, which were developed from these. He is editor of *ELT Journal*.

Barry O'Sullivan is deputy director of the Centre for Research in Testing, Evaluation and Curriculum at Roehampton University, London, England. His publications include the book *Issues in Business English Testing* in Cambridge University Press's Studies in Language Testing series. He works with and advises testing boards and education ministries around the world.

James Purpura is associate professor of linguistics and education in the TESOL and Applied Linguistics Programs at Teachers College, Columbia University, in the United States, where he directs the TESOL Program and teaches language assessment courses. Besides writing *Learner Strategy Use* and *Performance on Second Language Tests* (Cambridge University Press, 1999) and *Assessing Grammar* (Cambridge University Press, 2004), he has published in *Language Testing*, in *Language Learning*, and in edited volumes.

David D. Qian is an associate professor in the Department of English, Hong Kong Polytechnic University, where he supervises PhD theses in language testing and teaches language assessment and research methods. His research interests include large-scale performance testing, second language vocabulary learning and measurement, English learner corpora, and English for workplace communication.

Carsten Roever is a lecturer in the Department of Linguistics and Applied Linguistics at the University of Melbourne, in Australia. He earned his PhD in second language acquisition from the University of Hawai'i at Manoa. His research interests include interlanguage pragmatics, second language acquisition, and assessment.

Diane Schmitt is a principal lecturer in EFL at Nottingham Trent University, in England. She is the academic team leader for the Nottingham Language Centre and contributes to the MA in English language teaching. Her research interests are language proficiency standards for university entry, vocabulary acquisition and writing from sources.

Diane Strong-Krause, an associate teaching professor at Brigham Young University, in the United States, has been involved in language test development since the mid-1980s. Test development projects she has worked on include a computer-adaptive ESL placement exam (ESLCAPE), computerized speaking exams (using Oral Testing Software), and a set of achievement exams for a local intensive English program.

Carolyn E. Turner is an associate professor in the Department of Integrated Studies in Education at McGill University, in Canada. Her main interest is language testing/ assessment in educational settings. Her present research includes educational innovation and high-stakes tests and the assessment of co-constructed paired tasks. She is associate editor of the journal *Language Assessment Quarterly*.

Jean Turner is a professor in the School of Languages and Educational Linguistics at the Monterey Institute of International Studies, in the United States. Her current professional and research interests include the measurement of advanced language skills for language professionals and issues related to the integration of teaching and assessment. She has served as an assessment consultant for private and government agencies and companies. She is the author of articles or chapters in the *Annual Review of Applied Linguistics* and *The Content-Based Classroom*.

Gillian Wigglesworth is an associate professor and head of the Department of Linguistics and Applied Linguistics at the University of Melbourne, in Australia. Her research interests include first and second language acquisition, language testing and evaluation, and bilingualism, and she has published widely in these areas.

Index

Page numbers followed by *f* and *t* refer to figures and tables respectively. Page numbers in bold refer to the test reviews in this volume.

Also Available From TESOL

Assessment Practices
Christine Coombe and Nancy Hubley, Editors

Academic Writing Programs
Ilona Leki, Editor

Action Research
Julian Edge, Editor

Bilingual Education
Donna Christian and Fred Genesee, Editors

CALL Essentials
Joy Egbert

Collaborative Conversations Among Language Teacher Educators
Margaret Hawkins and Suzanne Irujo, Editors

Community Partnerships
Elsa Auerbach, Editor

Content-Based Instruction in Higher Education Settings
JoAnn Crandall and Dorit Kaufman, Editors

Distance-Learning Programs
Lynn Henrichsen, Editor

English for Specific Purposes
Thomas Orr, Editor

Gender and English Language Learners
Bonny Norton and Aneta Pavlenko, Editors

Grammar Teaching in Teacher Education
Dilin Liu and Peter Master, Editors

Intensive English Programs in Postsecondary Settings
Nicholas Dimmit and Maria Dantas-Whitney, Editors

Interaction and Language Learning
Jill Burton and Charles Clennell, Editors

Journal Writing
Jill Burton and Michael Carroll, Editors

Mainstreaming
Effie Cochran, Editor

Teacher Education
Karen E. Johnson, Editor

Technology-Enhanced Learning Environments
Elizabeth Hanson-Smith, Editor

For more information, contact
Teachers of English to Speakers of Other Languages, Inc.
700 South Washington Street, Suite 200
Alexandria, Virginia 22314 USA
Tel 703-836-0774 • Fax 703-836-6447
publications@tesol.org • http://www.tesol.org/